ॐ गण गणपतये नमः

गुरुर्ब्रह्मा गुरुर्विष्णुः

गुरुर्देवो महेश्वरः ।

गुरुःसाक्षात् परब्रह्म

तस्मै श्रीगुरवे नमः ॥

न अहं कर्ता हरि कर्ता हरि कर्ता हि केवलम् ।

BHRIGU NANDI NADI

|| Astrology Simplified ||

Saurabh Avasthi

Notion Press
USA | INDIA

Publisher:
Notion Press Media Pvt Ltd
#7, Red Cross Road,
Egmore, Chennai, Tamil Nadu 600008
Email ID: publish@notionpress.com
Phone Number: +91 44 46315631

Book Title:
BHRIGU NANDI NADI
Astrology Simplified

Genre: Astrology, Self-Help
Edition: 8, November 2024
Language: English
Country of Origin: India
Copyright © Author: Saurabh Avasthi

Other Books by Author:

VEDIC NUMEROLOGY || ANK JYOTISH ||
The Proven Methodology to Accurate Prediction

COMPATIBILITY IS A MYTH, 2024

The Art and Science of Signature Analysis: A Step-by-Step Guide to Deciphering
Nature, Behavior, Personality and Intent. 2023

Psychology of Doodles & Scribbles: Visual Expression of the Unconscious, 2023

Encyclopedia of Graphology: A Master Practitioner's Guide - Volume I: Gestalt
Method – Holistic Approach to Handwriting Analysis, 2023

Encyclopedia of Graphology: A Master Practitioner's Guide - Volume II: Trait
Method – Feature Analysis Approach to Handwriting Analysis (Letters A to Z,
Numerals), 2023

Basics of Graphology, 2023

Bespoke Sales Pitch: Date of Birth = Buying Behaviour = Sales Pitch, 2019

DEDICATED TO

**To my dearest parents,
I. C. Awasthi and Kiran Awasthi**

"The only true wisdom is in knowing you know nothing." - Socrates

"To know what you know and what you do not know, that is true knowledge." - Confucius

"Knowing is not enough; we must apply.
Willing is not enough; we must do." - Socrates

"The important thing is not to stop questioning. Curiosity has its own reason for existence." - Albert Einstein

"Human behavior flows from three main sources: desire, emotion and knowledge" - Plato

"Knowledge is of no value unless you put it into practice." - Anton Chekhov

"यदा संहरते चायं कुर्मोऽङ्गानीव सर्वशः |

इन्द्रियाणीन्द्रियार्थेषु वा बुद्धिः परिनामिनी ||"

"yadā saṁharate cāyaṁ kurmoṅgānīva sarvaśaḥ |
indriyāṇīndriyārtheṣu vā buddhiḥ parināminī ||"

"When a man dwells on the objects of sense, attachment to them is produced. From attachment springs desire and from desire, anger is born." - Bhagavad Gita (Chapter 2, Verse 62-63)

"न विद्यया न तपसा न दानेन न चेज्यया |

शुद्धेन हृदयेन विना न मुक्तिर्भवेत् ||"

"na vidyayā na tapasā na dānena na cejyayā |
śuddhena hṛdayena vinā na muktirbhavet ||"

"Knowledge is not obtained by mere scholarship or book-learning. It is obtained only by the practice of yoga and the realization of the Self." - Adi Shankaracharya

"यदा संसर्पमानो निवृत्तसर्वसंकल्पः |

शमो ह्यन्ते केवलं ज्ञानमवशिष्यते ||"

"yadā saṁsarpamāno nivṛttasarvasaṅkalpaḥ | śamo hyante kevalaṁ jñānamavaśiṣyate ||"

"The one who has controlled the mind and senses and has realized the Self, is eligible to attain the state of supreme peace and liberation." - Katha Upanishad (1.2.20)

"न च श्रुतेन न च स्मृत्या न चान्येनैव वेद्यं |

अहं ममेत्येव ज्ञानं स्वमात्मानमवेद्यं ||"

"na ca śruten na ca smṛtyā na cānyenaiva vedyam | ahaṁ mametyeva jñānaṁ svamātmānamavedyam ||"

"The Self is not known by the intellect, nor by the senses, nor by scriptures. It is known only by the one who says, 'The Self is mine'." - Ashtavakra Gita (1.14)

"समदुःखसुखः स्वस्थः समलोष्टाश्मकाञ्चनः |

तुल्यनिन्दास्तुतिर्मौनी संतोषेन च संतुष्टः ||"

"samaduḥkhasukhaḥ svasthaḥ samaloṣṭāśmakāñcanaḥ | tulyanindāstutirmounī santoṣena ca santuṣṭaḥ ||"

"The wise one, who has realized the Self, sees all beings as equal and does not differentiate between them." - Bhagavad Gita (Chapter 5, Verse 18)

"सुखदुःखे समे कृत्वा लाभालाभौ जयाजयौ |

ततो युद्धाय युज्यस्व नैवं पापमवाप्स्यसि ||"

"sukhaduḥkhe same kṛtvā lābhālābhau jayājayau |
tato yuddhāya yujyasva naivaṁ pāpamavāpsyasi ||"

"The one who has realized the Self, is not affected by
the dualities of pleasure and pain and is established
in the state of equanimity." - Bhagavad Gita (Chapter
2, Verse 56)

From a Student of Astrology

For other Students …..

Preface

Astrology is a field of never-ending learning, where each new insight adds a layer to an age-old science and each chart opens a fresh perspective. For every astrologer, the journey is one of continuous growth, where each horoscope encountered imparts unique wisdom and even after years of study, we remain students, forever curious. This unceasing curiosity keeps us questioning, pushing us to evolve and expand our understanding of the cosmos. It is this spirit of inquiry, the persistent *why* of human existence, that fuels the development of astrology and deepens our grasp of its mysteries.

In this book, I have strived to present Bhrigu Nandi Nadi (BNN) in a simplified, accessible way for practitioners and students alike. Unlike conventional texts, I have minimized the use of multiple charts, focusing instead on foundational theory. BNN is a profound science rooted in karmic philosophy, offering insights not just into the *what* and *when* of events but delving deeply into the *why*. This book addresses this pivotal question, exploring the metaphysical and karmic dimensions that make BNN such a powerful astrological tool.

To make the most of the concepts and insights shared here, I would urge readers to keep a few horoscopes at hand, testing each theory and principle as they progress. BNN shines when applied practically, its wisdom becoming apparent as each idea is tested and witnessed in real-life charts. This approach will help each reader appreciate the relevance and depth of BNN, experiencing its lessons firsthand.

This book is a humble offering of my accumulated knowledge, aiming to honor the principles of BNN to the best of my understanding. I am deeply grateful to my teachers for their invaluable guidance and to my students, whose support and encouragement have been pivotal in completing this work. My sincere apologies for any omissions or errors within these pages; I approach this offering with humility and an open heart and I seek forgiveness for any oversights in this endeavor. May this book be a useful guide on your journey into BNN, helping you explore astrology's endless depths and enriching your practice as much as it has mine.

INDEX

Bhrigu Nandi Nadi: A Masterpiece of Astrology

The Founding Father: Late Shri R.G. Rao

Late Shri R.G. Rao, a highly regarded astrologer and scholar, made significant contributions to the field of Nadi astrology by developing the system known as *Bhrigu Nandi Nadi* (BNN). His work uniquely blends elements from two prominent streams of Nadi astrology - *Nandi Nadi* and *Bhrigu Nadi*. Through extensive research and analysis of ancient texts, Rao devised this approach, which stands apart from traditional astrology by focusing on planetary significators (karaktatwas) rather than relying solely on the *lagna* or ascendant.

Background of Nadi Astrology

Nadi astrology, rooted in ancient Vedic wisdom, is believed to have originated thousands of years ago and centers on the idea of pre-recorded horoscopes. Nadi texts contain records for countless individuals, with descriptions of planetary configurations and predictions for specific types of karmic paths. The two key schools, Nandi Nadi and Bhrigu Nadi, each emphasize different approaches:

- **Nandi Nadi** often places emphasis on the Moon and the emotional and mental tendencies it reveals.
- **Bhrigu Nadi**, attributed to the sage Bhrigu, emphasizes Jupiter and its influence over karma and spiritual development.

Shri R.G. Rao's Approach in Bhrigu Nandi Nadi (BNN)

Shri R.G. Rao integrated these two perspectives, expanding the system by developing a method based on *karaktatwas*, or the essential significations of each planet. Instead of always referring back to the lagna or ascendant as a fixed reference point, he considered multiple starting points in a chart, depending on the specific planetary influence or area of life in focus. This makes BNN a flexible and insightful method, as it allows astrologers to study planetary interactions dynamically from different reference points, depending on the life aspect under examination.

Comparative Overview of Bhrigu Nandi Nadi (BNN) vs. Traditional Vedic Astrology

Primary Focus:

BNN: Emphasizes the *karaktatwas* (significations) of planets and signs. BNN interprets life events through the inherent qualities of each planet and Rashi, making the focus more qualitative.

Vedic Astrology: Focuses on planetary positions in relation to the Lagna (Ascendant) and houses. Each planet's influence is shaped by its lordship over houses, creating a more personalized approach linked to the native's individual chart structure.

Jeeva/Lagna:

BNN: Considers Jupiter as the *Jeev* (life force) and reference point, treating it as the Lagna for understanding karmic and life experiences.

Vedic Astrology: Uses the Ascendant (Lagna) as the central point, with the Lagna Lord representing the *Jeev* or core personality. This Lagna-based approach offers a more individualized perspective on the native's life journey.

Predictive Basis:

BNN: Relies heavily on transits, especially of Jupiter, Saturn, Rahu and Ketu, to time events. Transits reflect life's flow, focusing on the present influences on the native.

Vedic Astrology: Uses the Dasha system, which breaks time into planetary periods, providing a sequence of life events and a more detailed timeline of experiences.

Chart Usage:

BNN: Works with a single directional chart, simplifying analysis by focusing on the position and interactions of planets within one main chart.

Vedic Astrology: Utilizes multiple divisional charts (e.g., Navamsa, Dasamsa) to examine specific areas of life in detail, offering a layered and specialized insight into topics like relationships and career.

Birth Time Precision:

BNN: Less emphasis on exact birth time since Jupiter's position is the main focus. The native's karmic path and experiences can be interpreted broadly without requiring precise timing.

Vedic Astrology: Accurate birth time is essential, as it determines the Lagna and planetary placements within divisional charts, impacting the timing and specificity of predictions.

Comparison Summary

Aspect	Bhrigu Nandi Nadi (BNN)	Traditional Vedic Astrology
Primary Focus	Grah and Rashi Karaktatwas	Planets, Lagna and Houses
Jeeva/Lagna	Jupiter as Jeev/Lagna	Ascendant as Lagna, Lagna Lord as Jeev
Predictive Basis	Transits of Jupiter, Saturn, Rahu, Ketu	Dashas and Sub-Dashas
Chart Usage	Lagna/Directional Chart	Multiple Divisional Charts
Birth Time Precision	Less Emphasis	High Importance
Role of Rashi	Extensive Use	Supporting Role

The Role of Time, Place and Condition (Desh, Kaal, Patra)

A common question practitioners face is: If precise birth time is not emphasized in BNN, then do people born on the same day share identical fates? The answer acknowledges both *Yes* and *No*. BNN posits that people born on the same day may indeed experience similar planetary influences due to their shared planetary positions. However, the factors of *Desh, Kaal and Patra* - meaning time, place and condition - introduce unique variations to each individual's journey. This perspective upholds the following points:

1. **Time and Culture** (*Kaal*): The era or period in which a person is born affects how planetary energies manifest. Social norms, economic conditions and cultural perspectives play a crucial role in shaping how individuals experience similar influences.
2. **Geography and Surroundings** (*Desh*): The environment in which a person grows up - the country, city, neighborhood - brings nuances. For instance, a person born in a rural setting might experience career growth differently than someone born in an urban area, even with identical planetary configurations.
3. **Personal Condition or Capacity** (*Patra*): Each individual has unique inclinations, strengths, weaknesses and resources. Thus, people react differently to similar life events, which means identical charts manifest uniquely for each person according to their personal capacities, ambitions and perspectives.

This framework allows BNN practitioners to interpret horoscopes in a way that resonates with each client's personal context, emphasizing that the same planetary placements can play out uniquely depending on these critical factors.

Divine Choice in Guidance

An essential, spiritual concept in BNN is the belief that practitioners are divinely chosen to guide certain individuals. The interaction is seen as an act of destiny, where the practitioner is not randomly offering advice, but is chosen by a higher power to aid someone's journey. This underscores the importance of responsibility, humility and care in practice. It implies that every consultation is an opportunity for both guidance and growth, as it aligns with a larger cosmic plan.

The Approach to Logic and Faith in Practice

Another common doubt practitioners encounter is the desire to apply logic to every principle in BNN, often in an attempt to validate the science. BNN encourages practitioners not to engage in excessive skepticism but rather to gain experience by applying the system in multiple charts. As practitioners deepen their understanding, they are likely to observe the nuances of BNN unfold across different lives, enhancing faith through practice rather than theory alone.

This experiential learning approach suggests that by consistently applying the BNN system, the practitioner will witness a pattern of accuracy and depth in readings. This approach advocates openness and curiosity, guiding practitioners to experience BNN's effectiveness before forming conclusions.

Theory of Evolution - How are we Born?

The theory of **Samkhya Darshan** provides a profound understanding of the origin of the soul, the evolution of life and the connection between consciousness and material existence. According to Samkhya, everything in existence is an interplay of **Purusha** (pure consciousness) and **Prakriti** (material nature), which together form the foundation of the universe.

Let's break down how the **theory of evolution** and **astrology** are connected in this context:

Purusha and Prakriti:

- **Purusha**: Pure consciousness, often referred to as the **soul** or **Atma**, is the essence of all beings. It is passive, still and the observer of the material world. Astrologically, **Purusha** can be symbolized by the **Sun**, as the Sun represents the soul, the source of life and consciousness.
- **Prakriti**: Material nature or the cosmic energy that manifests into the physical world. This is the dynamic force that gives rise to all forms of life. It comprises of the **Manas, Ahamkara and The Three Gunas (Sattva, Rajas and Tamas)** The Moon can represent **Manas** (mind), which is an aspect of Prakriti. The Moon governs emotions, thoughts and mental processes.

The Duality of the Mind (Manas):

- **Manas**: It is the mental and emotional aspect of Prakriti. The **Manas** (mind) is symbolized by the **Moon** and its two extremes are represented by **Rahu** and **Ketu**.

Rahu: The ascending lunar node, associated with illusion, desire and worldly attachments. It signifies the material, unfulfilled desires and past karma.

Ketu: The descending lunar node, signifying detachment, liberation and the fruits of past karmas. It is the point where the soul begins to seek enlightenment and liberation.

These extremes show the soul's attachments and the forces that it must transcend to reach liberation.

Ahamkara (Ego or Sense of Self):

- **Ahamkara** represents the ego or the sense of self, which is the construction of identity. It is the principle by which the soul associates with the body and mind. The **Mars** energy represents **Ahamkara** and Mars is also the Deh or Body the physical form.
- Ahamkara helps in the identification with physical form, which ultimately leads to the cycle of birth and death (reincarnation) as the ego continuously tries to fulfill desires.

Formation of Jeeva (Individual Soul):

- The **Jeeva** is the soul that is influenced by Purusha (consciousness) and Prakriti (material nature). It is represented by **Jupiter** in astrology, symbolizing knowledge, wisdom and expansion. Jupiter brings the soul into the cycle of reincarnation, helping it grow through the experiences of life.
- The **Jeeva** is the combination of consciousness and material existence (Purusha and Prakriti), which is necessary for the soul to experience karmic cycles.

The Three Gunas:

- **Satva**, **Rajas** and **Tamas** are the three qualities or **Gun** that exist within Prakriti. These gunas influence the nature of the soul's actions, thoughts and evolution.
    - **Satva**: Purity, harmony, knowledge and goodness. The **Sun** can be associated with Satva, as it brings light and clarity.
    - **Rajas**: Passion, activity and desire. It is the principle of action and motion. **Mars** and **Mercury** can be associated with Rajas due to their connection with activity and the desire to achieve goals.
    - **Tamas**: Inertia, ignorance and darkness. **Saturn** is the planet that symbolizes **Tamas**, as it represents limitation, delay and the constraints that the soul must overcome to evolve.

Karma and Reincarnation:

- The soul is born with the **karma** (actions) accumulated from past lives. Depending on the nature of this karma, the soul may take a form influenced by one of the three **Gun**:
    - If **Satva** predominates, the soul is born in an environment conducive to peace, wisdom and spiritual growth.
    - If **Rajas** predominates, the person may be born with desires, attachments and ambitions that push them to fulfill worldly pursuits.
    - If **Tamas** predominates, the individual may face ignorance, apathy, or inertia, hindering progress.
- **Saturn** represents the manifestation of **Karma**, as it shows the limitations and lessons the soul must learn to evolve.

The Cycle of Birth and Death:

- The soul's cycle of birth and death continues until it has worked through all its karmas and transcended all the material desires. This can be seen in astrology when the planets align in specific ways to reveal past-life influences and current life lessons. The **Node positions** (Rahu and Ketu), along with the placement of **Saturn**, show the patterns of karmic debts.
- The goal is for the soul to stop generating new karma and cease to be influenced by the gunas. **Saturn** and **Rahu** show where the soul is still working through the effects of past karma.

Why are we born ?

To bear fruits of Past Life Karma.....

The Concept of Karma and Rebirth
In the realm of Astrology, Karma plays a significant role in shaping our lives. The question arises: Why are we born - to bear the fruits of our past life karma? The answer lies in the concept of karma and its connection to our past actions.

The Planet of Karma: Saturn
Saturn is considered the most important planet in the horoscope when it comes to karma. It is the planet that governs our past actions and their consequences. Saturn's position in our birth chart determines the type of karma we are born with and the lessons we need to learn in this lifetime.

Defining Karma
Karma is often misunderstood as simply being an action. However, karma is more than just an action; it is the intention behind the action that makes it a karma. Every

physical or mental action we perform with the intention of being the doer becomes a karma for us, producing a reaction that we will eventually have to experience.

Types of Karma

Sanchit Karma: Stored karma, represented by the **4th house**, which is the storage of all our past actions.

Prarabhdha Karma: Unavoidable karma, represented by the 6th house, which is the karma that we are born with and must experience in this lifetime.

Agami Karma: Planned karma, represented by the **12th house**, which is the karma that we plan to do in our thought process.

Kriyamana Karma: Action done in this birth that determines our next life, represented by the **10th house.**

Dridha Karma: Fixed karma, which is determined by the **dasha** (planetary periods)

Adrida karma: which is determined by the **gochar** (transits).

Dridha-Adridha Karma: which is determined by the **Yogas** in horoscope

We are born to bear the fruits of our past life karma because of the law of cause and effect. Our past actions, driven by our intentions, have consequences that we must experience in this lifetime. This is the fundamental principle of karma. By experiencing the consequences of our past actions, we can learn and grow and ultimately, achieve spiritual liberation.

"A child is born on that day and at that hour when the celestial rays are in mathematical harmony with his individual karma. His horoscope is a challenging portrait, revealing his unalterable past and its probable future results. But only men of intuitive wisdom can rightly interpret the natal chart : these are few."

"Charlatans" have brought the ancient science to its present disrepute. Astrology is too vast, both mathematically and philosophically, to be rightly grasped except by men of profound understanding. If ignoramuses misread the heavens and see there a scrawl instead of script, that is to be expected in this imperfect world. One should not dismiss the wisdom with the "wise".

Parmahansa Yogananda

Planetary Alliances and Conflicts: The Soul's Spiritual Journey

The concept of **planetary friendship and enmity** in Vedic astrology is deeply tied to both **mythological** and **philosophical** views. The relationships between the planets are often framed as lessons, challenges, or pathways that the soul experiences during its journey through life. These relationships aren't just seen as symbolic but also as energetic forces influencing the individual's growth, behavior and destiny. The **philosophical** interpretation of planetary relationships gives a deeper insight into the **spiritual journey** of the soul, including its struggles, desires and ultimate goal of **moksha** (liberation).

Here's a **philosophical approach** to the relationships of planets, as you mentioned, along with some detailed explanations:

Sun and Saturn: Enemies

- **Sun** represents the **Atma** (soul), the source of consciousness, energy and spiritual purpose. The Sun's primary goal is the achievement of **moksha**—liberation from the cycle of birth, death and karma. It seeks enlightenment and the purification of the soul.
- **Saturn** is the planet of **karma**, discipline, time and limitation. Saturn represents the **karmic cycles**—the consequences of past actions that bind the soul to the material world. Until the soul works through its karma, it cannot attain liberation.
- **Enmity** between Sun and Saturn exists because **Saturn represents the obstacles (karma) that** prevent the soul from reaching its ultimate goal of

liberation. **Saturn's energy keeps the soul bound** to the material realm, constantly reminding it of its unfinished karmic duties, making it a roadblock on the soul's path to **moksha**. The Sun (soul) seeks freedom, while Saturn (karma) seeks to bind the soul to material existence.

Sun and Venus: Enemies

- **Venus** represents **bhoga** (enjoyment, indulgence, sensual pleasures), material desires and comforts. It is the planet of **luxury** and **attachment** to the pleasures of the world.
- The **Sun**, as the soul's guiding force, desires to transcend material desires in pursuit of **spiritual growth** and liberation. Venus, which governs indulgence, sensuality and attachment to worldly pleasures, is a **roadblock** in this spiritual journey.
- **Enmity** exists because **Venus** (indulgence) distracts the soul from its higher purpose, pulling it into **attachment** to the physical world and delaying its evolution. **Venus** is concerned with enjoyment, whereas the **Sun** seeks liberation, which can only be attained when material attachments are overcome.

Sun and Rahu: Enemies

- **Rahu**, representing material desires, **illusion** and **unfulfilled cravings**, is the **north node** of the Moon. It is a shadow planet that represents **desires without boundaries**, attachment to the material world and often leads to **illusion** and **maya** (the illusion of the material world).
- The **Sun**, as the soul's center, seeks **clarity** and **truth** and its purpose is liberation through understanding and wisdom.
- **Enmity** exists because **Rahu** leads to an **unquenchable thirst for worldly experiences**, an

energy that drags the soul further away from its spiritual goals. While the **Sun** seeks spiritual illumination, **Rahu** promotes **material delusion** and obsession with desires.

Venus and Ketu: Enemies

- **Ketu** is the planet of **detachment**, **spirituality** and **moksha**. It is the tail of the **dragon**, representing the **past life karma** that the soul has accumulated and it is a key planet for **spiritual liberation**.
- **Venus**, on the other hand, is the planet of **bhoga** (material enjoyment) and attachment to the sensory world.
- **Enmity** exists because **Venus** is focused on indulgence and attachment to material pleasures, which distract the soul from **spiritual growth**. **Ketu**, the planet of detachment, calls for renunciation and a shift away from material attachments, opposing Venus' inclination toward enjoyment and indulgence.

Venus and Rahu: Friends

- **Rahu** and **Venus** share a common focus on **materiality** and indulgence. While **Venus** is the planet of sensual pleasures and luxury, **Rahu** represents desires that lead to obsession and materialism.
- **Friendship** exists because both planets work in the direction of **material desires** and pleasures, even if Rahu's approach is more extreme and irrational. **Rahu**, in its desire to break boundaries, often brings people into experiences of indulgence that are unorthodox, while **Venus** shows the path of pleasure and luxury.
- This dynamic is seen in individuals who seek **pleasure** in unconventional ways or have **unethical indulgences**, driven by both Venus'

attraction to enjoyment and Rahu's obsession with limitless desires.

Mercury and Moon: Enemies

- **Mercury** represents **intelligence, logic, communication** and **mental clarity**. Mercury's focus is on **disciplined thinking**, reasoning and analysis.
- **Moon**, the planet of **emotions, mind** and **subjectivity**, often wavers between moods, instincts and emotional responses. It represents the subconscious mind and emotional fluctuations.
- **Enmity** exists because **Mercury** seeks **clarity** and **focus**, while **Moon** is associated with the mind's tendency to **waver**, leading to distraction and lack of concentration. **Mercury** dislikes the **emotional instability** and subjectivity of the **Moon**, as the mind seeks to think and analyze clearly, while the Moon's influence is often irrational and swayed by emotions.

Mars and Mercury: Enemies

- **Mars** represents **action, energy, assertiveness** and **drive**. It is the planet of **impulsive action** and often acts without thinking.
- **Mercury**, on the other hand, is the planet of **intelligence, thoughtful analysis** and **communication**. It represents the mind's capacity to reason and plan.
- **Enmity** exists because **Mars** is all about **immediate action**, while **Mercury** wants to **analyze first** and then act. **Mars**'s impulsive nature often leads to hasty decisions, whereas **Mercury** seeks careful planning and thinking, which can be frustrating for the more **impulsive Mars**. The tension between action without thought (Mars) and intelligent planning (Mercury) creates this enmity.

Planets	Friends	Equals/Netural	Enemies
Sun	Moon, Mars, Jupiter	Mercury, Ketu	Venus, Saturn, Rahu
Moon	Sun, Mercury	Mars, Venus, Saturn, Ketu, Jupiter	Rahu
Mars	Sun, Moon, Jupiter	Venus, Saturn, Ketu	Mercury, Rahu
Mercury	Sun, Venus	Jupiter, Saturn, Mars, Rahu	Moon, Ketu
Jupiter	Sun, Moon, Mars	Saturn, Ketu	Mer, Venus, Rahu
Venus	Mercury, Saturn	Jupiter, Rahu, Mars	Sun, Moon, Ketu
Saturn	Mer, Venus	Jupiter, Rahu	Sun, Moon, Mars, Ketu
Rahu	Mercury, Venus	Jupiter, Saturn, Moon, Ketu	Sun, Mars
Ketu	Sun, Jupiter	Mercury, Moon, Mars, Rahu	Venus, Saturn

Compatibility with Other Systems

An additional consideration is whether one should adhere to BNN exclusively or integrate other astrological systems. BNN is not meant to replace other systems but to complement them. A practitioner with a foundational understanding of Vedic astrology or other methods will find that mastering BNN only enriches their insights.

Through BNN's unique framework and perspective on planetary interactions, a practitioner can reach similar conclusions as in other systems, but potentially with added simplicity and directness. Mastery of BNN can act as a filter, helping the practitioner synthesize insights from different systems to provide a holistic and multidimensional reading. The recommendation, therefore, is to start with BNN to gain mastery and later integrate other systems as the practitioner's skill and understanding evolve.

BNN Answers - Why we do What we do?

Bhrigu Nandi Nadi (BNN) stands out as an astrological approach that delves deeply into the *why* behind life's patterns and actions. While modern astrological practices like KP Astrology, Nadi Astrology and even classical Vedic Astrology often focus on delivering highly accurate predictions through intricate analysis of planetary positions, nakshatras and sub-lords, they may leave unanswered the question of *why* events and tendencies arise in the first place. In contrast, BNN prioritizes understanding the karmic and metaphysical influences behind these actions, answering *why we do what we do* in a way that reaches beyond surface predictions.

The Unique Depth of BNN

BNN goes beyond simply forecasting outcomes; it reveals the underlying karmic and spiritual layers that drive life events. Through its unique framework, BNN provides insights into the larger cosmic forces influencing one's journey, rooted in past life karma, spiritual imprints and karmic influences that shape the soul's path. This connection to karmic influences and metaphysical principles is what allows BNN to explore the *why* of each situation, offering individuals a clearer understanding of the deeper reasons behind their choices, tendencies and experiences.

BNN and Karmic Influences

BNN recognizes that our life paths are guided by prior life actions and choices. These karmic imprints, along with the planetary influences, reveal how our past-life karma plays a role in shaping the present. BNN interprets planetary configurations as mirrors of these influences, helping practitioners decode the *why* with a focus on karmic lessons and soul evolution. This karmic approach is unique to BNN, as it aims to interpret astrology not only as a tool for predicting events but as a map for understanding one's karmic journey.

How This Book Approaches BNN

This book attempts to provide a comprehensive overview of BNN's ability to answer the *why* in astrology. By explaining the concepts, tools and techniques unique to BNN, the book seeks to bring clarity to how karma and metaphysical principles manifest in the astrological chart. Through in-depth explanations and practical applications, the book offers practitioners insights into the spiritual dimensions of astrology, emphasizing BNN's capacity to guide not just through life's events but through life's purpose. While other astrological systems may excel in providing the *what* and *when*, BNN excels in illuminating the *why*. Its approach honors astrology as a profound science, one that connects individuals with their karmic history and spiritual path.

Key Aspects of Bhrigu Nandi Nadi

In Bhrigu Nandi Nadi, there are several key aspects that play a crucial role in understanding an individual's life and destiny.

Combination of Planets

One of the most important aspects of Bhrigu Nandi Nadi is the combination of planets. Each planet has its own nature, property, or karaktatwa, which influences the outcome of the combination.

Jupiter: The Jeeva Lagna

Jupiter is considered the Jeeva Lagna, or the planet of life. When Jupiter combines with other planets, it produces a specific result, regardless of the house it is formed in. However, it is essential to consider the Rashi (zodiac sign) in which the combination is formed.

Categorization of Planets

Planets are divided into three categories in Bhrigu Nandi Nadi:

- **Destiny Makers:** These planets shape an individual's destiny and include:
    - Sun
    - Mercury
    - Venus
- **Destiny Breakers/Obstructors:** These planets can obstruct or break an individual's destiny and include:
    - Rahu
    - Ketu

- **Destiny Modifiers:** These planets modify an individual's destiny and include:
  - Mars
  - Moon
  -

Special Roles of Jupiter and Saturn

Jupiter: Jeeva Karak: Jupiter is considered the planet of life or the individual self and plays a crucial role in shaping an individual's destiny.

Saturn: Karma Karak: Saturn is considered the planet of karma and plays a vital role in determining an individual's past life karma and its consequences.

Dev Grah and Danav Grah: Understanding Their Roles
In BNN, there are two types of planets: Dev Grah and Danav Grah. These planets play a crucial role in shaping an individual's life and destiny.

Dev Grah: Spiritual and Pious Gains
Dev Grah includes the following planets:
- Jupiter
- Sun
- Moon
- Mars
- Ketu

These planets do not provide materialistic gains, but instead, offer spiritual or pious gains. They are associated with a more spiritual and introspective approach to life.

Danav Grah: Materialistic Gains and Desires
Danav Grah includes the following planets:
- Saturn
- Mercury
- Venus
- Rahu

These planets are associated with materialistic gains and desires. They are responsible for fulfilling an individual's desires and providing them with worldly comforts.

Combination of Dev Grah and Danav Grah
When Dev Grah and Danav Grah combine, the results can be significant. Here are some key combinations:

Dev + Dev combination: This combination leads to a satvik life, where an individual prioritizes spiritual growth over materialistic gains. They may not experience materialistic gains, but their life will be filled with spiritual fulfillment.

Danav+ Dev Combination: Saturn + Venus or Mercury: This combination is essential for good materialistic gains. Saturn must combine with either Venus or Mercury to provide an individual with wealth and prosperity.
Exceptions and Special Combinations

There are some exceptions and special combinations to note:
Jupiter and Saturn: This combination is known as Mahabhagya yoga, which is a highly auspicious combination.
Jupiter + Mercury: This combination is beneficial, but the results may vary depending on the individual's birth chart.
Mars + Moon: This combination does not provide good results, as Mars and Moon get debilitated in each other's signs.
Sun + Mercury: This combination is beneficial and provides good results.

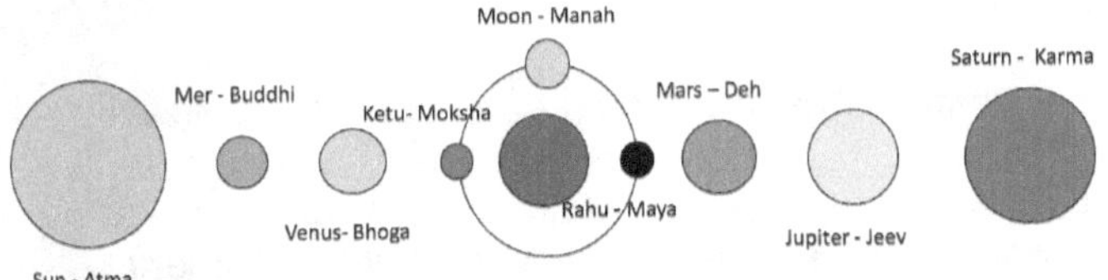

The Two Circles of Planets: Understanding Their Roles
The planets are divided into two circles: the Outer Circle
and the Inner Circle.

Outer Circle: Karma, Jeev and Deh
The Outer Circle consists of the following planets:
- Saturn (Karma)
- Jupiter (Jeev)
- Mars (Deh)

These planets are associated with karma, life and the
physical body.
- Moon (Man)
- Rahu (Maya)
- Ketu (Moksha)

These planets are associated with the mind, illusions and
liberation.

Inner Circle: Atma, Buddhi and Bhoga
The Inner Circle consists of the following planets:
- Sun (Atma)
- Mercury (Buddhi)
- Venus (Bhoga)

These planets are associated with the soul, intellect and
materialistic gains. They are considered destiny makers, as
they shape an individual's destiny and provide materialistic
benefits.

Combinations with Destiny Makers
When the planets from the Outer Circle combine with the
destiny makers from the Inner Circle

Saturn + Destiny Maker: Material benefits due to past life
karma.

Jupiter + Destiny Maker: Material benefits due to free will.

Jupiter + Saturn + Destiny Maker: Free will and karma
support each other, leading to enjoyment and fulfillment.

Mars + Destiny Maker: Enmity, hardships, ego, harassment and hastiness.

Moon + Destiny Maker: Deprivation or change in the effect, loss and blame.

Rahu + Destiny Maker: Illusions, reversals, or unethical means.

Ketu + Destiny Maker: Rejections, dissatisfaction and depression.

Directional Chart - Grouping of Planets

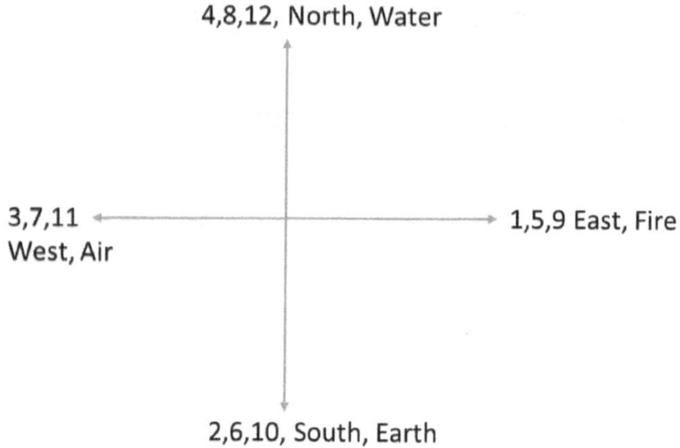

Key Points for Creating a Directional Chart and Grouping of Planets:

1. Grouping Planets by Signs, Not Houses:
In this system, planets are placed in groups based on signs rather than houses. The planets are categorized as per their positions in the signs 1, 5, 9; 2, 6, 10; 3, 7, 11; and 4, 8, 12.

2. Ascending Order of Degrees:
Arrange the planets within each group in ascending order of their degrees. This helps identify the significance of each planet's position relative to the others in the sign.

3. Planets Behind (Background):
Planets that are behind in degrees represent the native's past experiences or history. These planets show influences that have already been established.

4. Planets Ahead (Plan and Action):
Planets ahead in degrees indicate the future action plan and decisions that will be made by the native. They reflect where the person is headed.

5. Planets Opposite (Modifications/Support):
Planets positioned opposite each other modify the results of the other planet through aspects. A benefic planet can

improve the outcome of a difficult combination, while a malefic planet can worsen an already challenging situation.

6. Retrograde Planets Considered Twice:
For a retrograde planet, it will be taken into account twice in the directional chart. First, at its original placement in the sign as per the Lagna chart and second, in the previous sign, as retrograde planets influence both. When arranging the planets in ascending degrees within the directional chart, the retrograde planet will be included twice – once in its original position and once in the previous sign.

7. For exchange of planets (Parivartana Yoga), the planets involved in the exchange will also be considered twice in the directional chart, similar to the treatment of retrograde planets.

This means:
1. Each planet will be placed once in its original sign (where it resides in the Lagna chart).
2. The same planet will also be placed in the sign it exchanges with (as per the Parivartana Yoga).

Important: Rahu and Ketu are not considered as retrograde planets because their motion is generally retrograde by nature. A retrograde planet, by definition, is one that moves directly (forward) initially, then goes retrograde (backward) and eventually returns to direct motion. Since Rahu and Ketu are always retrograde in their movement, they do not follow this pattern of changing direction and hence, are not classified as retrograde planets

Example

Horoscope with no exchange and no retrograde planets

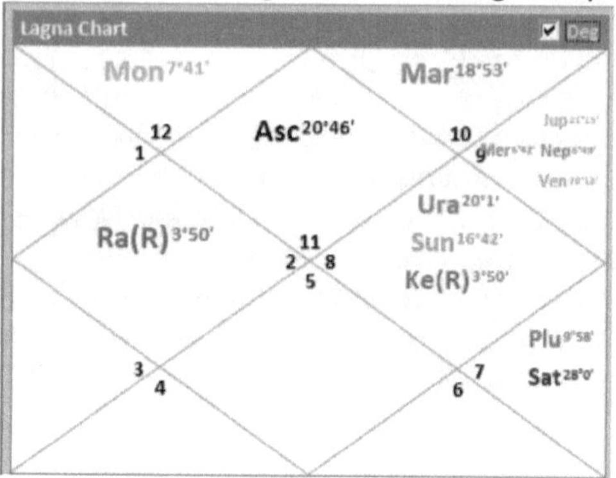

Directional Chart

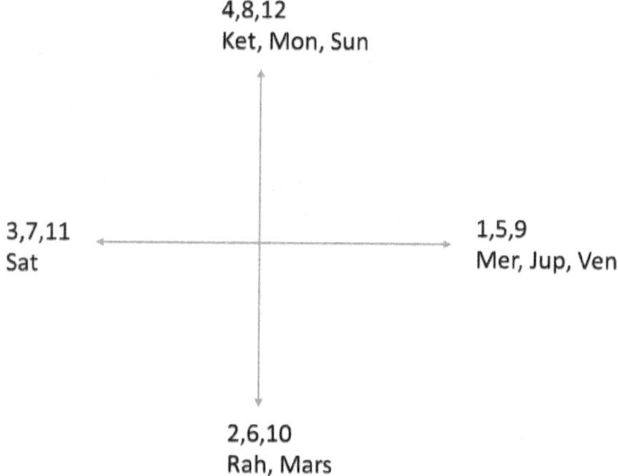

Example : With Retrograde Planets

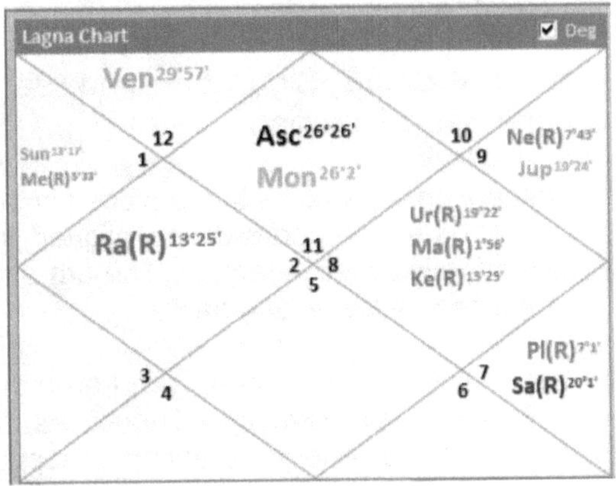

Retrograde Planets : Sat, Mar, Mer

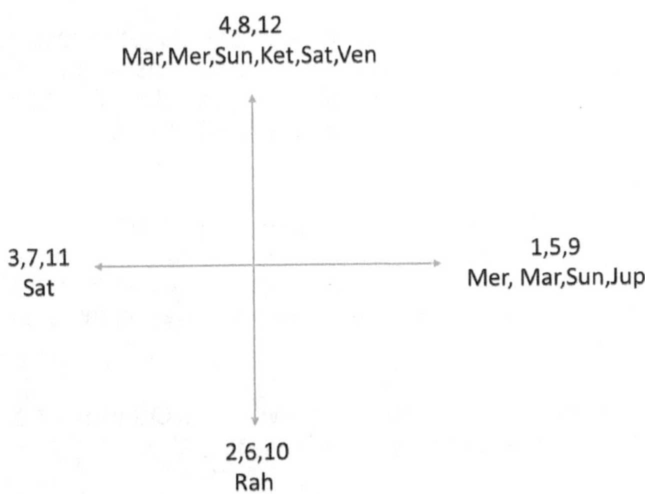

Rules for Interpretation

1. Planets in the Same Sign, 5th and 9th are Considered in the Same Direction

Planets in the same sign, as well as those placed in the 5th and 9th from each other, are considered aligned in the same direction, reinforcing their energies. The 5th and 9th houses are trine houses, representing harmony.

Example: If Mars is in Aries and Jupiter is in Leo (5th sign from Aries), both planets will have an influence as if they are in the same directional energy, creating a supportive synergy.

2. Planets in the 2nd, 12th and 7th Modify the Significations of the Matter Under Consideration

Planets in these positions (relative to the planet in focus) will impact or modify the main issue being considered in a chart. The 2nd house represents the next step, the 12th house the past or background and the 7th house external factors.

Example: If considering the 1st house (self), a planet in the 2nd house will show the next course of action, a planet in the 12th may reveal hidden factors and the planet in the 7th house will show external influence, like partners or competitors.

3. If Two or More Planets are Within a Quarter of a Star, They are Powerfully Associated

When planets are within a close range of a star (nakshatra)
- specifically, within a quarter (pada) of the same nakshatra
- they strongly influence each other's significations.

Example: If Venus and Mercury are both in the first quarter of Rohini Nakshatra, they will amplify each other's qualities, possibly showing artistic talents or intellectual pursuits related to Venus and Mercury.

4. Next in Order: Planets in the Same Star (Nakshatra)

Even if planets are in different quarters but within the same nakshatra, they are still considered to be influencing each other, but with slightly less intensity than if they were in the same quarter.

Example: If Sun and Saturn are both in Ashwini Nakshatra but in different quarters, there will still be an association between them, with Sun's authority being tempered by Saturn's discipline.

5. Next: Planets in the Same Sign

Planets within the same zodiac sign will influence each other, though not as strongly as if they were in the same nakshatra or quarter.

Example: If Moon and Mars are both in Taurus, they will still have some influence on each other, with Moon's emotions potentially fueling Mars' aggressive energy.

6. Degree-Wise: A Planet Ahead Gives Its Significations to the Planet Behind

A planet that is more advanced in degrees within a sign influences the planet that is following it (at a lesser degree). The planet ahead transfers its qualities to the planet behind.

Example: If Mercury is at $25°$ in Gemini and Venus is at $20°$, Mercury will pass its communication-oriented energy to Venus, possibly enhancing Venus's diplomatic and relationship-oriented behavior.

7. Planet in the 2nd: The Next Step in Action and Plan

The planet placed in the 2nd house from the main planet in consideration indicates what comes next in the sequence of events.

Example: If considering the Moon in the 1st house (signifying emotions), a planet in the 2nd house would suggest how these emotions lead to subsequent actions or decisions.

8. Planet in the 12th: The Background of the Matter, History

Explanation: A planet in the 12th house represents past influences, hidden aspects, or the background behind the issue under consideration.

Example: If Saturn is in the 12th from the Sun, it could indicate past responsibilities or restrictions that are influencing current circumstances regarding authority or personal growth (Sun).

9. Planets in the 2nd and 12th May Support or Oppose the Planet Under Consideration

The planets in the 2nd and 12th can either provide support or create obstacles for the planet under consideration. Their influence can help move things forward or cause delays.

Example: If Venus is in the 1st house and Mars is in the 2nd house, Mars may encourage boldness and passion. But if Saturn is in the 12th house, it may create some hesitations due to past limitations.

10. Planet in the 7th: Modification Due to External Influence

A planet in the 7th house (relative to the main planet) signifies external influences, partnerships, or opposition that will modify or impact the situation.

Example: If considering Mercury in the 1st house (self-expression), a planet like Jupiter in the 7th house would indicate external wisdom or advice influencing how one communicates or expresses ideas.

11. Planets in the Same Direction: Yoga Phala (Combined Results)

When planets are aligned in the same direction (as mentioned in point 1, including the 5th and 9th houses), they form a combination that produces a specific outcome (yoga phala).

Example: If Sun and Jupiter are in the 1st and 9th houses respectively, they create a beneficial yoga, leading to wisdom and prosperity in leadership roles.

12. A Retrograde Planet Influences the Previous Sign and the 12th House from Itself
When a planet is retrograde, it exerts its influence on the sign before it and the 12th house from its current position, acting as if it has "stepped back" into the previous sign.
Example: If Mars is retrograde in Taurus, its energy will also affect Aries (the sign before) and the house in which Aries is placed, leading to influences related to past actions or unresolved issues.

13. If a retrograde planet is under the influence of Rahu or Ketu: no effect
A retrograde planet's impact is usually diminished when it falls under the axis or influence of Rahu or Ketu, which disrupts the planet's normal functioning.
Example: If Jupiter is retrograde and aspected by Rahu, its ability to give its results related to wisdom, wealth, or children may not manifest as expected.

14. The results of a retrograde planet manifest in the later part of its transit, except for Saturn

Retrograde planets typically give their results in the later half of their transit through a sign or house, but Saturn is an exception to this rule.

Example: A retrograde Venus in a natal chart might delay relationship matters or wealth until the later years of life.

15. Saturn gives results in the first part of its transit, but if related to Jupiter, results accrue later

Saturn, unlike other retrograde planets, shows results early in its transit unless it has a connection with Jupiter. In that case, its results will be delayed.

Example: A retrograde Saturn in the 10th house might bring career challenges early on, but if it's connected to Jupiter, success may come later in life.

16. An exalted planet indicates the strength of its karakatva (significations)

An exalted planet is in its best position, which means it can fully express its significations such as wealth, career, relationships, etc., in a strong and positive way.

Example: An exalted Moon in Taurus gives a person strong emotional stability and wealth through real estate or land.

17. A debilitated planet indicates the weakness of its karakatva (significations)

A debilitated planet, being in its weakest position, struggles to manifest its significations.

Example: A debilitated Mars in Cancer may result in weak energy levels or issues with assertiveness and self-confidence.

18. If there is a Parivartana Yoga (exchange of signs between two planets), two directional charts should be made

When two planets exchange signs, they influence each other's houses, creating a powerful yoga. Analyzing both planets and the houses they rule is essential.

Example: If Mercury is in Mars' sign (Aries) and Mars is in Mercury's sign (Gemini), their areas of influence - communication and energy - will significantly enhance each other.

19. Planets in the 3rd, 7th and 11th from any sign are referred to as "Modifiers" or in opposite direction
Planets in these positions alter or modify the significations of the house or planet they are connected with.
Example: If Venus is in the 7th house, it can modify relationships and partnerships by bringing in the qualities of harmony, love and balance.

20. Planets in the 2nd, 6th and 10th from any sign indicate the native's action plan
These positions are related to efforts and work. Planets here indicate what actions the native will take to achieve goals.
Example: Mars in the 10th house can drive a person toward career success through hard work, determination and assertiveness.

21. Planets in the 4th, 8th and 12th from any sign indicate the native's past experiences
These houses relate to deeper, subconscious influences and karmic experiences. Planets here show past life influences or deep-rooted experiences that shape the present.
Example: The Moon in the 12th house can indicate past emotional traumas or spiritual experiences that influence a person's inner life.

How to Analyze: Select the subject for analysis and consider the relevant karaka planet
For analysis, focus on the key planet that rules over the area of life you want to study Example: If analyzing career, focus on Saturn (as the karaka for profession and hard work).

From the chosen planet, count 1st, 5th, 9th, 3rd, 7th, 11th and 2nd, 12th places and conjoin the planets positioned there degree-wise

Identify the planets in these key positions relative to the chosen karaka planet and combine their significations based on their degrees for interpretation.

For Rahu and Ketu, only consider the 1st, 5th, 9th and 12th houses

Sun

In astrology, the Sun is considered a Deva, or deity, representing our divinity, unity and central purpose in life. It symbolizes the light that we possess and aspire to expand.

The Sun as Atma: The Soul

The Sun is naturally associated with the Atma, or soul and is considered a Jeev Atma karak planet. It represents the cosmic intelligence, pure consciousness, or the enlightened mind.

Positive Traits of a Well-Placed Sun

A well-placed Sun in a birth chart can bring the following positive traits:

- Intelligence
- Perception
- Strength of will and character
- Endurance
- Stamina
- Vitality
- Positive spirit
- Direction
- Courage
- Conviction
- Confidence
- Leadership
- Independence
- Straight-forwardness

The Sun and the Heart

The Sun rules the heart and its nature in a chart reveals who we truly are in our hearts. It shows how we are with ourselves, in ourselves and by ourselves.

The Sun and Self-Manifestation

The Sun represents our sense of self and indicates the level of our self-manifestation. It shows where we shine, how we shine and in what we shine.

The Two Faces of the Sun

The Sun can represent two different aspects of our personality:

- Lower Level: Ego, power, prestige, fame, honor, respect, authority and control.
- Higher Level: Our soul, aspirations, creativity, seeking for light and truth and integrity.

The Sun and the Search for True Self

The Sun represents our true Self and is associated with the great enquiry "Who am I?" This inner search is the real basis for the psychology of astrology.

The Sun: Its Significance and Karakatwas in Astrology

The Sun is a fixed point in our solar system and all other planets revolve around it. Similarly, in a family, the family head is the central figure and in our culture, the father is often designated as the head. Therefore, the Sun is given the karakatwa (significator) of father.

The Sun is also associated with leadership, as it is the center of our solar system. In a nation, the leader or prime minister is the central figure and the Sun is given the portfolio of leader or minister.

The Sun's gravitational force keeps the planets in their orbits, preventing them from colliding with each other. Similarly, in the human body, the bones provide stability and balance to the organs. Therefore, the Sun is also given the karakatwa of bones.

The Sun is a luminous planet that gives light to all other beings and planets. Without light, nothing is visible and the Sun is given the karakatwa of eyes (right eye). The Sun's light is non-discriminatory, shining equally on all, regardless of wealth, social status, or species.

The part of the human body that receives the most sunlight is the head and inside the head is the brain. Therefore, both the head and brain are assigned to the Sun.

The Sun is associated with energy, activeness and vitality. Whenever there is sunlight, the body is active and energetic and whenever there is darkness, the body is passive. The Sun is essential for survival and many plants flower and produce food only in its presence. Therefore, the Sun is also given the karakatwa of life (Atma).

Jeev Karaktatwa of Sun : Father, Son, Atma (Soul)

Ajeev Karaktatwa of Sun

Personal Traits
Pious, Dignity, Self Respect, Ambition, Authority, Charisma, Clarity, Confidence, Consciousness, Courage, Creativity, Determination, Discipline, Ego, Energy, Enlightenment, Fatherhood, Focus, Glory, Honour, Leadership, Light, Inner fire, Masculine energy, Mobility, Power, Prosperity, Self-esteem, Self-expression, Self-realisation, Spirituality, Strength, Success, Vision, Vitality, Will power

Professional and Social Status
Administrator, Fair, Generous, Reliable, Popular, Success, Name & Fame, Prestige, Status, Promotion, Government, Govt. Jobs, Ministers, Politics, Administration, Government affairs

Emotions and Actions
Anger, Courage, Sacrifice, Punishment for betterment, Honesty

Divine and Cosmic Associations
Male, Bhrama, Shiva, Vishnu, Tejas, Pitta, Lotus colour, Gold colour, Fire

Sun: Other Significations

Category	Description
Planetary Cabinet	King
Lordship	Leo
Exaltation	Aries
Debilitation	Libra
Friends	Moon, Mars, Jupiter
Enemies	Saturn, Venus
Neutral	Mercury
Aspects	7th
Dasha Period	6 years

Time per sign	30 days
Direction	East
Vastu	Worship Place, Circle Shape, East, Fire Element, Copper Metal, Ruby, Orange Colour, Right side Window, Govt. Buildings, Royal Palaces, Forts, Forests, Open Fields, Courtyards allowing plenty of light, deserts
Mool Trikone	0-20° Leo
Sex	Male
Color	Orange
Guna	Sattva
Element	Fire
Varna	Kshatriya
Gemstone	Ruby
Metals	Gold, Copper
Energy	Tough, Noble
Dosha	Pitta
Chakra	Ajna/Third Eye
Height	Normal

Deity	Shiva
Nakshatras	Kritika, Uttar Phalguni, Uttar Ashada
Occupations	Administrators, Leaders, Politicians, Doctors
Body Parts	Vocal cords, Brain, Heart, Strength of bones, Upper spine, Vision, Head, Skeletal System
Nature & Personality	Royal Appearance, Golden Shine, Stout Body, Sparse Hair, Square shape, Well-proportioned body
Diseases	Heart problem, Problem related to bones
Food	Royal Food – Shahi Khana, Dry Fruits, 5-star food, Coffee, Wheat, Jaggery, Chapati, Roti, Poori, Upma, Bun, Bread, Biscuits, Pungent, Saffron, Pepper, Ginger, Cloves, Cinnamon, Cumin Seeds
Trees/Plants	Aak, bhilva, sandalwood, teakwood
Education	Political science, Social science, IAS/AFS, Medicine

Moon

Introduction to the Moon
The Moon is a Satvic or Spiritual planet and its influence on an individual's life is multifaceted. It is associated with faith, love, openness, humility, surrender, devotion, peace and happiness. The Moon also plays a significant role in childhood, procreation and inner happiness and is connected to intuition, comforts, well-being and inner calm.

Physical Characteristics and Movement
The Moon appears to be a bright, glowing orb in the night sky. It undergoes two distinct phases, known as Sukla Paksha and Krishna Paksha, which are closely observed in Indian astrology. The Moon's triple movement is a characteristic unique to it: it revolves around the Earth, rotates on its own axis and revolves around the Sun along with the Earth. This triple movement is a characteristic unique to the Moon. Along with the Sun, the Moon provides light and brightness to the Earth, although it only reflects the Sun's light.

Spiritual and Emotional Influence
The Moon makes individuals pliable, sensitive and contemplative and inspires them to do good for the sake of others. People with a strong, spiritual Moon often have a strong connection with traditional religion and may have had many monastic past lives. They tend to have sweet, tolerant and humane dispositions and are often saintly in nature. They are easy to be around and are the least critical, always tending to see the good in all.

Characteristics and Traits
A strong Moon in an individual's chart can indicate sensitivity, receptivity, a caring attitude towards others and a nurturing nature. It can also indicate emotional maturity, responsibility and the capacity to have a beneficial effect on society.

Physical Health and Associations

The Moon is responsible for the quality of blood, chest, stomach, lymph, lungs, left eye in a man and right eye in a woman, intestines, menstrual cycle, womb, nervous system, esophagus, glands and saliva. Its influence extends to the world's water resources, with approximately two-thirds of the planet's surface covered in water. The Moon's cycles have a direct impact on water levels, with a decrease in water levels observed during Amavasya and an increase during Purnima.

Influence on the Mind and Body The Moon's fast movement is mirrored in the human mind, which is constantly changing from moment to moment. This is why the Moon is said to govern the mind, or Manah, in Indian astrology. The Moon's influence on the mind is thought to shape our emotions, thoughts and behaviors. The Moon's cyclical pattern, taking approximately 28 days to complete one zodiac cycle, is mirrored in the menstrual cycle of women, which typically lasts around 28 days.

Association with Water and the Human Body

The Moon's association with water is also reflected in the human body, where it represents the fluid content, including blood. This connection is evident in the way blood pressure levels are affected by the Moon's cycles. For instance, individuals with low blood pressure tend to experience even lower levels during Amavasya, while those with high blood pressure may experience increased levels during Purnima.

Impact on Mental Health

The Moon's cycles also have a profound impact on mental health. Patients with mental disturbances often exhibit more erratic behavior patterns during Amavasya and Purnima, when the Moon is at its weakest and strongest points, respectively. Any adverse Moon position or strength can lead to fickle-mindedness, instability in decision-making and a lack of clarity.

Mythology and Additional Associations

The Moon's mythology reveals its association with cunningness and adultery, as it is said to have eloped with its guru's wife, Tara (Wife of Brihaspati), resulting in the birth of Mercury. The Moon is also linked to motherliness and nurturing and its cyclical pattern is mirrored in the menstrual cycle of women. The breasts, which symbolize a mother's ability to nourish her child, are considered a significator of the Moon. This connection extends to food and milk-related products, which are also attributed to the Moon's influence.

Beauty and Impermanence

The Moon's beauty is undeniable and its mesmerizing quality is reflected in its association with physical attractiveness. Individuals with a strong Moon in their horoscope are often known for their captivating presence, good imagination and appreciation for artistic beauty. The Moon's constant phase changes make it a symbol of impermanence and transience and easily perishable fruits and vegetables are attributed to the Moon's influence.

Vulnerability and Afflictions

The Moon is considered the most vulnerable planet in astrology and afflictions to it can have a profound impact on an individual's personality and emotional well-being. When the Moon is badly placed in a birth chart, it can lead to personality disorders, difficulties in relating to other people and emotional disturbances. In extreme cases, a badly placed Moon can even cause wrong imaginings, hallucinations and psychological turbulence, leading to numerous fears and phobias. This can also manifest as lunacy, bad heredity, poor family background, bad education and other traumas to the emotional nature.

Significator of Mother

The Moon is also considered the Significator of mother. This association can be understood by observing the similarities between a mother's behavior and the Moon's movements. Just as a mother's thoughts and eyes are always focused on her child, the Moon constantly follows the Earth, rotating around it without deviation, as if taking care of it like a child. This nurturing and protective quality of the Moon is reminiscent of a mother's love and care.

Significator of the Body The Moon is also associated with the human body in Indian astrology. As we previously discussed, the Moon has two distinct phases: Sukla Paksha and Krishna Paksha. During Amavasya, the Moon is not visible, but it gradually grows into a crescent shape and eventually becomes full on Purnima day. After that, it begins to diminish in size until it becomes invisible again. This cyclical pattern of growth and decay is reminiscent of the human body's development, from a single cell to a multi-cellular embryo, then to childhood, adulthood, old age and finally, death. The human body, like the Moon, undergoes phases of growth and decay, making the Moon the Significator of the body.

Gravitational Pull and Ayansha

The Moon is the closest celestial body to Earth and its gravitational pull is felt the strongest on our planet. This gravitational pull even causes a wobbling movement of the Earth, which is calculated as Ayansha in astrology. This unique relationship between the Moon and Earth has a profound impact on our lives and is reflected in the many ways the Moon influences our spiritual, emotional and physical well-being.

Influence of Other Planets

As a very sensitive and mutable planet, the Moon is easily influenced and can be overcome by other planetary energies. For example, Saturn's influence can darken or depress the Moon, leading to detachment and emotional numbness. Rahu's influence can cloud the Moon, causing individuals to lose power over their minds and leading to mental confusion and instability.

Jeev Karaktatwas : Mother, Elder sister, Mother in law

Ajeev Karaktatwas

Category	Details
Personal Traits	Mind, Imagination, Intuition, Memory, Mental clarity and focus, Mental peace, Subconscious, Psychic abilities, Adaptibility, Sensitivity, Receptivity, Calm/Fickle, Unpredictable, Changing, Cunningness, Lunatic, Mentally disturbed, , Peacefulness, Relaxation, Sleep
Professional and Social Status	Medicine, Medicines, Art, Creative expression, Food stuff, Nurturing, Comfort, Domestic life, Family, Feminine energy, Fertility
Emotions and Actions	Emotions, Feelings, Blames, act of cheating, loss, failures, dissatisfaction, eloping, Accusation, Dreaming
Divine and Cosmic Associations	Goddess Parvati, Water, White colours, All white things

Moon : Other Significations

Characteristics	Details
Lordship	Cancer
Exaltation	Taurus
Debilitation	Scorpio
Friends	Sun, Mercury
Enemies	None
Neutral	Mars, Venus, Jupiter, Saturn
Aspects	7th
Dasha Period	10 years
Time per sign	2.25 days
Direction	North West
Vastu	Water Bodies, Square shape, North west, water element, bell metal, pearl, left side windows, bathroom, Tap, Store Room, Vessels, Soap, Washing Machine, Fridge, Hotels, Washing place, Rivers, Water bodies, distilleries, swimming pools
Mool Trikone	3-30 Taurus
Sex	Female

Colour	White
Guna	Sattva
Element	Water
Varna	Vaishya
Gemstone	Pearl & Moonstone
Metals	Gold and Copper
Energy	Cold, humid, soft
Dosha	Kaph
Chakra	Ajna/ Third Eye
Height	Short
Diety	Shiva
Nakshatras	Rohini, Hasta, Shravan
Occupations	[Not specified]
Body Parts	Breast, Breast Milk, Menstrual cycle, Blood, B.P., Arteries, Urinary system, lungs, left eye
Nature & Personality	Circular shape, pleasing eyes, witty, unsteady, softness in appearance, dreamy look, attractive, stable/unstable mind

Diseases	Mental disorders, loss of memory, depression, anxiety, anemia, menstrual disorders in females,Cold, sinus, cough, bronchitis, measles, edema, swellings, loss of potency
Food	Generic for all food, milk and milk products, perishable food and vegitables, idly, dosa, rice items, ice food, tea and salt, curd, paneer, boiled rice, water
Mantra	Om Shram shreem shraum sah chandramasey namah
Trees & Plants	Palash, banana tree, drumsticks, paddy vegetables medicinal herbs
Education	Arts, astrology, psychology, chemistry, hotel, liquid/water related, dairy, grass, medicine, chemical, food, agriculture, juices, sea related, travel related

Mars

The Many Names of Mars
- Kuja
- Murugan
- Kartikeya
- Bhaum
- Krura
- Vakra
- Lohitanga
- Mangala
- Bhumiputra

The Energy of Mars
Mars is considered the embodiment of vital energy, electrifying all forms of terrestrial activities. It represents fire in all its forms, including:
- Flame hidden in matter (Urja or Energy)
- Tapas in Yogis (spiritual energy)
- Agni in Yagnas (ritual fire)
- Agni as Prakash (light)
- Agni as Ancha (Ushma) - Purusharth (energy for spiritual growth)
- Agni as Daha (burning energy)
- Agni as Agrani (Netritva - leadership energy)
- Agni as Kundalini (serpent fire or spiritual energy)
- Agni as Jatargani (stomach fire or digestive energy)

The Astrological Significance of Mars

In astrology, Mars is considered the son of Earth, or "Bhumiputra," as it is believed to have broken off from the Earth as a solid mass. This mythological origin story has led to Mars being associated with certain characteristics and objects.

Physical Characteristics

- Mars is composed of solid rocks and pointed structures, which is why rocks and sharp objects are attributed to Mars.
- Land property is also associated with Mars due to its connection to the Earth.

Family Ties

- As the son of Earth, Mars is considered a sibling to humans, who view the Earth as their mother.
- This familial connection leads to Mars being assigned the karakatwas (astrological influences) of brothers.

Visual Appearance

- When viewed from Earth, Mars appears reddish in color, which is why red-colored objects and red-cultured items are associated with Mars.
- Examples of these include blood, red coral and other red-hued objects.

Warfare and Industry

- In ancient times, humans used rocks to manufacture weapons and pointed objects, which were used for fighting. As a result, Mars represents all weapons, pointed objects and thorny plants.
- The production of fire from rocks is also attributed to Mars and injuries caused by fire are represented by Mars.
- Mars' association with sharp and pointed objects extends to surgical instruments, surgery, accidents and injuries.

Human Body

- Mars represents the strongest part of the human body, which is the teeth.

Asteroid Belt and Military Associations

- The asteroid belt between Mars and Jupiter is compared to an army of soldiers, with Mars as the commander-in-chief.
- As a result, Mars is associated with officer posts in the armed forces, bravery, adamancy, stamina and endurance.

Earth and Land Associations
- Mars also represents mud, which is the disintegration of stones. This association extends to bricks, agriculture, land business, stones, quarry and mud-related businesses.

Mars is a planet associated with various qualities, including power, strength, force, action, courage, aggression, will power, interests, passions, motivations and determination. When Mars is positively influenced, these qualities can manifest in a constructive manner, driving individuals to take bold action and pursue their goals with energy and enthusiasm.
However, when Mars is negatively influenced, these same qualities can manifest as competition, argument, domination, control, violence and injury.

Mars is also considered the general significator for various challenges, including injury, accident, conflict, enmity, misunderstandings, arguments and litigation. Its influence can create an environment of tension and strife, leading to conflicts and disputes with others.

Furthermore, Mars is associated with relationships, particularly with brothers, friends and alliances formed to achieve a common goal. It represents the energy and direction needed to apply energy towards a specific objective.

In addition to its influence on relationships and challenges, Mars is also linked to physical energy and vitality. It is associated with arms and muscles, providing individuals with physical power and strength. In males, Mars is also associated with sexual vitality and a weak Mars can cause impotence or a lack of manly characteristics.

Mars is a planet that represents our will, driving us to take immediate action and respond to situations instinctively. It is the planet of movement, prompting us to act quickly without hesitation, often relying on our reflexes to save us from harm.

Mars is also associated with our sense of right and wrong, guiding us to do what is correct and just. It is the planet of instinct, representing our primal brain and its automatic responses to stimuli.
In addition to its role in shaping our instincts and sense of morality, Mars is also linked to tools, weapons and machines, as well as their usage and development. It is the planet of work, effort and research, driving technological progress and innovation.

Mars is responsible for energizing us and motivating us to take action, but it does not necessarily provide the wisdom to use our power and energy wisely. Instead, it can sometimes lead us to regard power as an end in itself, rather than recognizing it as a means to achieve our goals.

Jeev Karaktatwas : Husband in female chart, Younger Brother, middle brother

Mars is associated with Body(Deh) in BNN
Jeev Karaktatwas : Husband in female chart, Younger Brother, middle brother

Mars is associated with Body(Deh) in BNN

Ajeev Karaktatwas

Category	Traits
Personal Traits	Egoistic, Selfish, Hasty, Stubborn, Foolish, Spendthrift, Adamant, Confident, Ambitious, Impatient, Impulsive, Disciplined, Enduring
Emotions/ Actions	Anger, Courage, Aggression, Domination, Quarrelsomeness, Irritation, Enmity, Failures, Power, Courageous, Brave, Competitive Spirit, Determination, Physical Strength, Fight, Adventure, Passion, Sexuality, Sexual Energy, Struggle, Violence, Disputes, Rivalaries, Masculine Energy, Bravery
Professional	Engineer, Police, Warrior, Machines, Technology, Metal
Social	Body (Deh), Cuts and wounds, Surgery, Debts, Construction, Litigation, Obstructions, Harassments
Divine & Cosmic	Kartikey (Hindu god),Fire, Heat in fire, Heat in blood, Red color, Areas where heat is produced, Rock, Energy

Mars : Other Significations

Characteristics	Details
Representations	Energy, Action, Aggression, Courage, Motivation, Anger, Argument, fights, conflicts, Physical strength, Younger siblings, Blood, Friends, Land, Logic, Surgery, Character, Weapons, men's sexual potency
Lordship	Aries and Scorpio
Exaltation and Debilitation	Capricorn (Exaltation), Cancer (Debilitation)
Friendships and Enemies	Friends: Sun, Moon, Jupiter; Enemy: Mercury; Neutral: Venus, Saturn
Aspects	7th, 4th, 8th
Dasha Period	7 years
Time per sign	45 days
Direction	South
Vastu	Kitchen, fireplace, Triangle shape, South, fire element, mined metals, coral, bedroom, bricks, oven, fire, energy meter, electronic transformer, meter boards, Electrical

	motors, Heaters, Stones, Stone pillars, Pillar Beams or Columns of the house, Minerals, Knife, Spears, Bullets, Sharp Items, Match box, Factory, Mines, Printing, Defence, Gym, Kitchen, Furnace, Battle fields, Operation theatre, Butcher shop
Mool Trikone	0-12deg Aries
Sex	Male
Colour	Red, Scarlet
Guna	Tamasik
Element	Fire
Varna	Kshatriya
Gemstone	Red coral
Metals	Iron
Energy	Male, Dry and fiery
Dosha	Pitta
Chakra	Solar plexus/Manipur
Height	Medium

Deity	Kartikeya/Hanuman
Nakshatras	Mrigshira, Chitra, Dhanishta
Occupations	Military men, police officers, Men in Uniform, builders, Chef/Cook, Mechanics, Designers
Body Parts	Blood, Reproductive organs, muscles, face, left ear, sense of taste, bone marrow, Eye brows, teeth, Blood, Semen, Bone Marrow, Bridge of nose, Red Blood Cells, Muscles, Capillaries, Testicles
Nature & Personality	Large stature, athletic and strong body, warlike attitude, independence, courage and self-respect
Diseases	Fever, Epilepsy, Piles (if connected with Rahu), tumors, high blood pressure, impotency, burns and cuts, body deformity, Bile, Wounds, Constipation, Thirst, Accident, Dog bite
Food	Spicy, Fried, Red chilli, hot food, tea, Any food which makes acid in stomach, Rich food, onion, garlic, hot chutney
Plants & Trees	Neem tree, thorn tree

Education	Techincal, Engineering, Mathematics, Agriculture, Manufacturing, Construction, Surgeon, Dentist, Army, Police, Security, Fire services, Mechanic, Carpainter, barber, Athlete, Sports, Body Stamina sports

Mercury

Mercury: The Swift and Social Planet

Mercury, the smallest planet in our solar system, is also the fastest, with a rapid movement that earns it a special significance in astrology.

Physical Appearance and Movement

Mercury appears greenish in color to the human eye. Its swift movement means it never strays more than 28 degrees or two houses from the Sun, resulting in more frequent retrogression and combustion than any other planet. However, some astrologers believe Mercury is immune to combustion.

Youthful Energy and Associations

Mercury's rapid movement makes it a planet associated with young people, who are often characterized by high energy levels. As the smallest planet, Mercury also represents children and the youthful spirit.

Social Nature and Companionship

Mercury's proximity to the Sun means it is always seeking companionship or a partner. It is uncomfortable with isolation and solitude. In human relationships, Mercury represents friendships and romantic relationships, particularly between young people who are close to each other.

Communication and Commerce

Mercury represents speech, communication and commerce on all levels, encompassing:
- Education and learning
- Writing and calculation
- Purposeful thinking and intellectual pursuits
- Trade and articles of trade, including money
- Post and messaging
- Computers and the internet

- Libraries and knowledge repositories
- Mobile phones and other communication device

Intellect and Mind
Mercury is associated with the intellect or informational mentality, influencing:
- The mind and nervous system
- Lungs and respiratory system
- Speech and expression

Characteristics and Traits
As the fastest-moving planet, Mercury is indicative of:
- Quick comprehension and reaction
- Changing character and adaptability
- Quicksilver thinking and expression
- Facility and ease in communication
- Rapid correlation of ideas and exchange of information
- Restlessness and a desire for mental stimulation

Life Skills and Abilities
Mercury's influence extends to:
- Degree of mental development in life
- Ability to manage daily affairs and mundane living
- Good research abilities and sound decision-making
- Effective communication and mutually beneficial friendships
- Ability to play games and engage in intellectual pursuits

Education and Clarity
Education is often likened to eyes, which require sunlight to see clearly. As the closest planet to the Sun, Mercury receives the maximum amount of sunlight, symbolizing the importance of clarity and illumination in the pursuit of knowledge. Therefore, Mercury is also known as the Vidya Karaka, or the planet of education and knowledge.

Connecting and Combining

As a combining or companion planet, Mercury represents the connections and bonds between individuals. In the human body, Mercury is associated with the fingers and hands, which connect people during handshakes and other forms of physical contact. Additionally, Mercury is linked to the throat, which connects the head and body, symbolizing the integration of thought and action.

Physical Associations

Mercury's proximity to the Sun means it receives the Sun's rays first, symbolizing its connection to the forehead, which is the part of the body that receives the most sunlight. Additionally, Mercury is associated with the skin, which is the part of the body that receives the most sunlight and is openly exposed.

Places of Gathering and Socialization

As a planet of combining or companionship, Mercury represents places where people gather and interact, such as:

- Libraries, Markets, Shopping malls, Parks, Party halls, Schools, Playgrounds. These places are all associated with Mercury's energy of connection and socialization.

Dual Nature

Mercury's unique position in the solar system, receiving complete sunlight on one side and complete darkness on the other, earns it the reputation as a planet of dual nature. This dual nature is also reflected in the attribution of eunuchs to Mercury, as they are often seen as embodying a mix of masculine and feminine qualities.

Wealth and Adaptability

While not a planet of wealth, Mercury is helpful in both acquiring and keeping wealth. Additionally, Mercury is a planet of adaptability, reflecting its ability to navigate and thrive in changing circumstances.

Jeev Karaks of Mercury:

Youngest Brother or Sister, Maternal Uncle, Father In Law, Friends (girlfriend or boyfriend), Second Wife, Mistress

Ajeev Karaks of Mercury

Category	Traits
Personal Traits	Intellect, Analytical skills, Communication, Versatility, Adaptability, Quickness, Agility, Youthfulness, Curiosity
Professional	Business, Commerce, Trade, Education, Learning, Accounting, Information technology (IT), Journalism, Writing and publishing, Negotiations, Problem solver
Social	Speech, Language, Diplomacy, Friend – male and female, Close friend, Social circle, Wit and humour
Divine and Cosmic Association	Astrology, Karak of Education, Gain of knowledge, Thoughts, Information, Tricks, Eloquence, Knowledge activity, Prince, Vishnu, Green colour
Emotions/ Actions	Emotional maturity, Sensitivity, Receptivity, Caring attitude, Nurturing nature, Emotional disturbances, Fickle-mindedness, Instability in decision-making, Lack of clarity

Mercury : Other Significations

Category	Details
Representation	Intelligence, Conscious Mind, Daughter, Sister, Business, Power of speech, Skill, Analytical ability, Wit, Sense of humor, Communication, Nervous system, Sense of Smell
Lordship	Gemini, Virgo
Exaltation	0-15 deg Virgo
Debilitation	Pisces
Aspects	7th
Dasha Period	17 years
Time per sign	30 days
Direction	North
Vastu	Play/Kids area,Arrow shape, North, Air element, quick, Silver, Emarald, Green colour, Hall, guest room, drawing room, study room, kubera sthan, books, pens, pencils, papers, photographs, wall paintings, book shelves, balcony, plastering of walls, parapet, garden, park green

	pads, green cuttings, crops, leaves, soil, land, mud walls, educational commercial places, libraries,recreation clubs, registration / passport office.
Mool Trikone	15-20 deg Virgo
Gemstone	Red coral
Metals	Silver
Dosha	Vaat
Chakra	Vishuddhi/Throat
Height	Tall
Sex	Eunuch
Colour	Green
Element	Earth
Varna	Kshatriya
Guna	Rajasik
Diety	Vishnu/Narayan

Occupations	Writers, Teachers, speakers, businessmen, astrologers, astronomers, scientists, people who possess secret of mantras
Body Parts	Hands, neck, shoulder, skin, forehead, tongue, vocal cord, throat, Nervous system, mouth, hair
Nature & Personality	Agile and tall body, Thoughtful orator, Intelligent and clever, Witty, Talkative, Looks younger than age
Diseases	Mental illness, neurosis, deafness, speech – stammering, acute depression, insomnia, tooth decay, cervical pain, allergy, bronchitis, leukoderma, sweating, leprosy, mental disorder, Nervous system, Brain, memory, childlessness.
Trees/Plants	Brahmi, green leaves, creepers
Nakshatras	Ashlesha, Jyeshtha, Revati
Food	Green vegetables, green dal and salads, sprouts, curry leaves
Education	Commerce, Planning, Astrology, Teaching., Exams, Media, Communication, Book writing, Lecturer, professor, scientist, research enginner, book publisher, accountant, auditor, poet, writer, comedian, lawyer, painter, correspondence

Venus

Venus, the brightest planet in the entire solar system, holds a unique place in astrology and mythology due to its extraordinary characteristics and symbolic representations.

Venus, also known as Shukra or Shukracharya, is neither too small nor too large in size. It rotates in an opposite manner compared to other planets, making it a non-conventional planet. Shukracharya, as per mythology, possesses the power to bring back the dead to life, an unconventional and miraculous capability, further emphasizing its unique status.

Known as the "morning star," Venus appears in the sky before sunrise, giving the illusion that it is responsible for bringing brightness, even though it is the Sun that causes daylight. Similarly, it is called the "evening star" as it appears in the sky before moonrise, creating an illusion that it illuminates the night, even though it is the Moon reflecting the Sun's light. This mimicry makes Venus a symbol of illusion, much like actors in cinema who portray roles and create an illusion on screen, despite these roles not reflecting their true selves. Hence, the entertainment industry, especially cinema, is assigned to Venus.

Venus, being the brightest planet, is also associated with the face. The face is the first feature people notice and whether a person is judged as bright, attractive, or dull often depends on the glow of their face. Particularly, the cheeks are represented by Venus as they play a significant role in facial expressions and makeup, highlighting beauty and allure.

In the human reproductive system, Venus, or Shukra, is linked to the sperm produced by males. The sperm is described as having a 'tejas' or glow, symbolizing life force. The sperm is usually deposited in the uterus of a woman, from where the development of an embryo begins. Thus,

Venus is considered the 'jeevakaraka' (life-giver) for females, representing fertility and the nurturing aspect of life.

Venus, the planet of beauty and luxury, is also connected to bright objects such as jewels, diamonds and all kinds of cosmetics and perfumes. These items enhance one's appearance and allure, reflecting the qualities of Venus. The planet's illusionary aspect extends to activities like horse riding or vehicle driving. In these activities, even though the individual may not be directly moving, the movement of the vehicle gives the sensation of travel, mimicking the illusory brightness of Venus.

Venus governs worldly fulfillment, loyalty and devotion. It represents our capacity for affection and the desire for harmony in life. As the goddess of love and beauty, Venus embodies qualities of love, art and aesthetics. In a male's chart, Venus represents the wife or lover and signifies sensitivity, refinement and gentleness. It is linked to our muse in life, our creative inspiration and the beloved that draws out our artistic expressions.

Venus shows our seeking for pleasure, comfort and luxury. It represents the pleasures of the senses and the comforts of the body, governing sexual attraction, sex appeal and attraction to the opposite sex. It is concerned with beauty, style and elegance, emphasizing quality over quantity. Venus desires not just the joy of possession but also the adulation and admiration of others. However, this desire for pleasure can turn into self-indulgence that dissipates, exhausts and debilitates, potentially leading to destructive behavior if unchecked.

Venus also denotes psychic abilities. On the positive side, it utilizes colors, gems and music, enhancing charisma and the power to inspire. On the negative side, it can be associated with black magic, hypnotism and self-destruction. This dual nature of Venus shows its potential to uplift and inspire or to mislead and harm, depending on how its energies are directed.

Jeev Karaktatwa of Venus : First Wife in Male Chart, Younger sister, Elder Daughter, Daughter in Law

Ajeev Karaktatwa

Category	Traits
Personal Traits	Beauty-Loving, Sensual, Passionate, Desirous, Artistic, Charm, Elegance, Grace, Sensitivity, Creativity, Diplomacy, Balance, Harmony, Pleasure-seeking, Indulgent, Enjoyment-oriented, Happiness-focused, Attractive, Comfort-seeking, Luxury-oriented, Beauty-conscious, Fashion-conscious, Scent-appreciative, Sweet-toothed, Intoxicant-prone, Oval-shaped (associated body/face shape)
Emotions/Actions	Love, Affection, Attachment, Desire, Attraction, Pleasure, Enjoyment, Happiness, Indulgence, Beautification, Entertainment, Socializing, Romance, Sex, Bed Pleasures, Passion, Sensuality
Professional	Designer, Secret Minister, Pandit (Scholar), Banker, Financier, Actor, Artist (Fine Arts), Poet, Musician, Dancer, Fashion Designer, Luxury Goods Dealer, Perfumer, Jeweler, Diplomat, Relationship Counselor, Beauty Professional, Entertainment Professional, Cultural Professional

Social	Marriage, Partnership, Relationships, Socializing, Entertainment, Culture, Wealth Display, Luxury Living, Fashion Trends, Art Appreciation, Music Appreciation, Dance Participation, Poetry Recitation, Romantic Pursuits, Sensual Experiences, Diplomacy in Relationships, Hosting Social Gatherings
Divine and Cosmic Associations	Venus (Planet), Morning Star, Evening Star, Shukracharya (in Hindu astrology), Jeev Karak for Women, Life-Giving Properties, Brightest Planet, Non-Conventional Rotation, Face of the Zodiac, Sperm Symbolism, Uterus Symbolism, Fertility, Progeny, Nectar of Life, Abundance, Prosperity, Affluence, Material Wealth, Luxury, Beauty in Nature (Flowers, Peacock colors), Vehicle of Desire, Sensual Cosmic Force, Artistic Inspiration, Embodiment of Love and Beauty

Venus : Other Significations

Attribute	Description
Represents	Spouse or sexual partner for Men, Love, Romance, Discretionary power, domestic happiness, Bed room, luxury, comforts, accumulated wealth, fixed assets, curd, cow
Lordship	Taurus and Libra

Exaltation	Pisces
Debilitation	Virgo
Friends	Saturn and Mercury
Enemies	Sun and Moon
Neutral	Mars, Jupiter
Aspects	7th
Dasha Period	20 years
Time per sign	30 days
Direction	South East
Vastu	Bedroom
Mool Trikone	0-15 deg Libra
Sex	Female
Colour	White, pink
Guna	Rajasik
Element	Water
Varna	Brahmin
Gemstone	Diamond, Quartz crystal
Metals	Silver
Energy	Feminine
Dosha	Kapha
Chakra	Anahat/Heart
Height	Short
Deity	Goddess Laxmi
Nakshatras	Bharani, Poorva Phalguni, Purva Ashadha

Occupations	Actors, artists, doctors, salesman, music, painting, poetry, singers, theatre and cinema, show business
Body Parts	Skin, throat, ovaries, veins, kidneys, reproductive system, Semen, Sperm, Uterus, Ovaries, Cheek, Right side of chin, Endocrine system (all glands producing different hormones), Womb, Face,
Nature & Personality	Plump body, round face, kind eyes, pleasant voice, beauty, sociability, grace, elegance, charm, hypnotic
Diseases	Skin related, allergies and sexual diseases,Thyroid, Diabetes, Veneral disease, sexual/uterus reproductive defects
Food	Presentable food, Juice, cold drink, rice in form of biryani, all sweets made from milk, junk food, microwave food, Luxurious meals/drinks, sour, pickles, tamarind, amla, lemon
Mantra	Om Dhram Dhreem Dhraum sah Shukraye namah ||
Trees/Plants	Mango, lemon, sour fruit trees
Education	Masters, Degrees expertise, performing arts, interiors, beauty, language of arts and poetry, acting, cinema

Jupiter

Jupiter: The Great Benefic of the Zodiac

Jupiter, often referred to as the "Great Benefic" in astrology, holds a position of paramount importance among the celestial bodies. Its influence extends across various aspects of human life, from spiritual growth to material prosperity. Let's explore the multifaceted nature of Jupiter's astrological significance:

Spiritual and Philosophical Influence:

- Known as "Guru" or the spiritual teacher
- Represents Dharma - the law of inner nature and self-realization
- Governs principles, morals, ethics, values and ideologies
- Symbolizes the guiding light of truth
- Influences law, religion, philosophy and spirituality
- Represents one's spiritual mission and divine spirit

Personal Growth and Optimism:

- Embodies joy in living and a positive spirit
- Known as the great optimist who always sees the good
- Helps overcome sorrow, depression and melancholy
- Transforms negative experiences into learning opportunities
- Indicates one's inner career and path to personal fulfillment

Luck and Prosperity:

- Planet of luck, favor, grace and fortune
- Brings wealth, abundance, prosperity and success

- Represents the daring optimist who ultimately succeeds
- Indicative of good karma and unexpected rewards
- Symbolizes divine grace and blessings that fulfill needs without seeking

Faith and Aspiration:

- Shows one's faith in life
- Can indicate the religion one follows
- Reveals the form of the divine one is naturally inclined to worship
- Represents devotion and dedication in life

Relationships and Family:

- Signifies progeny - their number, sex, health and one's relationship with them
- In a female's chart, represents the husband - his nature, health and her relationship with him

Physical Well-being:

- On a physical level, represents health, vigor and vitality
- Associated with a strong immune system

Generosity and Benevolence:

- Most helpful and generous of all planets
- Establishes goodness in life
- Through its influence, goodness comes to individuals

Astrological Significance:

- Considered the most benefic and saintly of all planets

- Its placement and aspects in a natal chart can indicate areas of life where one may experience expansion, growth and blessings

Physical Characteristics and Their Significance:

- Largest Planet: Jupiter is the biggest planet in our solar system, which translates astrologically to its association with expansion, growth and largeness in various aspects of life.
- Moderate Movement: Jupiter's orbital speed is neither too slow nor too fast, symbolizing balanced progress and steady growth in astrological interpretations.
- Color: Jupiter appears yellow when observed from Earth. This color association extends to its astrological significations.
- Soothing Rays: The light reflected from Jupiter is believed to have a soothing effect on Earth, making its astrological aspect generally considered benefic in a horoscope.

Life-Giving Properties:

- Jeeva Karaka: Just as the yellow yolk in an egg is the life-giving part, Jupiter is considered the 'Jeeva Karaka' or significator of life force in astrology.
- Oxygen Association: As the life-giver, Jupiter is also associated with oxygen, essential for breathing and cellular energy production, further emphasizing its role as a life-sustaining force.

Body Associations:

- Largest Organs: Reflecting its status as the largest planet, Jupiter is associated with the largest organs in the human body.
- External: The thighs, being the bulkiest external body part, are linked to Jupiter.

- Internal: The liver, the largest internal organ, is also under Jupiter's domain.
- Nose: In pranayama (yogic breathing exercises), the nose is the primary organ of breath control. Given Jupiter's association with breathing and life force, it's also linked to the nose.

Human Characteristics:

- Wisdom and Experience: Jupiter's large size is metaphorically associated with individuals who possess great wisdom and extensive life experience.
- Physical Size: People with larger body types or those who are obese are also associated with Jupiter's expansive nature.

Color Associations:

- Yellow Objects: Due to its yellowish appearance, Jupiter is associated with yellow-colored items in astrology and remedial measures.
    - Gemstones: Yellow sapphire
    - Spices: Turmeric
    - Metals: Gold

Animal Association:

- Elephant: As the largest land animal, the elephant is astrologically linked to Jupiter, the largest planet.

Jupiter : Other Significations

Represents	Wisdom, Clarity of mind and insights, prosperity, progeny, health, wealth, husband (in female chart), Jeeva, Teacher, Guru, Luck, Pitra, Gains, Higher education, Science and Law, Righteousness, Honour, Respect, Religion, Philosophy, Lord of words, Spirituality
Lordship	Sagittarius and Pisces
Exaltation	Cancer
Debilitation	Capricorn
Friends	Sun, Moon, Mars
Enemies	Mercury, Venus
Neutral	Saturn
Aspects	7th, 5th, 9th
Dasha Period	16 years
Time per Sign	12 months
Direction	North-East
Vastu	Locker, Valuables,Rectangle shape, North East, Ether, Water element, Yellow sapphire, Puja room, idol/photos, puja articles and tools, Treasury, ATM, peepal trees, temples, ashrams, mutts, Yoga centres, Meditation hall
Mool Trikone	0-10 degrees Sagittarius
Sex	Male
Colour	Green

Guna	Sattvik
Element	Ether or Space
Varna	Brahmin
Gemstone	Yellow Sapphire/Citrine
Metals	Gold & Platinum
Energy	Clean, generous
Dosha	Kaph
Chakra	Swadishthan/Sex
Height	Normal
Deity	Brahma, Indra, Shiva
Nakshatras	Purva Bhadrapada, Vishakha, Punarvasu
Occupations & Education	Spiritual teachers, brokers, doctors, scientists, judges, bankers,Audit, Banking, H.R.D, Religious study/ Sanskrit, trusts, planning, budgeting, Audit/Cash/Deposit/Saving/ Life Insurance, Ministers, Judge, C.E.Os, Professors, Advisory, Religious
Body Parts	Liver, blood, veins, arteries, hips, kidneys, fat,Lymphatic system (immune system) Fat, Index finger, thighs, Nose, Nostrils, Liver, Jaundice, Spleen, Back, large organs in body
Nature & Personality	Dignified appearance, sober appearance, obese, fair complexion, stout body
Diseases	Liver, sinus, tuberculosis, cancer, jaundice, enlargement of organs, kidney issues, cataract, hernia, diabetes, Obesity

Jeev Karaka of Jupiter : Self, Jeev karak of Male, Second Husband

Ajeev Karaka

Category	Traits
Personal Traits	Life force, Religious, philosophical, Respectable, noble, Humble, Honourable, Independent, Dutiful, Preacher, guide, Trainer, spiritual person, Honest, Patience, Maturity, High self-esteem, Optimism, Knowledge of love, Morality, Prosperity, Fulfillment of requirements, Fate, Yellow colour, Eminent person
Professional/ Social	Teacher, Presenter, Trainer, Spiritual person, Preacher, Education department/minister, Judge, E.D. department, Guide, Minister, Advisor, Counsellor, Consultant, Higher education, Enlightenment, Leadership, Influence, Authority, Abundance, Reputation, Growth, Development, Good cooperation, Good fortune, Philosophy, Morals, Ethics, Charity, Generosity, Minister, Guru or Mentor

Divine and Cosmic Associations	Jeev Karak for Male, Oxygen, Breathing, Divinity, High self-esteem, Patience, Maturity, Enlightenment, Fate, Yellow colour, Abundance, Expansion, Growth, Blessings, Higher education, Morals, Faith, Justice, Ethics, Breathing, Prosperity, Wisdom
Actions/ Emotions	Patience, Maturity, Experience, Success, Progress, Optimism, Morality, Charity, Blessings, Influence, Justice, Knowledge of love, Generosity, Good luck, Fulfillment of requirements, Self-efforts, Cooperation, Expansion, Abundance

Saturn

Saturn is often considered the most challenging planet in astrology and is known as the "legendary king of malefics." It represents the harsh realities of life, including death, disease, poverty, separation and ugliness. Saturn is seen as the God of Death, signifying endings and limitations. It teaches difficult life lessons through discipline, solitude and restrictions.

The energy of Saturn brings limitations to self-expression and self-realization, often leading to feelings of oppression and adversity. It rules old age and time, symbolizing the natural processes of aging and decay. When poorly placed in a chart, Saturn can cause premature aging, loss of vitality, depression and anxiety.

Physically, Saturn is connected to chronic and degenerative diseases, especially those related to aging, like arthritis and cancer. It signifies poverty and deprivation, binding individuals in servitude or under the control of external forces.

On a psychological level, Saturn governs fear, doubt and darkness, creating a sense of being trapped or unable to overcome life's obstacles. It amplifies feelings of self-doubt and makes people more susceptible to fears, fantasies and phobias. However, Saturn's influence also offers the opportunity for growth through perseverance, endurance and learning from hardships, ultimately shaping strong, disciplined individuals.

Saturn is known to bring bad luck, misfortune and challenging karma. It represents the planet of difficult karma or an unfortunate destiny. However, the hardships and suffering caused by Saturn often lead to deeper inner growth, prompting quicker spiritual evolution. Saturn's energy is one of delay and withholding, as it is the slowest-moving planet, causing obstacles and setbacks in life, including mental retardation in extreme cases.

It also symbolizes separation from loved ones and can result in the loss of love. In some instances, Saturn can bring out sexual perversions or unnatural actions. A strongly malefic Saturn is often seen in the charts of criminals, perverts, or those with an evil disposition, particularly when associated with Mars.

Despite its challenging side, Saturn is also regarded as the "grandfather spirit" and the lawgiver, serving as a guiding ancestor. It represents a yogi in meditation, offering the potential for complete detachment and independence. Saturn shows the way to transcendence, embodying the power of Shiva, the god of death and transcendence. Through Saturn, spiritual growth is possible and it plays a vital role in those seeking a spiritual path.

When well-placed, Saturn is essential for creating anything of enduring value in life. It fosters qualities such as discipline, austerity, detachment, patience and solitude. Saturn gives the focus, attention to detail and seriousness required to face life's challenges. It is the significator of life itself, indicating fate, longevity and the span of life. A strong Saturn offers protection and stability, even amid life's trials.

Saturn is the farthest planet from the Sun in the solar system, compared to the other nine planets. As it receives less sunlight and is colder than any other planet, Saturn represents darkness and cold, known as "Kapha" in Ayurveda.

Due to its large orbit, Saturn takes more time to complete its revolution than any other planet. This slow movement makes Saturn the significator of delay, slowness and lethargy. Elderly people, who naturally take more time to walk or perform activities, are associated with Saturn. As age comes with experience, experienced persons and wisdom are also linked to Saturn.

Since Saturn moves slowly, it is also connected with physically handicapped individuals, who are often slower in their physical movements. The planet's cold nature, due to its distance from the Sun, represents the "Kapha" humor in Ayurveda. Kapha is responsible for coldness and stagnation in the body and an excess of it leads to death. Thus, Saturn becomes a natural indicator of longevity and the end of life.

In terms of sunlight, Saturn receives the least of it. Similarly, the legs, which are less exposed to sunlight in the human body, are represented by Saturn. Darkness, in general, is associated with Saturn and as such, all black things such as charcoal, iron and other dark materials are assigned to Saturn.
Human destiny, which is often uncertain and "dark," is also linked to this planet.

Places that are dark or lack sunlight, such as caves, mortuaries, charcoal quarries and dark rooms, are ruled by Saturn. Since the night is a time of darkness, Saturn governs sleep as well.
People who live in poverty often face delays and slow progress in stabilizing their lives. Hence, poverty, slow pace and deprivation are karakatwas (significators) of Saturn, representing the struggles faced by the less fortunate.

Saturn Other Significations

Represents	Longevity (life expectancy), Discipline, Hard work, House, Construction, Servants, Cunningness, Storage, Shoes, Doctor, Duty, Sorrow, Laziness
Lordship	Capricorn and Aquarius
Exaltation	Libra
Debilitation	Aries

Friends	Mercury, Venus
Enemies	Sun, Moon, Mars
Neutral	Jupiter
Aspects	7th, 3rd, 10th
Dasha Period	19 years
Time per sign	30 months
Direction	South
Vastu	Store room, Dirt & Filth
Mool Trikone	0-20° Aquarius
Sex	Eunuch
Colour	Black
Guna	Tamsik
Element	Airy
Varna	Shudra
Gemstone	Blue Sapphire
Metals	Iron, Steel
Energy	Cold, Dark
Dosha	Vaat
Chakra	Mooladhara (Root)
Height	Short
Deity	Brahma, Bhairon, Shiva
Nakshatras	Uttar Bhadrapad, Pushya, Anuradha
Education & Occupations	Workers, Artists, Organizers, Practical oriented studies, coal industries, servicing industries, labor contracting, watchman, cleaners, peon, sweeper, cobbler, brick layers , 2nd hand old used good dealing

Body Parts	Teeth, Bones, Spleen, Right ear, Sense of hearing, Feet, Knees, Hair, Nails, Bone marrow, Lower waist
Nature & Personality	Deep set eyes, Slenderness, Large teeth and nails, Rheumatic and Lazy
Diseases	Cough, Vision problems, Arthritis, Hysteria, Pains and chronic illness, Paralysis, Cancer
Food	Raw Pulses, Karela, Amla, Neem, Bitter food (Kasaila), Stale food, Dhaba (cheap places to eat), Black pepper, Oil foods, astringent, oil, til, coffee, fried items
Vastu	Bow shape, West, Air element, blue sapphire, dining hall, steps of the front of the house, box, container, carry bag, doormat, dustbin, dining table, factories, dilapilated/remote places, Dump yard, store room, woolen clothes. Iron, lead, whirling wind, storm, oil mines,

Saturn Jeev Karak : Elder Brother , Third Husband, Husband brother

Ajeev Karak

Category	Traits
Personal Traits	Fear, Focus, Inner strength, Introversion, Isolation, Justice, Loneliness, Maturity, Obstacles, Patience, Perfectionism, Prudence, Self-control, Wisdom
Social Associations	Low-paid servant, Poverty, Poor people, Co-worker, Slum, Adversity, Grief, Misery, Gloomy, Separation, Authority, Delayed rewards, Traditional values
Professional Associations	Profession, Work, Karma, Career, Service, Industry, Workload, Dedication, Consistency, Challenge, Effort, Diligence, Discipline, Endurance, Hard work, Structural integrity, Responsibility, Delay, Karmic results, Delayed benefits, Pessimism, Determination, Steady
Divine Associations	Karma (action and consequences), Transformation, Lessons and growth, Limitations and restrictions, Order (divine order), Spiritual growth, Purity, Death

Rahu

Rahu, the son of Maya, symbolizes material energy and illusion. It drives us toward immersion in worldly life, making us feel as though we are kings in this material realm through its deceptive energy.

Unlike the other seven planets, Rahu and Ketu are not visible through the naked eye or astronomical instruments. For this reason, they are known as shadow planets or **Chhaya Grahas**. These shadow planets don't have physical form, size, or shape like other planets because they don't have a physical existence. Instead, Rahu and Ketu are purely mathematical points, formed at the intersections of the Sun and Moon's orbits.

These points are important because they block the rays of other planets that fall on the Earth. Therefore, Rahu acts as a **blocker in living things**, while Ketu blocks **materialistic aspects**.

In celestial mythology, Rahu and Ketu are often compared to a snake. Rahu is like the **head of the snake**, always with its mouth open, representing consumption and obsession. On the other hand, Ketu is the **tail of the snake**, representing endings, spirituality and detachment. Therefore, they are often viewed as the **head and tail of the snake**, symbolic of desire (Rahu) and liberation (Ketu).

Rahu and Ketu, like other entities that lack a physical form, are believed to exist in a **sookshma (subtle)** form. Just like the human soul is said to exist in a subtle form after death and rituals are performed to honor it, other celestial beings also exist in this subtle form. This includes gods, demigods, rakshasas, demons, devils, yakshinis, mohini and ghosts.

Rahu, associated with **demons and evil forces**, belongs to the rakshasa group, while Ketu is linked to **devas and siddhars** (spiritual beings).

Characteristics of Rahu:

As Rahu is symbolized by a wide-open snake's mouth, anything that resembles an open form is linked to its karakatwas (significations). Examples include the mouth, large intestine, ponds, lakes, rivers, oceans, dried wood, plastic, rubber, etc. These forms all share the expansive, consuming nature that Rahu represents.

Habits and Intoxication: Rahu is linked to all forms of intoxication, such as alcohol and drug addiction. In a metaphorical sense, alcohol can be seen as a liquid manifestation of Rahu.

Public Professions: Rahu is essential for success in professions that require public influence, such as film stars, journalists, artists and TV presenters. It grants the ability to capture and maintain the attention of large audiences, fueling creativity, imagination and inspiration.

Spying and Secrecy: As a shadow planet, Rahu governs covert activities such as spying and detective work.

Demonic Combinations: Certain combinations, like the Moon with Rahu and Jupiter with Ketu, can lead to destructive tendencies rooted in selfishness, envy and pride, as seen in figures like Hitler.

Fame and Success: There is no planet like Rahu when it comes to sudden, unexpected fame, prestige and political success. It can propel individuals into the spotlight unexpectedly.

Intuition and Clairvoyance: Rahu is also responsible for intuition and in some cases, it can even lead to clairvoyance. People in professions that require deep insight, such as psychologists, psychotherapists, fortune-tellers, astrologers, philosophers and scientists, all benefit from a strong Rahu.

Rahu represents all things unnatural, including artificial light like electricity. It governs areas like corruption, sexual slavery, trafficking of women and divorce.

Politics and Technology: Rahu holds sway over politics, especially in connection with media, the internet, publicity and technology, making it influential in shaping modern society.

Revolution and Change: As the planet of revolution, Rahu is constantly seeking change and disruption. It often creates figures like Robin Hoods, who fight for justice and challenge existing systems.

Intelligence and Wit: Similar to Mercury, Rahu is associated with sharp intelligence, intuition, wit and communication skills. It provides a keen sense of humor, often laced with sarcasm. When Rahu is linked with Mercury or Jupiter in a chart, it can be positively controlled, balancing its more chaotic energies.

Reflective Nature: Rahu absorbs the energy of any planet it is associated with, making its effects unpredictable. During Rahu's period, one can expect tendencies towards lewdness, pornography, promiscuity and   sexual perversions.

Speech and Behavior: Rahu influences criticism, arguments, swearing, vulgarity and black humor. It can also lead to excessive sleep, extreme risk-taking and participation in dangerous sports.

Foreign Influence: Rahu has a strong connection with foreigners and foreign governments, emphasizing a global or non-traditional influence in life.

Unorthodox Passion: Rahu embodies intense passion and obsession, driving people to pursue unorthodox, non-traditional paths with deep attachment. This "madness" for something unconventional is Rahu's defining feature.

Rahu and Ketu two Opposites

Rahu is attachment, Ketu is detachment:
Rahu makes us crave material possessions, success and worldly experiences, binding us to the physical world.
Ketu, on the other hand, signifies detachment from these desires, leading to spiritual growth, inner reflection and renunciation of worldly attachments.

Rahu likes to learn, Ketu likes to teach:

Rahu is curious and eager to explore the unknown. It seeks knowledge from various sources, always looking for new ideas and experiences.

Ketu, having already attained wisdom through past experiences, prefers to share that knowledge, making it a teacher or guide for others.

Rahu is the planet of knowledge, Ketu is the planet of wisdom:

Rahu represents worldly knowledge, intellectual curiosity and the pursuit of information, especially through unconventional or modern means.

Ketu represents deeper, intuitive understanding and spiritual wisdom, gained through introspection and past life experiences.

Rahu is worried about the future, Ketu is attached to the past:

Rahu is always projecting forward, concerned about future goals, ambitions and desires. It drives individuals to think about what lies ahead.

Ketu is reflective of past experiences and memories, focusing on what has already been learned or achieved, sometimes leading to nostalgia or regret.

Rahu is risk-taking, Ketu treads the known path:

Rahu is bold, adventurous and willing to take risks to achieve its goals. It thrives on uncertainty and seeks new opportunities.

Ketu prefers safety and comfort in what is familiar. It tends to avoid risks, choosing paths that are well-trodden and proven.

Rahu represents the future, Ketu represents the past:

Rahu is future-oriented, always pushing us toward new horizons, innovation and the next step in life.

Ketu draws its energy from past experiences and karmic lessons, grounding individuals in what has been previously learned or experienced.

Rahu is expansion, Ketu is compression:

Rahu encourages growth, expansion and the accumulation of more - whether it's material wealth, knowledge, or experiences.

Ketu, conversely, represents minimalism, contraction and focusing on the essence rather than the excess. It pushes for simplification and letting go of what is unnecessary.

To be in the present moment (Now) harmonizes Rahu and Ketu:

Both **Rahu** and **Ketu** pull in opposite directions - Rahu toward the future and Ketu toward the past. To balance their energies, one must stay centered in the **present moment**, integrating the lessons from both the past and the future while focusing on the "now." This brings harmony between material pursuits and spiritual evolution.

Functions of Rahu and Ketu: Rahu signifies taking things inward (consumption or intake), while Ketu represents expulsion (excretion or removal). For instance, the mouth represents Rahu as food is ingested through it and the anus represents Ketu as waste is excreted through it.

Gender Representation: In human reproduction, the male, who transfers the seed, represents Ketu, while the female, who receives it, is symbolized by Rahu.

Breathing: Breathing through the nose (associated with Jupiter and Ketu) increases longevity, while breathing through the mouth (associated with Rahu and Jupiter) reduces it.

Exaltation and Debilitation of Rahu and Ketu

There are various views on the exaltation and debilitation of Rahu and Ketu:

1. **First View**: Both are exalted in Taurus and debilitated in Scorpio.
2. **Second View**: Both are exalted in Scorpio and debilitated in Taurus.
3. **Third View (Most Convincing)**: Rahu is exalted in Taurus and debilitated in Scorpio, while Ketu is exalted in Scorpio and debilitated in Taurus.

Exaltation of Rahu in Taurus:
Rahu is exalted in the 20 degrees of Taurus, particularly in Rohini Nakshatra, ruled by the Moon. Taurus, ruled by Venus, represents luxury, wealth, pleasure and enjoyment - perfect for Rahu, the "bhoga karaka" (indicator of worldly pleasures). Moon in this placement also emphasizes beauty, lust and indulgence, which align with Rahu's desire for material fulfillment. People with this influence tend to pursue luxury and have a heightened sense of pleasure-seeking.

Debilitation of Ketu in Taurus:
In contrast, Ketu, the spiritual seeker, feels discomfort in Taurus as its focus is wisdom and detachment, making the materialistic nature of Taurus less suitable. Hence, Ketu is debilitated here.

Exaltation of Ketu in Scorpio:
Ketu finds its exaltation in 20 degrees of Scorpio, specifically in Jyeshta Nakshatra, ruled by Mercury. Scorpio, ruled by Mars, is associated with obstacles, challenges and deep transformation. These traits align well with Ketu's role as the seeker of wisdom, making it comfortable here as Scorpio requires one to overcome hardships, much like the spiritual pursuit for knowledge. Studying difficult sciences like Vedic knowledge or astrology is a long and challenging journey, resonating with Ketu's energy.

Debilitation of Rahu in Scorpio:
On the other hand, Rahu, which seeks enjoyment and pleasure, feels out of place in Scorpio's intensity and focus on challenges and obstacles. Thus, Rahu is considered debilitated in Scorpio as its focus on indulgence clashes with Scorpio's deeper, transformative nature.

This balance between the material and spiritual natures of Rahu and Ketu helps illustrate their contrasting roles in human life and destiny

Ketu is symbolized by structures resembling a snake's tail, such as nerves, hair, fingers, creepers and other thread-like structures. Additionally, it is associated with parts like the male genital organ, small intestine, anus and narrow water channels.

Functions of Rahu and Ketu: Rahu signifies taking things inward (consumption or intake), while Ketu represents expulsion (excretion or removal). For instance, the mouth represents Rahu as food is ingested through it and the anus represents Ketu as waste is excreted through it.

Gender Representation: In human reproduction, the male, who transfers the seed, represents Ketu, while the female, who receives it, is symbolized by Rahu.

Breathing: Breathing through the nose (associated with Jupiter and Ketu) increases longevity, while breathing through the mouth (associated with Rahu and Jupiter) reduces it.

Rahu Karaktatwas in BNN

- **Illusions & Deception**: Associated with falsehoods, confusion and unclear realities. Rahu creates situations that seem real but are deceptive.
- **Artistic Imagination**: Inspires creativity, particularly in arts, film and imagination.
- **Dishonesty & Fraud**: Linked with unethical behavior, manipulation and deceit.
- **Sins & Doubts**: Creates moral dilemmas, spiritual confusion and unclear boundaries between right and wrong.
- **Hardships & Challenges**: Known for causing struggles, obstacles and adversities.
- **Shadow Deals & Hidden Agendas**: Rahu represents covert, secretive actions that are done away from the public eye.
- **Fear & Insecurities**: Generates inner fears, uncertainties and anxieties, often rooted in the unknown.
- **Extreme Behaviors**: Pushes individuals to extremes - obsession, addiction and breaking conventional norms.
- **Foreign & Unfamiliar**: Represents foreign lands, other religions and unconventional approaches.
- **Cinema Actors & Impostors**: Associated with film, drama and disguises, where reality and illusion blend.

- **Death & Dark Entities**: Rahu is connected with death, demons, ghosts and other negative or dark energies.
- **Expansion & Chaos**: Brings growth, but often in chaotic and unmanageable ways, causing disruptions.
- **Eclipses & Shadows**: As a shadow planet, Rahu governs eclipses, symbolizing blocked light and hidden truths.
- **Innovation & Breakthroughs**: Drives technological advancements, unconventional thinking and transformation.
- **Desire for Fame & Power**: Fuels an intense hunger for fame, material success and control.
- **Sudden Events & Unpredictability**: Rahu brings unexpected changes, surprises and sudden twists of fate.
- **Escapism & Addiction**: Encourages tendencies to escape reality through addictions or distractions.
- **Restlessness & Rebellion**: Instills rebellion against traditional norms and constant inner restlessness.

Jeev Karaktatwa

- **Paternal Grandparents**: Rahu is associated with paternal lineage, particularly grandparents.

Body Parts:

- **Mouth, Lips, Ears, Intestines, Rectum**
- **Health Issues**: Causes various health problems such as inflammation, seizures, mental disorders and black patches on the skin.
- **Accidents & Past Sins**: Often linked with misfortunes, poisonings and diseases that are hard to diagnose.

Vastu (Home and Space):

- **Southwest Direction**: Governs this direction in Vastu Shastra, representing stability but also hidden dangers.
- **Elements**: Linked with air and fire, symbolizing volatility and energy.
- **Objects & Places**: Rahu is associated with items like lead, electronic gadgets, broomsticks, foreign embassies, airports, tombs and more.
- **Unusual Spaces**: Terraces, garages, mosques and unconventional areas are connected to Rahu.

Food:

- **Non-Vegetarian & Foreign Foods**: Represents exotic, foreign and indulgent foods, as well as intoxicating drinks.
- **Specific Ingredients**: Items like hing (asafetida) and mustard are linked with Rahu's energy.

Trees/Plants:

- **Durva, Bamboo, Babool**: Trees and plants associated with Rahu's shadowy and mysterious influence.

Deity:

- **Durga**: Rahu is connected with the goddess Durga, symbolizing power, protection and the ability to overcome obstacles.

Education and Occupation:

- **Nuclear Physics & Electronics**: Fields involving advanced technology, energy and hidden forces are governed by Rahu.
- **Secretive or Unethical Work**: Rahu encourages work that involves secrecy, espionage, or even underworld dealings.

- **Cinema & Technology**: Careers related to the film industry, computers and electronics are influenced by Rahu's energy.
- **Import/Export & Foreign Relations**: Involvement in international trade, research and global affairs are common under Rahu's influence.

Ketu

General Characteristics:

- **Unworldly & Superstitious**: Connected with otherworldly matters, often leading to mystical beliefs and superstition.
- **Fault-Finding & Reclusive**: Tends to be overly critical and prefers solitude, avoiding social interactions.
- **Depression & Rejection**: Associated with feelings of sadness, rejection and isolation from society.
- **Adamant & Stubborn**: Exhibits rigid behavior and an unwillingness to change or adapt.
- **Endings & Blockages**: Ketu symbolizes conclusions, blockages in materialistic pursuits and detachment from worldly matters.
- **Dev Gan & Siddha**: Represents divine beings and those who have achieved spiritual mastery, like yogis and saints.
- **Thread-Like Structures**: Governs things such as wires, nerves, ropes, pipes and other thin, thread-like structures.
- **Liberation & Moksha**: Ketu is the planet of spiritual liberation, emphasizing quitting worldly attachments and achieving enlightenment.
- **Obstructions & Failures**: Causes obstacles and failures, especially in materialistic or worldly pursuits.
- **Small & Subtle**: Ketu is connected with small, delicate matters and subtle energies.

- **Suicidal Tendencies**: Can lead to extreme mental distress, which may lead to thoughts of quitting life itself.
- **Detachment & Isolation**: Encourages letting go, disconnection from worldly affairs and spiritual isolation.
- **Hidden Knowledge & Mysticism**: Governs occult, hidden and mystical knowledge. Ketu promotes inner wisdom and insight.
- **Psychic Abilities & Intuition**: Enhances psychic talents, intuition and deep spiritual awareness.
- **Transformation & Rebirth**: Associated with spiritual rebirth, deep inner transformation and karmic evolution.
- **Non-Attachment & Non-Materialistic**: Encourages detachment from material gains and worldly possessions.
- **Transcendence & Spirituality**: Ketu guides one towards spiritual growth, transcendence of worldly desires and mystical experiences.
- **Unpredictability & Withdrawl**: Ketu brings sudden changes, often leading to feelings of withdrawal and isolation from the world.

Jeev Karaktatwa

- **Maternal Grandparents**: Ketu is related to one's maternal grandparents, representing ancestral wisdom and connection.

Body Parts:

- **Excretory System & Waste**: Ketu rules the lower bodily functions and waste elimination.
- **Hair, Nails, Private Parts**: Governs body parts like hair, nails, beard, moustache and private areas.
- **Health Issues**: Associated with diseases like cancer, depression, skin problems and immobility.

- **Suicidal & Mental Distress**: May cause psychological struggles and suicidal thoughts due to extreme detachment.

Vastu (Home and Space):

- **Flag Shape & Central Areas**: In Vastu, Ketu is connected with flag shapes and central areas like the Brahmasthana.
- **Fire Element**: Ketu represents the fire element, symbolizing purification, but also destruction.
- **Narrow Spaces & Rope-Like Items**: Associated with staircases, narrow entries, ropes and thread-like items.
- **Places of Healing or Confinement**: Hospitals, medical shops, courts, jails and graveyards fall under Ketu's domain.
- **Religious Temples**: Temples associated with ascetic or monastic traditions like Vinayaka, Buddhist, Jain and Christian churches.

Food:

- **Chinese Food & Roots**: Foods connected to Ketu include roots, Chinese cuisine and spiced/seasoned food.
- **Soda & Seasonings**: Ketu governs items like soda, seasoning and pepper.

Trees/Plants:

- **Thatch Grass, Aloe, Banyan**: Plants such as thatch grass, aloe and the banyan tree represent Ketu's energies.

Deity:

- **Ganesh, Saints, & Monks**: Ketu is linked to deities like Lord Ganesh, saints, monks and other spiritually ascended beings.

Education and Occupation:

- **Medical & Theology**: Governs subjects such as medical sciences, theology and occult sciences.
- **Occult & Divination**: Ketu encourages pursuits like astrology, energy healing and other mystical practices.
- **Handicrafts & Weaving**: Associated with craftsmanship, including weaving, tailoring and knitting.
- **Law & Pathology**: Also influences legal professions, pathology and research into diseases.
- **Energy Healing & Divine Services**: Ketu promotes work in spiritual and healing fields such as divine service and energy healing.
- **Telecommunication & Leather Industry**: Linked with professions in telecommunication, mobile technology and the leather industry.

Rashis - Zodiac Signs

Fire Signs: Aries, Leo, Sagittarius (1, 5, 9)

- **Element**: Fire
- **Direction**: East
- **Trikone**: **Dharma Trikone** (Triangle of Destiny)
- **Role**: Destiny Promoter
- **Explanation**:

Fire signs are driven by passion, energy and strong inner conviction. The Dharma Trikone (1, 5, 9 houses) is considered the *triangle of destiny*, representing actions that are naturally supported by the universe or destiny itself. People with planets in these fire signs often find that their goals and desires are naturally aligned with their life's purpose.

Destiny Promoter: This means that fire signs promote success that seems to come from within - almost as if destiny supports these individuals with less external struggle. For instance, having the Sun (the planet of self and success) in one of these fire signs indicates that success is attainable, provided the person channels their strong willpower and self-confidence.

Examples:

Aries: Initiation, leadership, pioneering new projects - success often comes by acting on strong desires and courageously pursuing goals.

Leo: Self-expression, charisma, creativity - destiny aligns to bring recognition and leadership opportunities with minimal obstacles.

Sagittarius: Adventure, expansion of knowledge, exploration - success is attained through optimism, exploration and following one's philosophy.

Key Concept: Fire signs represent *self-driven success*, where destiny naturally supports individuals to achieve their goals, provided they remain committed to their path with passion and enthusiasm.

Earth Signs: Taurus, Virgo, Capricorn (2, 6, 10)

- **Element**: Earth
- **Direction**: South
- **Trikone**: **Karma Trikone** (Triangle of Action)
- **Role**: Destiny Manipulator
- **Explanation**:

Earth signs are grounded in practicality, stability and hard work. The Karma Trikone (2, 6, 10 houses) represents the triangle of action, meaning success comes through the consistent application of effort and strategic thinking. People with planets in these signs must actively work to *shape their destiny* through material pursuits and deliberate action.

Destiny Manipulator: Unlike fire signs, where destiny seems to support automatically, earth signs require individuals to manipulate or work toward their goals. Success doesn't come easily; it requires effort, persistence and careful planning. However, the reward for hard work is often substantial and long-lasting.

Examples:

Taurus: Success through persistence, financial security and stability - achieved through a strong focus on material comfort and steady effort.

Virgo: Achievement through meticulous planning, attention to detail and problem-solving - success comes by applying the mind and perfecting skills.

Capricorn: Success through discipline, long-term planning and hard work - destiny is achieved through perseverance and steady progress toward long-term goals.

Key Concept: Earth signs demand *dedication and effort*. Destiny is something to be shaped through practical actions, strong willpower and methodical planning. These signs reward persistence, effort and a strong sense of responsibility.

Air Signs: Gemini, Libra, Aquarius (3, 7, 11)

- **Element**: Air
- **Direction**: West
- **Trikone**: **Karma and Luck Trikone**
- **Role**: Destiny Promoter (Gemini & Libra), Effort Promoter (Aquarius)
- **Explanation**:

Air signs are associated with intellect, communication and social interaction. The Air Trikone (3, 7, 11 houses) represents *karma and luck*, where success is tied to one's ability to interact with others, gather information and use intellect or networking to achieve goals.

Destiny Promoter (Gemini and Libra): These two signs promote success through efforts that involve communication, relationships and networking. However, unlike fire signs, success isn't automatic - it requires continuous, logical and intellectual effort. Emotional sensitivity may act as a barrier in these signs, as air signs rely more on mental agility and interaction rather than emotional depth.

Effort Promoter (Aquarius): Aquarius promotes success through effort alone, without the added benefit of luck or destiny. Success for Aquarians requires innovation, out-of-the-box thinking and consistent, relentless effort in unconventional ways. There's no easy path to success in this sign - it has to be earned.

Examples:

Gemini: Success through communication, adaptability and learning - achieved through curiosity, gathering information and social interaction.

Libra: Success through partnerships, harmony and diplomacy - achieved by balancing relationships and working with others for mutual benefit.

Aquarius: Success through innovation, social causes and unconventional thinking - achieved by breaking away from tradition and consistently working toward unique goals.

Key Concept: Air signs require *intellectual effort and interaction*. Success is gained through communication, social interaction and adaptability. For Aquarius, success comes through innovation and effort, without luck or easy gains.

Water Signs: Cancer, Scorpio, Pisces (4, 8, 12)

- **Element**: Water
- **Direction**: North
- **Trikone**: **Moksha Trikone** (Triangle of Liberation)
- **Role**: Destiny Manipulator
- **Explanation**:

Water signs are connected to emotions, intuition and deep inner experiences. The Moksha Trikone (4, 8, 12 houses) represents *liberation*, where success comes through emotional and spiritual transformation. People with planets in these signs need to *manipulate their mental and emotional energy* to achieve their goals.

Destiny Manipulator: Water signs indicate that success and destiny are deeply intertwined with the individual's emotional and mental state. Mental resilience, emotional intelligence and spiritual insight are critical. Luck comes when these individuals align their emotional and intuitive power with their goals. However, without mastering their inner world, water signs can struggle with emotional overwhelm.

Examples:

Cancer: Success through nurturing, emotional security and home life - achieved by creating emotional balance and a secure environment.

Scorpio: Success through transformation, intensity and deep emotional insight - achieved by confronting inner fears and using personal power for change.

Pisces: Success through intuition, imagination and spirituality - achieved by connecting with higher consciousness and transcending material desires.

Key Concept: Water signs represent *emotional and spiritual success*. Destiny is manipulated through inner transformation, emotional resilience and intuitive power. Those with planets in water signs must use their emotional intelligence and spiritual awareness to achieve success.

Each group of signs brings a different approach to how destiny and success are achieved, whether through natural support (fire), effort (earth), intellect (air), or emotional transformation (water).

Important: Jeev Tatva Adopts the Characteristics of Each Sign It Occupies

ARIES

CORE QUALITIES
Personality: Passion, Enthusiasm, Energetic, Courageous, Confident, Self-centred
Temperament: Short tempered, Hasty, Impatient, Aggressive, Quarrelsome
Leadership Style: Administrator, Quick decision maker, Protector, Pioneers

BEHAVIORAL TRAITS
Communication: Harsh words, Outspoken
Social Nature: Obedience to elders, Recognition and respect in society
Approach: Discriminative at times, Ruthless, Practical
Mindset: Egoistic, Materialistic, Spirit of competition

ACTION & MOVEMENT
Activities: Movement, Action, Active
Challenging: Friction, Perverse
Professional: Army, Police

MATERIAL ASPECTS
Domain: Land and land produce
Field: Agriculture, Cultivation

EMOTIONAL STATES
Positive: Enthusiasm, Confidence, Courage, Recognition
Challenging: Sadness, Aggression, Impatience, Friction

KEY CHARACTERISTICS
Leadership Style: Pioneering, Administrative, Protective
Decision Making: Quick, Hasty, Sometimes impulsive
Social Status: Respectable, Recognition-seeking
Work Approach: Competitive, Action-oriented, Energetic

TAURUS

TAURUS CHARACTERISTICS

CORE QUALITIES
Personality: Patient, Dependable, Caring, Reliable, Physical and Emotional strength
Temperament: Stubborn, Forceful, Determined, Pleasure loving
Leadership: Masterly behaviour, Productive, Enduring

BEHAVIORAL TRAITS
Communication: Pleasant, Pleasing manners
Social Nature: Appearance conscious, Beauty-oriented, Fashion-focused
Approach: Determined, Strive to achieve goals
Mindset: Materialistic, Sensual, Luxury-loving

ACTION & MOVEMENT
Activities: Commerce, Trade, Arts
Challenging: Permanence of things, Stability, 'Sthir' nature
Professional: Fine arts, Drama, Show business, Finance

MATERIAL ASPECTS
Domain: Wealth, Jewellery, Precious stones
Field: Built-up house, Vehicles, Treasury

EMOTIONAL STATES
Positive: Caring, Reliable, Patient, Artistic
Challenging: Stubborn, Lavish spending, Boastful

KEY CHARACTERISTICS
Leadership Style: Dependable, Productive, Stable
Decision Making: Patient, Determined, Goal-oriented
Social Status: Beauty conscious, Fashion-oriented
Work Approach: Enduring, Reliable, Commerce-focused

GEMINI

CORE QUALITIES
Personality: Jovial, Talkative, Adjustable, Curious, Expressive
Temperament: Restless, Confused, Flexible, Indecisive
Leadership: Clever, Analytical, Knowledgeable

BEHAVIORAL TRAITS
Communication: Expressive, Speech-oriented, Communicative
Social Nature: Selfish, Hypocritical, Secret moves
Approach: Creative, Versatile, Highly analytical
Mindset: Intelligence, Presence of mind, Good memory

ACTION & MOVEMENT
Activities: Travel, Research, Education
Challenging: Indecision, Restlessness, Contest
Professional: Computers, Mathematics, Tailoring, Cloth manufacturing

MATERIAL ASPECTS
Domain: Skills, Creative intelligence
Field: Educational institutions, Landed property

EMOTIONAL STATES
Positive: Creativity, Intelligence, Clarity
Challenging: Confusion, Hypocrisy, Selfishness

KEY CHARACTERISTICS
Leadership Style: Analytical, Creative, Intelligent
Decision Making: Flexible, Sometimes indecisive
Social Status: Knowledgeable, Skilled
Work Approach: Versatile, Creative, Skill-oriented

SPECIAL SKILLS
Artistic: Music proficiency, Sculptor, Painter
Technical: Mathematical proficiency, Computer skills, Creative

CANCER

CORE QUALITIES
Personality: Care taker, Emotional, Sensitive, Intelligent
Temperament: Moody, Unstable, Wavering, Wandering
Leadership: Knowledgeable, Prosperous, Mother-like

BEHAVIORAL TRAITS
Communication: Sarcastic, Ridiculing nature
Social Nature: Emotional bondage, Female folk oriented
Approach: Escaping, Changing, Reflective
Mindset: Greedy, Mirror-like reflection, Sensitive

ACTION & MOVEMENT
Activities: Travel, Change in place, Foreign residence
Challenging: Unstable nature, Scandals, Elopements
Professional: Army, Police, Agriculture, Dairy

MATERIAL ASPECTS
Domain: Food, Eatables, Drinks
Field: Agriculture, Dairy cattle products, Cereals and grains

EMOTIONAL STATES
Positive: Caring, Intelligence, Prosperity
Challenging: Moodiness, Cheating, Deceit, Thievery

KEY CHARACTERISTICS
Leadership Style: Nurturing, Care-taking, Emotional
Decision Making: Wavering, Changing, Unstable
Social Status: Foreign connections, Prosperous
Work Approach: Agricultural, Food-related,
Chemical-oriented

SPECIAL ASPECTS
International: Overseas travel, Foreign residence
Creative: Flowers, Art and art-related
Products: Chemicals, Dairy products, Cereals
Relationships: Emotional bonds, Female associations

LEO

CORE QUALITIES
Personality: Royal, Loyal, Righteous, Energetic, Ambitious
Temperament: Egoistic, Boastful, Rigid, Forceful
Leadership: Dominative, Leader, Creator, Responsible

BEHAVIORAL TRAITS
Communication: Command in office and society
Social Nature: Famous, Political connections, Celebrity status
Approach: Practical thinking, Fast decision making
Mindset: Materialistic, Practical, Optimistic, Honest

ACTION & MOVEMENT
Activities: Foreign travel, Government service
Challenging: Plays with emotions, Vanity, Arrogance
Professional: Doctor, Surgeon, High posts, Authority positions

MATERIAL ASPECTS
Domain: Fire, Chemicals
Field: Medicine, Drugs

EMOTIONAL STATES
Positive: Generous, Success to endeavours, Brilliance
Challenging: Ego, Discrimination, Dominating nature

KEY CHARACTERISTICS
Leadership Style: Ruling, Authoritative, Responsible
Decision Making: Fast, Practical, Discriminative
Social Status: Highly placed, Name and fame
Work Approach: Dharmic, Righteous, Dignified

VIRGO

CORE QUALITIES
Personality: Perfectionist, Practical, Sincere, Intelligent
Temperament: Critical, Insistent, Tolerant, Strenuous
Leadership: Shrewd, Methodical, Knowledgeable

BEHAVIORAL TRAITS
Communication: Good speaking ability, Writing skills, Pleasant conversationist
Social Nature: Friendly, Agreeable nature
Approach: Highly analytical, Methodical, Selective
Mindset: Creative, Concentrated, Business-oriented

ACTION & MOVEMENT
Activities: Travel, Research, Business
Challenging: Perfectionism, Critical nature
Professional: Commerce, Law, Accountancy, Photography

MATERIAL ASPECTS
Domain: Dry land, Landed property
Field: Printing, Publishing, Show business

EMOTIONAL STATES
Positive: Intelligence, Creativity, Concentration
Challenging: Critical nature, Insistence, Strenuousness

KEY CHARACTERISTICS
Leadership Style: Analytical, Methodical, Practical
Decision Making: Shrewd, Concentrated, Selective
Social Status: Knowledgeable, Professional
Work Approach: Perfectionist, Business-oriented, Creative

SPECIAL SKILLS
Academic: History, Geography, Geology
Professional: Legal knowledge, Mathematical knowledge, Accountancy
Creative: Photography, Drama, Cine field, Business

LIBRA

CORE QUALITIES
Personality: Loving, Cheerful, Enthusiastic, Patient, Balanced
Temperament: Sensitive, Casual, Bold, Frank
Leadership: Methodical, Enterprising, Judicial, Learned

BEHAVIORAL TRAITS
Communication: Frank opinion, Expression without reservation
Social Nature: Friendly, Pleasant, Harmonious
Approach: Balanced, Comparative, Justice-oriented
Mindset: Artistic, Equality-focused, Organized

ACTION & MOVEMENT
Activities: Arts, Drama, Show business
Challenging: Indulgence, Casual nature
Professional: Lawyers, Judge, Cinema field

MATERIAL ASPECTS
Domain: Chemicals, House
Field: Vehicles, Beauty-related

EMOTIONAL STATES
Positive: Cheerful, Enthusiastic, Pleasant
Challenging: Over-indulgent, Overly sensitive

KEY CHARACTERISTICS
Leadership Style: Balanced, Just, Methodical
Decision Making: Comparative, Equality-based
Social Status: Prosperous, Learned
Work Approach: Artistic, Organized, Pleasant

SPECIAL ASPECTS
Artistic: Eye for beauty, Artistically inclined
Professional: Judicial, Legal
Personal: Cleanliness, Pleasing manners
Social: Harmonious relationships, Flexible approach

SCORPIO

CORE QUALITIES
Personality: Mystifying, Sensitive, Psychic, Adventurous
Temperament: Jealous, Hateful, Revengeful, Coward
Leadership: Forceful, Technical, Controlled

BEHAVIORAL TRAITS
Communication: Interrupting, Secretive, Spy-like
Social Nature: Suppressed ego, Harmful, Blemished
Approach: Mystic, Root-seeking, Core-focused
Mindset: Sinful, Passionate, Violent

ACTION & MOVEMENT
Activities: Mining, Technical work, Agriculture
Challenging: Violence, Revenge, Jealousy
Professional: Police, Armed services, Engineer

MATERIAL ASPECTS
Domain: Machinery, Metals
Field: Land, Watery wet land, Agricultural implements

EMOTIONAL STATES
Positive: Controlled emotions, Technical skills
Challenging: Sadness, Venomous nature, Passion

KEY CHARACTERISTICS
Leadership Style: Forceful, Secretive, Technical
Decision Making: Mystical, Root-cause oriented
Social Status: Professional, Technical
Work Approach: Adventurous, Technical, Precise

SPECIAL SKILLS
Technical: Engineering, Machinery, Instruments
Professional: Accountancy, Police work, Armed services
Agricultural: Pumpset operation, Land management
Investigative: Spy work, Secret professions

SAGITTARIUS

CORE QUALITIES
Personality: Pious, Religious, Honest, Wise
Temperament: Energetic, Truthful, Patient, Conventional
Leadership: Advisor, Guide, Guru, All-rounder

BEHAVIORAL TRAITS
Communication: Straight forward, Preaching, Academic
Social Nature: Respect for elders, Respected in society
Approach: Philosophical, Idealistic, Conventional
Mindset: Ascending from material to spiritual plane

ACTION & MOVEMENT
Activities: Study, Research, Religious matters
Challenging: Fanaticism, Turbulent and struggling
Professional: Priest, Teacher, Academic, Spiritual guide

MATERIAL ASPECTS
Domain: Forest products
Field: Spiritual, Academic, Religious

EMOTIONAL STATES
Positive: Prosperity, Success, Luck
Challenging: Mid-life materialistic struggles

KEY CHARACTERISTICS
Leadership Style: Guiding, Advisory, Spiritual
Decision Making: Wise, Philosophical, Patient
Social Status: Famous, Respected, Academic
Work Approach: Slow and steady, Research-oriented

SPECIAL ASPECTS
Career Path: Slow and steady rise
Life Phases: Challenging mid-life, Peaceful later life
Spiritual: Religious matters, Adherence to rituals
Academic: Research, Study, Philosophy

CAPRICORN

CORE QUALITIES
Personality: Loyal, Responsible, Sincere, Strong-willed
Temperament: Shy, Tensed, Stubborn, Orthodox
Leadership: Service-oriented, Dependable, Reliable

BEHAVIORAL TRAITS
Communication: Truthful, Reserved
Social Nature: Hates bossism, Serving nature
Approach: Workaholic, Conventional
Mindset: Set frame of mind, Devotional

ACTION & MOVEMENT
Activities: Construction, Production, Achievement
Challenging: Dull nature, Tension, Stubbornness
Professional: Politics, Judge, Research, Teaching

MATERIAL ASPECTS
Domain: Dry land, Landed property
Field: Mining, Metals, Hardware, Paints and oil

EMOTIONAL STATES
Positive: Determination, Mental strength, Persistence
Challenging: Tension, Shyness, Orthodox nature

KEY CHARACTERISTICS
Leadership Style: Responsible, Service-oriented, Reliable
Decision Making: Strong-willed, Patient, Determined
Social Status: Dependable, Truthful
Work Approach: Persistent, Preserving, Workaholic

SPECIAL NOTE
Mars can exercise power despite being in enemy sign
Jupiter is debilitated despite being in friendly sign

AQUARIUS

CORE QUALITIES
Personality: Eccentric, Metaphysical, Mentally evolved, Spiritual
Temperament: Liberal, Noncommittal, Inquisitive, Secretive
Leadership: Sacrificing, Accomplished, Procuring

BEHAVIORAL TRAITS
Communication: Friendly, Liberal, Unexposed
Social Nature: Friendship with folks on any level, Miser
Approach: Research-oriented, Intuitive
Mindset: Higher thinking, Interest in occult, Hidden knowledge

ACTION & MOVEMENT
Activities: Research, Broadcasting, Space
Challenging: Secretive nature, Noncommittal attitude
Professional: Psychology, Medicine, Drugs

MATERIAL ASPECTS
Domain: Space, Broadcasting
Field: Drinks, Drugs, Medicine

EMOTIONAL STATES
Positive: Extraordinary understanding, Intuition
Challenging: Miserly nature, Concealed emotions

KEY CHARACTERISTICS
Leadership Style: Liberal, Sacrificing, Understanding
Decision Making: Intuitive, Research-based
Social Status: Friendly with all levels
Work Approach: Delving into unknown, Occult research

SPECIAL ASPECTS
Spiritual: Higher thinking, Metaphysical interests
Research: Occult, Hidden knowledge
Understanding: Extraordinary level of comprehension

PISCES

CORE QUALITIES
Personality: Highly Intuitive, Metaphysical, Philanthropic
Temperament: Moody, Sensitive, Pleasure-loving
Leadership: Teacher, Saint, Preacher

BEHAVIORAL TRAITS
Communication: Preaching, Silence, Mystical
Social Nature: Philanthropic, Escapist
Approach: Regretting, Rectifying
Mindset: Infinite understanding, Spiritual

ACTION & MOVEMENT
Activities: Teaching, Research, Spiritual life
Challenging: Temptations, Escapism, Moodiness
Professional: Teacher, Saint, Spiritual guide

MATERIAL ASPECTS
Domain: General prosperity
Field: Success with less effort

EMOTIONAL STATES
Positive: Rejoicing, Extraordinary understanding
Challenging: Regret, Sensitivity, Perishing feelings

KEY CHARACTERISTICS
Leadership Style: Teaching, Preaching, Mystical
Decision Making: Intuitive, Metaphysical
Social Status: Prosperous, Philanthropic
Work Approach: Less effort, High success

SPECIAL ASPECTS
Spiritual: Mysticism, Metaphysical understanding
Understanding: Extraordinary level of comprehension
Success Pattern: Prosperity assured, Less effort required
Emotional Range: From excitement to silence
Mental State: From rejoicing to regretting

70 TWO PLANET COMBINATIONS

Key points for 2 planet combinations:

- **Planetary Relationships**: Consider planets that are in 1-5-9, 2-12 and 1-7 relationships with each other.
- **Degree-Based Sequence**: The planet with the lower degree is considered the first planet and the planet with the higher degree is considered the second.
- **Karaka Matching**: While interpreting the results, match the **jeev karaka** (life-related significations) of one planet with the **ajeev karaka** (non-life-related significations) of the second planet.
- **Energy Transfer**: The planet with the higher degree has crossed the planet with the lower degree, thereby transferring its influence and energy to the planet with the lower degree.
- Native's horoscope is formed after the birth of native and hence all combination interpretation is from the time of birth of native.

Combination 1 : Sun-Moon Combination (Moon Degree > Sun Degree):

- This combination shows that the Moon has crossed the Sun in degree. The jeev (life-related aspect) of one planet is combined with the ajeev (non-life-related aspect) of the other.
- The native will have a strong sense of self-respect, high confidence and pious thinking. However, there may also be signs of ego and attitude.
- A significant change in the father's life is indicated after the birth of the native. This could involve a change in residence, job, or even city.
- The father may travel frequently and be an emotional person.

- The native may experience difficulties in learning initially due to a lack of focus or a fickle-minded nature.
- The native's mother may come from a high-status or prestigious family and may have a dominating nature.

Combination 2 : Moon-Sun Combination (Sun Degree > Moon Degree):

- The Sun has crossed the Moon in degrees, bringing its influence to the Moon. The **jeev** (life aspects) of one planet interacts with the **ajeev** (non-life aspects) of the other.
- The native is **ambitious**, focused on **gaining name, fame and status**. There may be strong signs of **ego** and **attitude**.
- Before the birth of the native, the **father** might have experienced a **loss** or significant **change** in life.
- After the native's birth, the **mother** becomes more **dominating** in the household. She will be a **truth-seeker**, have a **royal nature** and hold a strong influence over the family dynamics.

Combination 3 : Sun-Mars (Mars Degree > Sun Degree):

- Mars has crossed the Sun in degrees, influencing the Sun. The **jeev** (life aspects) of one planet interacts with the **ajeev** (non-life aspects) of the other.
- After the birth of the native, the **father** may face an **accident** or undergo **surgery**.
- The father might also experience significant **problems** in life after the birth of the native.
- Additionally, the father could buy **property** following the native's birth.
- The native's **husband or brother** will come from a **prestigious family** and may display **dominance**,

ego and **attitude**. However, they will also be **pious** and **good-hearted**.

- The native's **son** is likely to have **anger issues**, prone to **disputes** and could be **short-tempered**.

Combination 4: Mars-Sun (Sun Degree > Mars Degree):

In this case, **Sun's degree is higher than Mars**, so Sun has crossed Mars, giving its energy to Mars.

Father:

- The father may have faced **an accident or surgery** before the birth of the native.

- The father might have **purchased property** before the native's birth.
- He may experience **problems in life** early on.

Husband:

- The native's husband will achieve **name and fame after marriage**.

- He will be **successful, dominating**, with **ego and attitude**.
- However, he will also be **pious** and **good-hearted**.

Brother:

- The brother will be **proud and successful** and will gain **recognition in society**.

Son:

- The native's son may experience **initial problems in learning** and may struggle with **bad company**.

General Influence:

Mars and Sun are both fiery planets and their combined intensity will depend on the sign where the combination occurs.

The best results will be observed if this combination happens in fiery signs (1, 5, 9), which can enhance the fiery nature of both planets.

Combination 5: Mercury-Sun (Degree of Mercury > Degree of Sun)

- **Native's Education**:
    - The native is likely to receive an **education from a government institution**.
    - They will inherit **intelligence and common sense** from their father.
    - There are **bright prospects in the educational field** for the native, particularly if **Mercury is not afflicted** by planets like **Mars or Ketu**.
- **Father**:
    - The father is **intelligent**, with excellent **communication and business skills**.
- **Neighbours/Relatives**:
    - The native's **neighbours or relatives** may be **influential**, of **high status**, or even **powerful and famous**.
- **Sister/Daughter**:
    - The native's **sister or daughter** will be **dominating** and may have some **connection with the government**.
- **Subjects of Education**:
    - The native's education may involve **recognized subjects** such as **mathematics, science, history, political science, administration services, or even MBA**.
- **Father's Influence**:
    - The native will share several **traits with their father** and may inherit an interest in their **father's favorite subjects**.

- o They will likely **gain proficiency** in whatever their father undertook or excelled in.

In this combination, Mercury (which rules intelligence, communication and learning) dominates over the Sun (representing father, authority and government), suggesting a strong intellectual inheritance from the father and a bright academic future for the native.

Combination 6: Sun-Mercury (Degree of Sun > Degree of Mercury)

- **Father**:
  - o The father comes from an **intelligent background** and is **well-educated**.
  - o He receives **support from relatives and neighbours** in his endeavors.
- **Son**:
  - o The son will have a **natural intelligence** from birth.
  - o He will be proud of his **intellectual abilities** and quick to **grasp knowledge**.
- **Sister/Daughter**:
  - o The native's **sister or daughter** will be **famous**, **egoistic** and **dominating**, showing strong leadership qualities.
- **Native**:
  - o The native will achieve **name, fame and status** through their **education, intelligence** and **communication skills**.

In this combination, with the **Sun** having a higher degree than **Mercury**, the native's **father** plays a strong role in shaping their intelligence and educational background. The native's **success** and **recognition** are likely to come through their **mental abilities** and the way they communicate and learn.

Combination 7: Sun-Jupiter (Degree of Jupiter > Degree of Sun) (Atma-Jeev Sam Yoga)

- **Father**:
    - The father becomes **religious** or **spiritual** after the birth of the native.
    - He may become a **public figure**, involved in **public activities** or **social service**.
    - He will be seen as a **good advisor, wise** and an excellent **guide** to others.
- **Native**:
    - The native will **resemble the father**, both in physical appearance and certain qualities.
    - The native inherits the **creditworthiness** and **reputation** of their ancestors.
    - There will be **support and success** in the native's endeavors, often receiving **assistance from others**.
- **Son**:
    - The native's son will be **polite, humble** and **honest**.
    - He will also be **knowledgeable**, with a strong moral foundation and respect for values.

In this combination, **Jupiter**, being of a higher degree than **Sun**, signifies that the native will inherit **spirituality** and **wisdom** from their father. The native's **success** is likely to come from their **reputation**, **guidance** and the **respect** they have in society.

Combination 8: Jupiter-Sun (Degree of Sun > Degree of Jupiter)

- **Native**:
    - The native will embody **Sun-like qualities**, being **bright, truthful** and **radiant** in personality.

- They will have a sense of **ego** and may appear **dominating**, but with a **good heart** and genuine intentions.
    - The native is likely to **lead with confidence** and strive for **honesty** in all dealings.
- **Father**:
    - The father has a **religious** or **spiritual background** or holds a spiritual disposition.
    - He is seen as **wise, honest** and respected for his **upright character**.
- **Son**:
    - The native's son will be blessed with **previous life merits**, which will lead him to **prosper** in life.
    - The son will receive **help from divine grace**, ensuring **success** and **favorable outcomes** in his endeavors.

Combination 9: Sun-Venus (Degree of Venus > Degree of Sun)

- **Native**:
    - The native is likely to **earn money through government channels** or by associating with **luxurious** or prestigious sources.
    - There may be **challenges in progeny** due to the **fiery nature of the Sun** and the connection of **Venus to fertility (sperms)**. The heat from the Sun may **dry or burn** the reproductive essence, creating potential issues in having children.
    - The native prefers **posh areas** for living and enjoys the possession of **luxurious vehicles, branded items** and overall **high-end lifestyles**.
- **Wife**:

- o The native's wife comes from a **high-status family**, likely to be associated with **government organizations**.
  - o She may be **egoistic** and **dominating**, but she has a **pure heart** and genuine intentions.
- **Father**:
  - o The father is likely to be **good-looking** and fond of **comforts and luxuries**.
  - o He will have a penchant for keeping things **neat, clean** and aesthetically pleasing.
  - o The father will also be financially well-off and may be involved in **business ventures** or **profitable activities**.

This combination indicates that **Venus's** influence on the native brings a desire for **luxuries** and **comforts**, while the **Sun** adds an element of **prestige** and **association with government** or high-profile matters. There could be **tension** due to the **Sun-Venus** dynamic when it comes to **progeny**. The native's surroundings and relationships are marked by **wealth, elegance and strong status**.

Combination 10: Venus-Sun (Degree of Sun > Degree of Venus)

- **Father**:
  - o The father is already in possession of **money, luxuries and comforts** before the birth of the native.
  - o He is likely to have a **female-oriented nature**, enjoying the **company of women**.
  - o The father will **spend money** on enhancing his **status**, indulging in **luxuries** and seeking **pleasures**.
- **Son**:
  - o The native (son) will be heavily influenced by **sensual pleasures** and driven by a desire for **physical comfort** and indulgences.

- **Wife**:
    - After marriage, the wife becomes **dominant** and gains **name and fame**.
    - She is likely to be **proud**, authoritative and will assert her dominance in the relationship and social life.

This combination suggests a strong influence of **Venus** in the native's life, creating an atmosphere of **luxury, sensuality and dominance**. The father is materially comfortable and may be indulgent, while the native is focused on **sensual gratification**. The wife, post-marriage, ascends in **social status** and plays a **dominant role**.

Combination 11: Saturn-Sun (Degree of Saturn > Degree of Sun)

- **Father**:
    - The father may hold a **low-grade job**, likely related to the **government** or a **government-related institution**.
    - He may have faced **hurdles and difficulties** throughout his life.
    - The father might appear **older than his actual age** and may exhibit **lethargy** or lack of energy.
- **Native**:
    - The native will be influenced by their father's profession and may follow a **similar career path**, often related to **government work** or a **reputed institution**.
    - The native's **past life** may have been filled with **pain** and hardships.
    - In their present life, the native may face **initial struggles**, dealing with **hurdles** and challenges, especially in their **early years**.
    - There is a tendency for the native to associate with people from **lower socioeconomic backgrounds**.

- **Profession** may involve work in **government sectors** or **institutions with authority**.
  - **Elder Brother**:
    - The native's elder brother will be **dominant**, **egoistic** and assertive in the family.
  - **Son**:
    - The native's son is likely to be **lazy** and will tend to befriend people from **lower social classes**.
    - He may continue to face **hurdles** during his early years of life.
    - The son may have experienced significant **pain** or struggles in a **previous life**.

Influencing Factors:

- If **Mars** is in the **2nd house**, it worsens the situation, leading to more problems and challenges in life, amplifying the native's difficulties.
- If **Venus** is in the **2nd house**, then things improve after the initial struggles, bringing **relief** and better circumstances later in life.

This combination emphasizes **hardships**, particularly related to the father's struggles, which seem to echo into the native's life as well. The involvement of Saturn brings a strong influence of **discipline, delay and hurdles** and the native's early life may reflect this energy. However, the presence of **Venus** could offer some reprieve after initial difficulties.

Combination 12: Sun-Saturn (Degree of Sun > Degree of Saturn)

- **Father**:
  - Experiences significant **hardships and difficulties** before the native's birth

- o Prone to **health issues** and various forms of **suffering** in early life
  - o Notable turning point occurs after native's birth
  - o Achieves **recognition and status** in profession following native's birth
  - o The birth of the native appears to be auspicious for father's fortune
- **Native**:
  - o Strong **ambition** and desire for professional recognition
  - o Natural inclination towards **Sun-influenced careers** such as:
    - Government service
    - Administrative positions
    - Political roles
    - Leadership positions
    - Authoritative roles
  - o Possesses drive to achieve status and recognition
  - o May face initial obstacles but has capacity to overcome them
- **Professional Characteristics**:
  - o Drawn to positions involving:
    - Authority
    - Public visibility
    - Administrative responsibility
    - Government sectors
    - Management roles
    - Positions requiring leadership

Combination 13: Rahu-Sun (Degree of Rahu > Degree of Sun)

- **Rahu as Venus:**
  - o In this combination, **Rahu** can be treated as the disciple of **Venus**, often bringing **initial struggles** but offering **great**

rewards later in life. While Rahu is known for causing **confusion** and challenges at first, it eventually leads to significant growth and success.

- **Paternal Grandparent:**
    - The paternal grandparent (likely the grandfather) will have been a **spiritual**, **famous** and **powerful** person.
    - The native's paternal line (grandfather, father, son) may share a resemblance, including **similar physical features**.
- **Father:**
    - The father may face **initial struggles** in life, but after overcoming these obstacles, he will experience a **new beginning** and **prosperity** in the latter part of life.
    - There may be challenges related to **male progeny**, indicating **difficulty** in having a son or complications during pregnancy.
    - In some cases, there may even be instances of **untimely death** among male family members.
- **Native:**
    - The native may have a tendency toward **showing off** or engaging in **exaggerated displays** of wealth or status.
    - They are likely to face **obstructions** and may be drawn toward **unethical behaviors** or actions that bend the rules.

Combination 14: Sun-Rahu (Degree of Sun > Degree of Rahu)

- **Father:**
    - The father experiences **problems** and **difficulties** before the birth of the native.
    - There is a **new beginning** in the father's life before the birth, signaling a shift or transformation, often tied to struggles that lead to growth or new opportunities.

- **Native:**
  - This combination suggests that the native may have had an **early death** in a **past life**, possibly through **suicide** or **accidental means**.
  - Rahu's influence here may indicate unresolved karmic patterns from the previous life, bringing these past-life experiences into the present incarnation.

Combination 15: Sun - Ketu (Degree of Ketu > Degree of Sun)

- Father is the youngest in the family, representing the end of the lineage.
- If the firstborn is a son, there may be no further children; a daughter before the son is possible.
- Father experiences constant tension throughout life.
- The Maternal family (Maternal Grand Parent) has a strong reputation, name and status.
- Father and son do not share a good relationship; there may be constant friction or distance.

Combination 16: Ketu - Sun (Degree of Sun > Degree of Ketu)

- Father is the eldest sibling; no child was born before him.
- Father is spiritual and may have experienced tension before the birth of the native.
- The native has a spiritual background from a previous life.
- The Maternall family (Maternal Grand Parents) gains name and fame after the birth of the native.
- There may have been a miscarriage before the native's birth, particularly if the native is a son.

Combination 17: Moon-Mars

- **Mother**: Stubborn, rough, rigid nature; may face fire danger, accident, or surgery before the native's birth. Likely to buy property or land.
- **Native**: Courageous mind, possible land purchase near water bodies.
- **Husband**: From a distant place, may have an affair or experience changes and blame before marriage.
- **Brother**: May suffer losses or face blame, leading to a change in location; caring by nature.
- **Daughter**: Stubborn, short-tempered.

Combination 18: Mars-Moon

- **Mother**: Likely to experience an accident or surgery before the native's birth; may suffer from ongoing mental problems.
- **Husband**: Fickle-minded, may change places or travel after marriage, enjoys changes.
- **Native**: Likely to be born through C-section, prone to sexual thoughts, irritability and mood swings; possible land near water, changes in property.
- **Brother**: May travel or change places, faces initial challenges.
- **Sister/Daughter**: Exhibits rough behavior and aggression stemming from a previous birth.

Combination 19: Moon-Mercury

- **Mother**: Intelligent, educated, business-minded and possibly the younger sibling in her family.
- **Native**: Highly intelligent with an excellent memory, intuitive and may have many friends. Could exploit friends for personal gain, leading to a bad reputation. Changes in education or business are likely to be beyond their control, forcing adjustments such as changing subjects or schools. Despite this, they excel in studies and gain knowledge in many fields.
- **Sister/Daughter**: Well-educated and intelligent.

- **Education**: The native is quick to learn, grasp new topics and apply skills effectively. A topper in studies, but should choose subjects of personal interest for success.

Combination 20: Mercury-Moon

- **Mother**: Intelligent, elder sibling in her family, with a highly intellectual mind.
- **Native**: Intelligent, with emotions guiding their thought process.
- **Sister/Daughter**: Intelligent from a past life, likely to change places after completing education.
- **Education**: Native may travel for education or experience changes in their schooling or subjects. They might pursue education related to psychology, the mind, travel, liquids, or other fields that involve frequent changes.
- **Business**: Business changes are likely, but by the native's choice.
- **Chal Kapat Yoga**: The native may face betrayal, deceit, or defamation in life. They are likely to be cheated, possibly by friends or romantic partners and should be cautious when choosing romantic connections. If Saturn aspects this combination, the native could both deceive others and be deceived themselves.

Combination 21: Moon-Jupiter

- **Mother**: Resembles the native in looks and nature, religious, acts as an advisor, has a pious nature, comes from a good family and gains recognition or becomes a public figure after the native's birth.
- **Native**: Has a spiritual and religiously inclined mind, guided by higher beliefs. There may be significant changes in the family before the native's birth. The native could face severe health issues, nearing death, at the time of birth.

- **Travel**: The native will travel extensively, especially every 12 years and is likely to settle far from their birthplace.

Combination 22: Jupiter-Moon

- **Mother**: Spiritual, religious and knowledgeable before the native's birth, comes from a respected family.
- **Native's Mind**: Receives inner guidance for religious and spiritual activities, often seeking higher knowledge. Changes in the family are seen after the native's birth.
- **Likes and Health**: Fond of dairy products, sweets and food in general. The native may face health issues related to **Kapha** (like congestion or weight gain).
- **Character**: The native can adapt easily to different situations but might face allegations or accusations about their character.

Combination 23: Moon-Venus

- **Mother**: Beautiful and money-minded, may be the younger sister to the native's maternal aunt.
- **Wife**: Life experiences significant changes before marriage, may have faced challenges or blemishes prior to marriage. She might be from a distant place or have traveled extensively before marriage.
- **Money**: Native is likely to inherit money from the mother. Venus, representing residence, indicates a home near a water body.
- **Native**: Money-minded, there is a possibility of having a relationship with the wife's younger sister.
- **Daughter/Sister**: Luxury-oriented and may elope for settling in life.

Combination 24: Venus-Moon

- **Mother**: Comes from a wealthy and luxurious background, money-minded, with an interest in fine arts.
- **Wife**: Younger sister present. The wife experiences significant life changes after marriage.
- **Native**: Money flows in and out and the native struggles to save. Constant thoughts about women. Spendthrift, often for sensual pleasure, with an artistic nature. Residence changes after marriage.
- **Daughter/Sister**: Desirous by nature, prone to fickle-mindedness and subject to blames.

Combination 25: Moon-Saturn

- This combination is considered one of the worst, associated with **Punarphu Dosha** in KP astrology.

Nature of the combination:

Bad for both the native and the mother. The fast-moving Moon contrasts sharply with the slow-moving Saturn, creating internal conflict. The mind moves quickly but feels restricted and unable to find space, leading to frustration.

Moon-Saturn (Retrograde): This makes the situation even worse, causing a head-on collision between fast and slow movement.

Saturn (Retrograde)-Moon: Slightly better, as the planets are moving in opposite directions, offering some balance.

Moon and Saturn at the same degree: The worst-case scenario. The fast-moving Moon crashes into the slow-moving Saturn, amplifying frustration.

- **Mother**: Likely to have faced many struggles and problems after the birth of the native, including possible depression.
- **Native**:
- The mind becomes negative and frustrated.

- Profession may be related to liquid or work as a servant, likely in a foreign land or a place with different cultures.

Combination 26: Saturn-Moon

- **Mother**: Life was problematic before the birth of the native, indicating struggles or hardships.
- **Native**:
- **Profession**: The native will experience dissatisfaction and constant desire for change in their profession. Their mind will frequently seek professional shifts, indicating a lack of fulfillment.
- Likely to travel for work, with a profession related to **travel or the hotel industry**.
- **Health**: There is a possibility of developing a **chronic disease**, often attributed to **past life karma**. This could manifest as ongoing physical issues due to unresolved karmic debts.

Combination 27: Moon-Rahu

- **Mother**: Her life will face problems and struggles immediately after the birth of the native.
- **Native**:
- The native will have a **daydreaming** nature, often lost in illusions and fantasies.
- Likely to be **psychic** or highly intuitive, but also prone to **delusions** and irrational fears.
- The native may struggle with **mental health** issues, especially if not supported by benefic planets in the chart, leading to risks of **mental illness** or being easily affected by **black magic**, **witchcraft**, or the **evil eye** ("nazar lagna").
- The presence of a **water well** or water body near their residence may also be significant.
- **Paternal Grandparents**: Likely to have **migrated** and settled in a different place from where they originally lived.

Combination 28: Rahu-Moon

- **Paternal Grandparents**: There will be significant **life changes** in the paternal grandparents' life after the birth of the native.
- **Mother**: The mother will face **life-threatening situations** before the birth of the native and will overcome them, leading to a **problematic life** in general.
- **Native**:
- The native's **mind is deeply intuitive**, often remembering or connecting with **past life** experiences.
- Possesses **premonitions** and can foresee things, but this intuitive ability is mixed with **illusion** and confusion.
- There is a tendency toward a **cheating mentality**, thinking and acting in **unethical** ways.
- May struggle with issues of **adultery** or develop **adulterous tendencies**, largely driven by the mind's illusions and manipulative nature.

Combination 29: Moon – Ketu

- **Maternal Grandparents**: The maternal grandparents will likely be from a **far-off place**, indicating distant roots or migration.
- **Mother**:
- The mother will face **lifelong tension**, always burdened with worries or stress.
- She could be the **youngest sibling** in her family.
- The mother will have a strong inclination toward **spirituality**, particularly focusing on **liberation** or **moksha**.
- **Native**:
- The native's **mind will be spiritual**, often contemplating **liberation** or detachment, but will always carry a sense of **tension** or unease.

- May have **strained relationships with females**, particularly not getting along well with women in their life
- If the native has a **sister** or **first daughter**, there could be no children after tha.t
- A **Mother Goddess temple** may be located near the native's birthplace, symbolizing spiritual protection or connection.
- The native may have deep thoughts about **renouncing life** or feel drawn toward a path of **moksha** or spiritual liberation.

Combination 30: Ketu – Moon

- **Mother**:
- The mother is likely the **eldest sibling** in her family.
- She would have experienced **tension before the birth** of the native, possibly related to family or personal stress.
- The mother may **resemble her maternal grandparent**, either in appearance or personality traits.
- **Native**:
- The native's **mind recalls past life experiences**, possibly carrying memories or emotions from previous incarnations.
- The native has an **intuitive** nature, often able to **read the thoughts of others** or catch onto subtle vibrations, giving them psychic-like abilities.
- Highly **spiritual**, with a tendency to contemplate deeper existential questions.
- If the native has a **daughter**, she could be someone the native had a connection with in a **previous life**.
- The native might have a **gloomy or sadistic tendency**, often feeling **dejected** or depressed due to emotional difficulties or disappointments in life.
- There could be a strong inclination to **quit a job** or withdraw from professional commitments, especially when feeling overwhelmed or frustrated.

- **Ketu's Influence**:
- Ketu, being the **significator of endings**, can mark the end of **bad** periods or transitions into **better phases**. However, it can also signify the **opposite**, where good phases may come to an end, leading to challenges. This duality of Ketu's influence will often bring **unpredictable shifts** in the native's life.

Combination 31: Mars – Mercury

- **Brother/Husband**:
- The **brother or husband** of the native is likely to be **intelligent** and **educated**, with a sharp mind and good analytical skills.
- **Native**:
- The native's **land or property** will likely have a **commercial purpose**, such as being a part of a **commercial place** or **educational institute**.
- The native's **education** will be influenced by **Mars**, leading to interests or career paths related to **Archaeology**, **technical subjects**, **History**, **engineering**, or **real estate and property business**.
- **Neighbours**:
- The native's **neighbours** will be challenging to deal with - **uncontrollable** and **non-cooperative**. They may be involved in **policing**, **real estate**, or work as **property dealers**.
- **Sister/Daughter**:
- The native's **sister or daughter** may have **died in an accident** in a past life. This karmic connection could influence their relationship in the current life, with possible implications for protection or unresolved issues related to past events.

Combination 32: Mercury – Mars

- **Education**:
- The native will face **breaks or disruptions** in their education unless they pursue **Mars-related**

subjects, such as **engineering, technical studies, archaeology**, or **real estate**.

- They will encounter **hurdles and challenges** in their education, requiring **extra effort** to succeed. It's essential for them to stay physically active, as **physical exertion** helps maintain their mental balance and **intellectual focus**, preventing setbacks in academics.
- **Sister/Daughter**:
- The **sister or daughter** of the native may experience an **accident** or **undergo surgery** at some point in their life.
- **Native**:
- The native is likely to own **commercial property** and at least **two properties are assured** in their life.
- **Brother**:
- The native's **brother** is intelligent, but there may be **disputes or misunderstandings** between them, potentially leading to tension.

Combination 33: Mars – Jupiter

- **Native**:
- The native may carry **hidden anger** or latent frustration.
- They are likely to have **land** near a **religious place, institution**, or **public area**.
- In their **past life**, they may have experienced an **accident** or **surgery** and they might have a **birthmark** as a reminder of that past incident.
- The native is likely to have been born via **C-section**.
- **Brother**:
- The native's **brother** may become a **public figure** or someone who is recognized in society.
- **Husband**:
- The husband is likely to be of a **religious nature**, with a **noble** and righteous personality.

Combination 34: Jupiter – Mars

- **Native**:
- The native will have a **short temper**, may be **harsh** and **adamant** in nature, often acting in a **hasty** manner.
- They may suffer from **blood-related issues**, such as **acidity**, **headaches** and **high blood pressure** - all signs of potential health concerns.
- An **accident** or **surgery** is indicated in the native's life at some point.
- The native is likely to **gain land** and **property**.
- **Husband**:
- The husband may come from a **noble** and **religious family**.
- The native's husband may have a **big brother**, indicating the presence of an elder male figure in the family.

Combination 35: Mars – Venus

- **Husband and Wife**:
- If there are no planets between Mars and Venus, the **husband and wife** may have been connected in a **previous birth**.
- The **wife** will have a **birthmark** on her body due to an **accident or surgery** from her past life.
- Mars behind Venus indicates **tension before marriage**, leading to **ego clashes**, **aggression** and a **possessive** nature in the wife.
- The **wife** is likely to have a **big brother**.
- **Native**:
- The native, whether male or female, will be **beautiful**.
- The native's **brother** will be **handsome** and will be able to make **money**.
- **Land and Property**:
- The native's land is likely to be located near a **bank, ATM,** or **medical shop**.

Combination 36: Venus – Mars

- **Brother and Wife**:
- The **brother** may have an **elder sister**.
- The **wife** may have a **younger brother** and could face an **accident or surgery** after marriage, with a possible risk of **miscarriage**.
- **Husband**:
- The **husband** will have a **passionate** and **luxurious** attitude, possibly with **artistic tendencies**.
- **Wife**:
- The **wife** will be **short-tempered**, with a likely physical appearance of **exposing teeth**, a **high nose bridge** and **reddish eyes**.
- She will have **anger issues** after marriage.
- There is a possibility that the wife was the **same spouse in a previous birth**, returning to cause **trouble** for the husband.

Combination 37: Mars – Saturn (Engineer Combination)

- **Native Profession**:
- Profession will likely involve **technical fields** such as **agriculture**, **weapons**, **machines**, or **engineering** (Yantra Yoga).
- If Mars is not involved in the profession, there will be **problems**.
- Native will face **competition** and **enemies** in their career, with hurdles to overcome in professional life.
- **Siblings**:
- **Brother** born after the native's birth will face a **problematic life**.
- **Elder brother** may have had a **hard struggle** in life and might not have a good relationship with the native.
- **Married Life**:
- **Problems in married life** for females, with difficulties adjusting in the family.

- If benefic planets influence later, the marriage will **succeed**.
- If malefic influences (e.g., **Ketu**), there could be a risk of **divorce**.
- The initial years of marriage will be **difficult**.

Combination 38: Saturn – Mars

- **Professional Life**:
- Native will face **problems** in their profession due to **hasty decisions** and mistakes.
- The profession should involve **Mars significations** (e.g., technical, machinery, engineering) or the native will encounter **struggles** and **stiff competition** in their career.
- **Relationships**:
- This combination is **problematic** for the **native**, **brother**, **elder brother** and **husband**.
- Expect challenges and difficulties in their professional and personal lives.

Combination 39: Mars – Rahu

- **Personality & Behavior**:
- **Courage expands** greatly, leading to excessive boldness (**may do extraordinary things**).
- Native is daring, **strong** and does not easily show anger but suppresses it, converting it into **jealousy** and heartache.
- **Bad deeds** may arise from excessive courage and thinking/comprehending power decreases.
- There is a **danger** from vehicles, metals and **disputed land**.
- The native's **grandparents** may have owned land, likely dilapidated or disputed.
- **Family**:
- The **brother** will face **initial struggles** but will experience a new beginning, with issues getting resolved later.

- In female charts, this combination is **not favorable for marriage**, often indicating **inter-caste marriage** or **problems after marriage**.
- **Husband** may live in a **foreign land** and if the marriage is inter-caste or abroad, the problems may be lessened.
- There is a possibility of the **untimely death** of a brother and there may be **no elder brother**.
- **Female Chart**:
- In charts of females, this combination (Me+Ve+Mars+Rahu) increases the possibility of **molestation** or **rape**.

Combination 40: Rahu - Mars

- **Personality & Behavior**:
- Native lives in **illusions** with a great sense of **imagination**.
- Will have tendencies to **fight without reason** and there are **dangers** in life that may be suppressed or hidden.
- Has a **secretive nature** and an interest in **shadowy activities**.
- The native's land may be near a **park** but likely not in a good or desirable place.
- **Family**:
- **Husband** may come from a **foreign land**, a **different culture**, or a distant place and may have an **unethical past**.
- The **brother** might have had a **troubled past** or not a good life in a previous incarnation.
- The **paternal grandparent** purchases property after the native's birth and may have been **aggressive**.
- There may be an **accident or surgery** after the birth of the native.

Combination 41: Mars - Ketu

- **Personality & Behavior**:

- The native will be **adamant** and strongly opinionated, often trying to **prove their point**, regardless of whether it's valid.
- Exhibits an **argumentative nature** and does not have good relations with **siblings**.
- **Family**:
- If the native has a **brother**, there will be **no younger sibling** after him.
- The **husband** will be the **youngest child** in his family and will experience **lifelong tension**.
- The **maternal grandparent** may have had an **accident or surgery** and purchased land before the native's birth.
- **Female Chart**:
- This is one of the **worst combinations** for females regarding marriage.
- The native will face **problems getting married**, a **break in marriage**, or a **difficult married life**.
- Three possible outcomes are likely after marriage:
    1. **Death** of a male family member in the husband's family.
    2. **Miscarriage**.
    3. **Separation**.
- At least one of these events is highly probable. In a **female chart**, if this combination is seen, the marriage should ideally take place when **Jupiter transits** over this combination (houses 1, 5, or 9), forming the **Mangal Sutra Yoga** (Mars = beads, Ketu = thread). The female should always wear **married symbols** like sindoor, mangal sutra and bangles to avoid serious issues in marriage.
- **Divorce**:
- If a **female chart** has Mars-Ketu and a **male chart** has Venus-Ketu, it strongly indicates a **high chance of divorce**.
- However, if the **male chart** has **Venus + Jupiter**, the male will try to **save the marriage** and will not initiate a divorce.
- **Male Chart Considerations**:

- If a male's chart shows a combination of **Venus + Ketu**, especially alongside this Mars-Ketu combination in the female's chart, **divorce is almost certain**.
- However, if the male's chart also includes **Venus + Jupiter**, it indicates a higher likelihood of him attempting to **preserve the marriage**, even in difficult circumstances, reducing the chances of divorce.

This combination highlights **marital challenges**, familial tensions and strong indications of **difficult outcomes in married life**, particularly for women.

Combination 42. Ketu - Mars:

- **Maternal grandparents** may undergo **surgery** or **accident** after the native's birth, may **purchase property** or **land**.
- **Brother** connected from a **past life**; possible **untimely death** of brother in the past life.
- **Husband** is also linked from a **past life**.

Combination 43. Mercury - Jupiter:

- **Native intelligent by birth**, uses **intelligence** to become **wise**.
- **Greenery, gardens, trees, jungle** around the **place of birth**.
- **Knowledge from previous birth** will surface in this life.
- Will **master multiple branches** of knowledge.
- Befriends a **matured girl** with a **good heart**, **truth-seeker** and **practical**, but **marries a different woman**.
- **Good education**, born **intelligent**, even without formal education.
- **Education in religious subjects**, frequent **nose touching**, should live in a house with **proper ventilation**.

- **Sister/Daughter** is **religious, knowledgeable** and a **public figure**.
- **Male child** after a **daughter**.

Combination 44. Jupiter - Mercury:

- Native may have a **younger sister**, intelligent, with **good grasping power**.
- Promises **good education**, especially if **Sun** is present - **meritorious student**.
- **Guided education**, supported by a **good teacher**.
- Close friendships with **females**, may be involved with them.
- **Female native** comes from a **noble family**, is **spiritual**.
- Education spans **many subjects**, supported by **past life knowledge**.
- **Sister/Daughter** is **religious and spiritual**, connected from a **previous birth**.

Combination 45. Mercury - Venus:

- **Smoothness in life** - comfortable education and lifestyle.
- If **Jupiter** is involved, life is even **more comfortable**, with less stress.
- **Education** may be related to **finance, fine arts, music, dance, medicine, fashion design, interior design, gemstones business and finance**.
- Native can **increase wealth** through **continuous learning** - the more informed they are, the more they will **earn**.
- **Sister/daughter** will be **good-looking**, connected to **luxury and finance**.
- **Wife** could be a **businesswoman** before marriage, may have an **elder sister** and is **intelligent**.
- Native is **sweet-talking**, **courteous** and easily makes **friendships with the opposite sex**.
- Native may build a **house surrounded by greenery**.

Combination 46. Venus - Mercury:

- **Wife's younger sister** is significant in the native's life.
- **Native's sister** may be **wealthy**, carrying over prosperity from a **previous life**.
- The native will likely have received an **education in an expensive or luxury school**, possibly in a **private institution**.
- The native's **daughter** may have a strong inclination or **talent in fine arts**.
- The native may have **affairs outside of marriage** but is careful in managing them, avoiding situations that could lead to **blame or scandal**.

47. Mercury - Saturn: Kumbhakaran Yoga / Idle Yoga

- The native is prone to **laziness** and enjoys being **idle** or sleeping a lot.
- **Education** becomes challenging as the native lacks interest in studying and requires **repeated effort** to grasp concepts. Progress in education will be **slow**.
- The native may lean towards subjects involving **practical applications**.
- The **elder brother** likely has a **commercial background** and might have **chosen his own life partner**.
- **Sister/daughter** may also face **life challenges**.
- The native may pursue a **business** profession and will likely show an interest in it at least once in life.

Combination 48. Saturn - Mercury:

- **Education** is steady and **not problematic**, often pursued in **old or traditional buildings**.
- The native applies **intelligence in their profession** and may form a **romantic connection at work**.
- **Elder brother** is also **intelligent** and may be involved in **business**.

- The native's profession is likely linked to **business, teaching, communication**, or **commercial activities** where **communication** is essential.
- **Sister/daughter** may have **challenges carried from a past life**.

Combination 49. Mercury - Rahu:

- **Education** may occur in a **foreign land** and tends to be **research-oriented**. The native is **extraordinarily intelligent** and may face **initial challenges** in their educational path.
- This combination suggests **problems in education** but also the potential for **advanced degrees** like a Ph.D. or **multiple master's degrees**.
- **Income** might be delayed due to prolonged education, but earnings will **increase significantly later**.
- **Rahu energies** should be channeled into learning, making the native an **expert in online learning** and possibly more inclined toward **studying abroad**.
- Fields like **photography** and the **film industry** can lead to **lifetime achievements** for this native.
- Education may also involve **esoteric subjects** like **tantra** and **mantra** or other **secret knowledge**.
- The native may live or work near **Muslim cemeteries** or places with **Muslim cultural influence** and might have a **Muslim friend** who provides support. They may have **marks or disfigurement on their head or forehead**.
- **Sister** may have **secret relationships**.
- **Grandfather** is likely from an **intellectual background** and may own **substantial landed property**.

Combination 50. Rahu - Mercury:

- **Photographic Memory**: The native has a **visual memory** and remembers things in **pictures**.

- **Self-Perception**: Believes they are **very intelligent** and uses **reverse thinking** to persuade and benefit from others.
- **Education**: May have studied **tantra and mantra** in a previous life and tends to believe they know subjects thoroughly, though there may be a **cheating aspect** in their studies. To make the most of this combination, the native should **study away from their hometown**.
- **Land Matters**: Likely to face **hurdles** in matters related to **land**.
- **Smoking Tendency**: Many natives with this combination are inclined toward **smoking**.
- **Sister/Daughter**: Likely had an **untimely death in childhood** in a past life but is **blessed with a long life** in this one.
- **Grandparents**: Intelligent, likely to **start a business after the native's birth** and may **acquire landed property**.

Combination 51. Mercury - Ketu:

- **Education**: The native may experience **breaks and hurdles** in their education, often leaving it **incomplete**.
- **Personality**: Tends to be **unworldly**, **aloof** and may face **rejections** or feel detached from societal norms.
- **Health**: There may be **hearing issues** or **skin ailments**.
- **Interests**: Likely drawn to **astrology, occult sciences, law, Ayurveda**, or **allied medical sciences**.
- **Intellectual Development**: **Regular meditation** can help enhance the native's intellect and they have an advanced **sixth sense**.
- **Sister/Daughter**: Likely the **youngest sibling** with no younger siblings and may have a **spiritual inclination**.

- **Maternal Grandparents**: Likely come from a **business-oriented family** background.

Combination 52. Ketu - Mercury:

- **Education**: The native's education has a **spiritual foundation**, likely influenced by **spiritual pursuits in a previous life**.
- **Writing**: The native should focus on **writing** as a path to excellence. Practicing academic or vocational tasks through writing can help **resolve mental blockages**.
- **Schooling**: May have attended a **convent school** or one with a spiritual or religious background.
- **Sister/Daughter**: May have experienced **suicidal tendencies or an unnatural death in a past life**.
- **Maternal Grandparents**: Known for their **intelligence**.

Combination 53. Jupiter - Venus: Sanjeevni Yoga

- **Appearance**:
- **Male native** will have a **beautiful wife**.
- **Female native** will herself be **beautiful**.
- **Wife**:
- Likely from a **religious** and **noble family**.
- May have an **elder brother**.
- **Native**:
- **Money-minded**, with an interest in **fine arts**.
- Likely to own a **large and beautiful house**.
- **Daughter**:
- Expected to be **fortunate** and bring luck to the family.

Combination 54. Venus - Jupiter:

- **Wife**:
- Becomes **religious after marriage** and may gain recognition as a **public figure**.
- Has a **younger brother**.

- **Native**:
- Likely has an **elder sister** born before them.
- Comes from a **wealthy family** with a background in **fine arts**.

Combination 55. Jupiter – Saturn: Maha Bhagya Yoga

- **Maha Bhagya Yoga**: This unique combination occurs in the **Kal Purush Kundli** where **Jupiter** and **Saturn**, as the 9th and 10th lords, form a powerful yoga. If **Jupiter's degree is higher than Saturn's** in any single sign, which happens approximately once every 20 years, it creates the **Maha Bhagya Yoga**. Those born under this yoga are considered **highly fortunate (ati bhagyashali)**.
- **Prosperous Life**: This combination promises a **prosperous and successful life**, especially when Jupiter and Saturn are in **conjunction**.
- **Challenges and Traits**:
- **Life Challenges**: Despite the luck associated with this combination, the native may still experience **difficulties and problems** in life, which they will likely overcome.
- **Physical Appearance**: Attractive **cheeks and nose**.
- **Desires and Success**: The native desires **good things in life** and will likely achieve **mastery** in their profession, gaining **recognition and fame**.
- **Career Inclination**: They may pursue a profession with a **religious background**, often choosing paths related to **teaching, preaching, or spirituality**.

Combination 56. Saturn - Jupiter

- **Physical Traits**: Native may have a **straight, long and thick nose** with **medium cheeks**.
- **Personality**: Known for being **hardworking** and **efficient** in their tasks, with a strong inclination toward seeking **truth**.

- **Profession**: Likely to pursue careers involving **religious activities**, **teaching**, **coaching**, or **consulting** by choice, indicating a preference for meaningful, knowledge-based professions.
- **Past Life**: The native may have had an **ordinary or challenging past life**, which fuels their current life's dedication to personal growth and purpose.

Combination 57. Jupiter - Rahu

- **Birth and Early Life**: The native may be born in a place with a **different culture** than their family background. After the native's birth, they may experience a **near-death situation** or face **serious health issues and difficulties**.
- **Social Circle and Challenges**:
- Around ages **24-25**, the native may fall into **bad company**, associating with **people from lower social backgrounds**.
- Despite these challenges, the native has the resilience to **overcome obstacles** and may eventually **reach a high position or success**.
- **Interests and Learning**:
- The native may be drawn to **non-traditional** or unconventional activities, with a possible interest in **learning occult, evil, or unethical techniques**.
- Believed to be the **incarnation of a great-great-grandfather**, carrying forward certain ancestral traits.
- **Grandparents**:
- They likely come from a **religious family**, with **similar faces and nature** as the native, symbolizing continuity in family values and traits.

Combination 58. Rahu - Jupiter

- **Grandparent**: Develops a **religious inclination** after the native's birth, becoming more spiritually oriented.
- **Past Life and Present Life**:

- In a **past life**, the native had an **unnatural death** at a young age, but in this life, they are blessed with **long life**.
- Likely born in a **famous or well-known place**.
- **Health and Constitution**:
- Around age **11**, the native may face **serious health issues** and generally has a **weaker constitution**.
- There's a tendency toward **bad habits**, yet a strong, almost unseen **power supports them**, helping to overcome various life challenges.
- **Interests and Skills**:
- Drawn to **research** and **exploration** of knowledge.
- A natural **storyteller** or **writer**, skilled at weaving **illusions** and **narratives** that may be far from factual, but captivating in their creativity.

Combination 59. Jupiter – Ketu

- **Birth and Life Path**:
- Native may be **born in a lane** or **nursing home**.
- This combination is considered a **moksha combination**, indicating that it might be the native's **last birth** before achieving spiritual liberation.
- **No younger siblings** are likely and the native may experience **lifelong tension**.
- **Spiritual Inclination**:
- The native will be deeply **spiritual** and inclined toward **mysteries, the occult and spiritual realms**.
- There may be a struggle to **balance the material and spiritual worlds**, often finding it challenging to adjust between the two.
- **Maternal Grandparents**:
- Likely have a **religious and spiritual background**, adding to the native's inherent spiritual leanings.

Combination 60. Ketu - Jupiter

- **Maternal Grandparents**: Develop a **spiritual inclination** after the native's birth, deepening their connection to religious practices.
- **Past Life**:
- The native may have experienced an **untimely or suicidal death** in a previous life.
- They are **reconnected with the same family** from their past life, symbolizing unfinished karmic ties.
- **Family Position**: The native is the **eldest child**, with no older siblings.
- **Birthplace**: Likely born **near a Devi temple** or a place of spiritual significance.
- **Personality and Material Inclination**:
- Shows **reluctance toward material pursuits** but may have an underlying tendency to **accumulate possessions** despite disinterest in materialism.

Combination 61. Venus – Saturn

- **Male Progression**: The native (male) is likely to experience **career and personal progress after marriage** with this combination, whether it appears as **Venus-Saturn** or **Saturn-Venus**.
- **Wife's Characteristics**:
- The wife is likely to be a **professional** with her own **income**.
- She may face **initial adjustment issues** in the marriage and it is beneficial if she is **working** to ensure a smoother marital relationship.
- **Native's Profession**:
- Progresses significantly after marriage, with possible involvement in **finance, banking,** or working in **high-rise buildings**.
- The native's workplace is likely to be **beautifully located** and may be in a **prestigious office** environment.
- This combination is favorable for **professional success** but may bring challenges at the **personal (jeev) level**.

Combination 62. Saturn - Venus

- **Profession**: The native's career is likely to involve **fine arts**, **finance**, or other areas related to **Venusian qualities** (beauty, luxury, creativity).
- **Wife's Characteristics**:
- The wife may face **challenges or issues before marriage**.
- She may have a **slow, deliberate approach**, often taking time to start tasks but ensuring they are **completed** once begun.

Combination 63. Venus – Rahu

- **Paternal Grandparents**: Likely **wealthy and prosperous** before the native's birth.
- **Wife's Characteristics**:
- **Extremely beautiful** and attractive.
- Faces **challenges or difficulties initially after marriage**, but experiences a **new beginning** or positive changes later.
- **Male Chart (Flirt Yoga)**:
- Indicates a **flirtatious nature**; the native may be inclined to flirt frequently.
- **Wealth and Material Gains**:
- This combination promises **significant wealth** and **at least two vehicles**.
- There are chances for **sudden financial gains** through **speculations, gambling, unethical means, or betting**.
- The native will likely prosper in **Rahu-related professions**.
- **Physical Markers**:
- **Fish-shaped line** on the palm.
- **Wide, dark birthmark** on the body.
- **Nature of Rahu-Venus Combination**:
- Rahu, in this context, acts as an **illusive Venus** on the malefic side, bringing desires and materialism, while Venus is grounded in practicality. This duality

often creates **initial struggles** but leads to success over time.

Combination 64. Rahu - Venus

- **Parental Grandparents**:
- Likely to experience **financial gains, increased luxuries and comforts** after the native's birth.
- **Wealth and Relationships**:
- This combination does not typically bring **sudden wealth**, but the **flirtatious tendencies (flirt yoga)** are prominent.
- The native has **strong desires for females** and may have **secret affairs**.
- Tends to earn money through **unethical means**, often involving hidden or deceptive activities.
- **Wife's Characteristics**:
- **Faces difficulties before marriage** and may have a **secretive and suspicious nature**.

Combination 65. Venus – Ketu

- **Maternal Grandparents**: Likely from a **wealthy, rich family** background.
- **Male Chart (Challenges)**:This combination is challenging, potentially leading to one of the following issues:
- **Death of a male family member**.
- **Miscarriage**.
- **Separation**.
- If **Jupiter aspects this combination**, it may help prevent separation.
- **Wife's Characteristics**:
- **Spiritual** and knowledgeable in **occult matters**.
- Faces **lifelong tension** or struggles.

Combination 66. Ketu – Venus

- **Maternal Grandparents**: Experience **progress and prosperity** after the native's birth.

- **Wife's Characteristics**:
- Likely connected from a **previous life**.
- The wife is probably the **eldest sibling** in her family.
- **Low chances of separation** in marriage, as both planets are moving in opposite direction.

Combination 67. Saturn - Rahu

- **Intelligence**: The native will be **highly intelligent**, despite the challenging Saturn-Rahu combination.
- **Professional Success**: Achieves **success in profession** after facing initial hurdles, often using **unethical or easy means** to earn money. The native is resourceful, with a talent for **finding shortcuts or "jugaad"** to solve problems and achieve goals.
- **Financial Inclinations**: Has a strong desire for **quick and easy money**.
- **Saturn + Rahu + Venus + Mercury**: This combination is particularly **beneficial for professional success**.
- **Paternal Grandparents**: Likely to experience **suffering due to past life karma**.

Combination 68. Rahu - Saturn

- **Profession**: The native's profession may be **connected to their past life**, particularly in fields related to **tantra or mantra**.
- **Challenges**: Likely to face **problems and obstacles in their professional life**.
- **Intelligence**: The native is **intelligent** and resourceful.
- **Professional Success**: This combination alone is generally **unfavorable**; however, if **Venus and Mercury** are also connected, it becomes **beneficial for career success**.

Combination 69. Saturn – Ketu

- **Professional Challenges**: This combination brings **professional tension** and is generally **unfavorable for career success**, potentially leading to an **unsuccessful professional life**.
- **Career Path**:
- For success, the native should **integrate Ketu's significations** into their profession, such as roles that involve **healing or resolving pain** (e.g., doctor, lawyer, military, occult practitioner, healer).
- If Ketu-related fields are not pursued, the native may face significant **professional struggles**.
- Has difficulty working under others and dislikes taking orders, suggesting a preference for **independent work**.
- **Maternal Grandparents**: Likely endured **problems and suffering**, possibly connected to **past life karma**.

Combination 70. Ketu – Saturn

- **Professional Environment**: This combination leads to a **challenging work environment** where the native may feel **disinterest** in their profession and often prefers to **work alone**.
- **Disputes and Arguments**: Ketu, acting in a manner similar to Mars (**Kujavat Ketu**), brings a tendency for **arguments and disputes** in the professional sphere, resulting in frequent **misunderstandings** and conflicts.
- **Challenges**: The native may experience **ongoing issues and misunderstandings** in their career due to Ketu's influence, making harmonious collaboration difficult.

Prashna (Horary) Technique Using 70 Combinations

This approach to Prashna (horary astrology) is unique because it directly interprets the native's query and its answer through the planets involved in a combination based on a chosen number. Here's how it works:

1. **Ask the Querent to Choose a Number**:
   - The querent picks a number from **1 to 70**.
   - Each number correlates to one of the 70 astrological combinations.
2. **Interpret the Chosen Combination**:
   - Locate the chosen combination and analyze it.
   - The **first planet** represents the **question** or **issue at hand**.
   - The **second planet** provides the **answer or outcome**.
3. **Positive or Negative Outcome**:
   - **Malefic or challenging combinations** (those involving planets like Saturn, Rahu, Ketu, or Mars in problematic combinations) suggest a **negative outcome** or obstacles related to the query.
   - **Benefic combinations** (those involving planets like Jupiter or Venus in favorable alignments) indicate a **positive outcome** or solution.
4. **Examples**:
   - **Example 1**: Querent picks **number 45**.
   - **Combination**: Mercury - Venus
   - **Interpretation**:
   - **Question (Mercury)**: Likely related to **education, finance, communication, or relationships**.
   - **Answer (Venus)**: Positive outcome - success in matters of **luxury, comfort and financial gain**.
   - **Outcome**: Positive. If the querent's question was about finances, the answer suggests a comfortable financial situation or success through Mercury-Venus areas like finance, fine arts, or education.
   - **Example 2**: Querent picks **number 68**.

- o **Combination**: Rahu - Saturn
- o **Interpretation**:
- o **Question (Rahu)**: Likely about **career, ambition, or unconventional approaches**.
- o **Answer (Saturn)**: Difficulties and challenges, possibly **delays, struggles, or obstacles in career**.
- o **Outcome**: Negative. This combination is often challenging, indicating a career path requiring resilience to overcome obstacles or potential delays.

Practical Application:

This method provides **quick insights** for a querent's query without requiring a detailed chart analysis.

It's especially useful when immediate guidance is needed, using the qualities of each planet in the chosen combination to provide a **concise answer** to the query.

The Radiant Source: Understanding the Sun

Sun in Different Houses from Jupiter: Detailed Explanation

1st House (Sun with Jupiter in Lagna):

The native has a **powerful and spiritually inclined personality**, with a **practical outlook** on life. The Sun's influence here gives a **strong physical build** and a **healthy body** (unless negatively impacted by malefic aspects). The native may resemble their **father in appearance** or embody certain paternal traits. The **sign** is less significant here as the combined influence of Sun and Jupiter highlights **inner strength and purpose**.

2nd House (Sun in the 2nd House from Jupiter):

Known for **straightforward and direct speech**, the native experiences **financial instability** with money flowing in and out quickly, which can affect long-term financial stability. **Marriage and family life are delayed**, often starting later in life, regardless of gender. This delay often brings maturity and life experience to the native, shaping their relationships in unique ways.

3rd House (Sun in the 3rd House from Jupiter):

The Sun brings **inner strength, courage and powerful communication skills**. The native may be an **effective orator** and often a natural **leader** in communication-related fields.Strong inner resilience is accompanied by a desire for **pilgrimage** or spiritual journeys, indicating an inclination toward spirituality or religious exploration.

4th House (Sun in the 4th House from Jupiter):

This placement brings blessings to the **mother, academics and overall happiness**. The native may excel in **studies** (unless affected by malefic aspects) and is likely to have a **strong-willed mother** who may hold a ruling position within the household.The home will have a **spiritual or peaceful aura**, often imbued with a sense of harmony and positivity.

5th House (Sun in the 5th House from Jupiter):

Here, the Sun acts as a **malefic**, possibly leading to **delays in childbirth** and prohibiting **negative habits** in the native. It often leads the native toward disciplined and righteous behavior.There may be a **curse of a Brahmin** or **family deity** affecting the native, which could stem from **past-life deeds** or unfulfilled obligations. However, children born to the native will have a **bright future** as the 5th house (purva punya bhava) reflects blessings of Jupiter's wisdom and good fortune.

6th House (Sun in the 6th House from Jupiter):

This placement can cause **eye problems** since the Sun governs **vision**. The **relationship with the father** may suffer due to challenging aspects (6-8 axis).The native will likely have **strong and efficient servants** and may encounter **powerful adversaries** or enemies. Pets, especially those considered dangerous, may play a role in their life as well, reflecting the Sun's strength in this house of challenges.

7th House (Partners/Day-to-Day Activities/Friends):

The native attracts **powerful and influential friends**, often older or more experienced. Friends may have **political ties** or high-status connections, providing the native with a broad network of support.Daily activities are approached with **discipline** and organization, helping maintain a structured routine and stability in relationships.

8th House :

With the Sun in the 8th house from Jupiter, the native may experience **financial losses** throughout life due to Sun's aspect on the 2nd house of money.However, this placement also brings **name and fame**, possibly due to involvement in profound or transformative pursuits, often elevating the native's public image despite financial instability.

9th House (Fortune, Education, Travel, Children):

The native enjoys **honors and awards** and is inclined toward **long-distance travel**, especially for pilgrimages or spiritual purposes.Higher education (such as post-graduate studies) may be pursued in a **different region or country**, indicating the search for knowledge beyond local borders.The **second child** of the native is likely to be successful, adding a layer of positivity to this house.

10th House (Father and Profession):

There is a strong resemblance between the **father and grandfather** in appearance or character.The native's **professional life** is positive, with a likelihood of reaching a **high-ranking position** - possibly in government or a similar structured field.

11th House (Profits and Friends):

This placement brings **good profits** and financial gains, with support from **powerful friends** who may assist the native in reaching goals or expanding influence.Social networks are beneficial, enhancing both status and financial stability.

12th House (Secret Enemies and Health):

The native may face a **powerful secret enemy** who subtly works against them or attempts to **sabotage their progress**.Potential **enmity with the father** could arise, indicating underlying tension in their relationship.

Sun in Different Rashis: Effects on Father and Son

Rashi impact can be seen on the Jeev Tatva represented by the planet and not much on the native

Aries (Sun Exalted):

Father: Gains a **higher position** after the native's birth, bringing **name and fame**. Exalted Sun enhances the father's reputation and may result in **prominent status**.

Son: Will experience similar benefits, born into a **favorable environment**. Native will be **self-willed**, acting with **independence and authority**, often making decisions based on personal will.

Taurus:

Father: **Financially stable**, with likely success in **financial matters** or businesses.

Son: Career is likely in a **financial institution** or related field, inheriting a natural inclination toward wealth and financial security.

Gemini:

Father: Grows and succeeds through **intelligence** and adaptability, thriving in fields that value **mental acuity**.

Son: Likely to create a career in **arts, commerce**, or **communication**, with both father and son known for their **intelligence and creativity**.

Cancer (Moon's Rashi, Creative Influence):

Father: Displays a **love for art** and creativity, possibly enjoying pursuits or hobbies that express this affinity.

Son: To achieve career success, it's beneficial for him to **leave his birthplace**. Likely to travel extensively or settle far from his origin.

Leo:

Father: Possesses a **stout, authoritative** presence, enjoying **prestige and royal or governmental favors**. Known for **clear, direct communication**, he carries authority naturally.

Son: Resembles the **grandfather's characteristics** and is likely to enjoy similar **royal or governmental support** in life.

Virgo:

Father: Known for **intelligence and resourcefulness**, with a reputation for **receiving help and cooperation** from others.

Son: Follows a similar path, benefiting from **intellectual pursuits** and **supportive networks** that assist him in personal growth and prosperity.

Libra (Sun Debilitated):

Father: Faces **challenges and struggles** after the native's birth, undergoing a **difficult period**. Despite hardships, he may **rise from the grassroots level** later in life, gradually achieving stability. He endures a **tough career path**.

Son: Experiences similar **struggles** and likely pursues a career in **financial institutions**.

Scorpio:

Father: Encounters **struggles** throughout three stages - going into, being in and emerging from **debilitation**. His career may relate to **machinery or land dealings**.

Son: Also faces similar **hardships** and may enter professions related to **machinery or real estate**.

Sagittarius:

Father: Holds a **philosophical outlook** and often engages in **divine contemplation**, with moderate prestige in his career. His life's purpose is **spiritual growth**.

Son: Will likely lead an **honorable life** with a focus on spirituality or higher knowledge, much like his father.

Capricorn:

Father: Achieves **gradual growth**, with occasional fits of **anger** and frustration. He enjoys **traveling**.

Son: May also have a career involving **travel or machinery**, following a similar professional path to his father.

Aquarius:

Father: Known for his **discretion and intelligence**, particularly in challenging situations. He enjoys **prestige** and may have knowledge of **occult matters**.

Son: Reflects similar qualities of **intellect and reputation**, with an interest in the **occult**.

Pisces:
Father: Honorable, spiritually inclined and known for his good looks. He is often respected within the community.
Son: Likely to share his father's spirituality and respectable standing in society, receiving favors from influential people.

Conjunction of Sun with Different Planets Irrespective of Degrees

Sun + Moon:

Family Deity: Female Goddess.

Traits: Highly **intelligent**, with the ability to **overcome troubles using intellect**. Gains **wealth later in life** and **achieves name and fame** in a different land.

Sun + Mars:

Family Deity: Hanuman or Kartikeya.

Traits: Skilled in **surgery, arts, music, or sports**. Strong limbs and **physical prowess**. Gains **recognition for talents**. Elderly or powerful people may help them **overcome obstacles**.

Sun + Mercury:

Family Deity: Vishnu or Laxmi Narayan.

Traits: May have a **delicate constitution** with **elite eating habits** and potential **skin issues**. Strong in **academics, spiritual studies and languages**. Likely to excel in **design, media and communication**, achieving **fame**.

Sun + Venus:

Family Deity: Goddess Laxmi.

Traits: Enjoys **costly vehicles** and a **healthy, delicate body**. Gains **recognition in career** and is admired wherever they go. In male charts, the **wife may be the family leader** and is likely **spiritual, values tradition** and enjoys **traveling to spiritual and joyful places**. Tends toward **high expenditures**.

Sun + Saturn:

Family Deity: Kal Bhairav or Shakti.

Traits: Achieves **high-ranking positions** and a **good salary** unless influenced by Rahu. Known for **stability in business** (especially large-scale) and **health**. Gains **prestige and respect** in their profession.

Sun + Rahu:

Family Deity: Snake God.

Traits: Health issues may include **gastric and skin problems**; the father might be **speculative, imaginative**, or prone to illusions. Gains **fame in foreign lands** for creative work. The father is likely to enjoy a **long life**.

Sun + Ketu:

Family Deity: Ganesh.

Traits: Father could be the **eldest, youngest, or last child**. May have **allergies** or **electricity-related issues**. Achieves **fame with the blessing of family deities** and ancestors. Potential danger of **death within the first year of life**, surrounded by strong **spiritual energies** and **intuition**. This is an especially **good combination for astrologers**.

Sun Combinations and Their Effects:

- **Sun + Mars**:
- **Father's Life**: Accident or surgery after native's birth; possibility of land purchase.
- **Sun + Mercury**:
- **Father's Traits**: Intelligent, may start a business after the native's birth.
- **Sun + Jupiter**:

- **Father's Role**: Becomes religious, public figure; strong bond with the native.
- **Sun + Venus**:
- **Father's Wealth**: Gains wealth, luxury and comfort after the native's birth.
- **Sun + Saturn**:
- **Father's Challenges**: Faces struggles and problems after the native's birth.
- **Sun + Rahu**:
- **Father's New Path**: Begins a non-traditional venture after native's birth.
- **Sun + Ketu**:
- **Father's Spirituality**: Grows interested in occult; may indicate his last life.

Sun's Secrets

- **Sun in Taurus**: Mother of native will be very faithful to her husband as Moon is exalted in Taurus.
- **Sun + Saturn in Gemini and Mercury in Cancer**: Native may become a talented painter.
- **Sun hemmed/placed between 2 inimical planets (Venus, Rahu, Saturn)**: Father may have a short lifespan.
- **Sun in Gemini or Virgo**: Father may be a trader.
- **Sun in Taurus with Venus**: Father is likely to be wealthy.
- **Sun between Saturn and Mars**: Father faces many challenges and obstacles.
- **Sun + Ketu in Virgo or Gemini**: Father may work as an advisor to others.
- **Enemy planet in 12th to Sun**: Indicates a short lifespan for the father.
- **Sun in Libra and Mars in Capricorn**: Father may struggle with managing household responsibilities.
- **Sun + Mars + Rahu + Saturn**: Father may earn a low salary.
- **12th House from Sun aspected by Saturn**: Father may encounter problems due to bad company.
- **Sun in Cancer**: Father may settle with in-laws.
- **Sun in Aries and Venus in Taurus**: Father may be a master of fine arts.
- **Sun + Venus + Rahu in 2nd House**: Father may have a mistress.
- **No planets in 2nd and 12th Houses from Sun**: Father may face significant challenges.
- **Sun + Venus + Moon**: Native may be the child of the father's second wife.
- **Mars in 12th from Sun, Jupiter in 2nd**: Native's brother may achieve fame.
- **Venus + Sun**: Native's wife is likely a devotional or spiritually inclined person.

- **Sun in 11th from Saturn**: Indicates potential for a government job.
- **Sun + Venus + Mercury (in consecutive houses)**: Father may have had two wives or a mistress.
- **Sun + Mars + Moon**: Father receives rental income or benefits from landed property.
- **Venus in 2nd from Sun (aspected by Jupiter)**: Native and father may share the same profession.
- **Sun + Mercury + Jupiter in 2nd House**: Born into an educated family; father and grandfather are well-educated.
- **8th Lord from Sun in 3rd House with Mars and/or Saturn**: Father may face early death.
- **Sun + Venus**: Unhappy married life; wife may have ego, attitude, or authority issues.
- **Mars in 7th from Sun**: Father may have a bad temper.
- **Sun and Jupiter exchange + Transiting Saturn or Jupiter over Sun or Jupiter**: Brings name, fame and promotion to the native.
- **Sun in 3rd from Jupiter**: Native will experience parental happiness.
- **Sun in 12th from Jupiter**: Native's father may not take care of the native during childhood.
- **Sun exalted with no planet in 12th House**: Father struggled to achieve a high position.
- **Sun + Rahu + Saturn in Aries or Scorpio (Mars sign)**: Father may possess old ancestral property.
- **Sun in debilitation with Rahu in Leo**: Father might face danger during Jupiter's transit over Rahu.
- **Venus + Rahu + Mars**: Native may elope with a woman or have relationships with another woman.

House Placement from Jupiter

- **12th House from Venus**: Difficulty saving money (if Venus is alone).
- **3rd House from Saturn**: Government influence.

- **6th House**: Argumentative and prone to frequent disputes.
- **10th House**: Wealth and suspicious nature.
- **Lagna**: Represents self-made wealth.

Body Significance of Sun in Different Signs

- **Sun in Aries**: Prone to **headaches or migraines**.
- **Sun in Taurus**: **Reddish face** and **harsh voice**.
- **Sun in Gemini**: **Powerful shoulders** and **muscular arms**.
- **Sun in Cancer**: **Healthy heartbeats** but may experience **chest problems**.
- **Sun in Leo**: **Good appetite**.
- **Sun in Virgo**: **Strong intestinal muscles**, possibly with **six-pack abs**.
- **Sun in Libra**: **Good-looking body** despite Sun's debilitation.
- **Sun in Scorpio**: Prone to **excessive urination**.
- **Sun in Sagittarius**: **Well-shaped thighs and hips**.
- **Sun in Capricorn**: Potential for **knee problems** or **large knee caps**.
- **Sun in Aquarius**: **Strong calf muscles**.
- **Sun in Pisces**: **Strong feet**.

Understanding Moon : Cycles of Emotion and Reflection

Moon in Different Houses from Jupiter

Moon in 1st House from Jupiter:
The **malefic impact of the Moon is minimized**. The native has a **pious and gentle mind** and may **resemble their mother**. The **mother is likely religious** and may hold a **public or socially respected position**. Positive, progressive changes are common in the native's mindset, with an **affinity for traveling to religious sites**.

Moon 2nd from Jupiter:
This position often leads to **early marriage**. The native's speech is **sweet, soft and quick** but can sometimes seem irrelevant. Financially, there's a **continuous and fast inflow and outflow of money**, resulting in **fluctuating finances without crisis**. Some **differences of opinion** may arise with the mother, who might spend significantly on **religious activities**.

Moon 3rd from Jupiter:
The native may experience **blame or scandals** for actions they didn't commit. There is likely to be a **younger sister** and **sudden, short trips** are common. Relationships with the mother are generally **friendly** and she may have a **good network of friends** and an **elder brother**.

Moon 4th from Jupiter:
The **mother's profession** may be connected to **teaching or preaching**. Her father (the native's maternal grandfather) is likely **pious** and **religious**. The native enjoys a **generally happy life** and may **change residences and vehicles** a couple of times over their life.

Moon 5th from Jupiter:
This position often indicates a **girl child** for the native, who will **bring good changes**. The native is considered **lucky for the mother**, as this arrangement brings **blessings** and Jupiter's position in the 9th house from the Moon supports the mother's well-being.

Moon 6th from Jupiter (6-8 relationship):
Relationships with the mother may be **strained** and the native may **not get along well** with her. **Illnesses tend to be short-lived** and come and go quickly. However, if **Jupiter or Saturn** influences this position, it can lead to **longer-term or chronic health issues**. Despite potential challenges, the **mother's longevity remains strong**.

Moon 7th from Jupiter:
The native's **partner has positive thoughts** and approaches **day-to-day activities in a fast, unplanned manner**.

Moon 8th from Jupiter:
The native has **good longevity**. However, if the **mother falls ill**, it may be a **long-term illness** as Jupiter, representing longer durations, is in the 6th house from the Moon.

Moon 9th from Jupiter:
Brings **sudden good fortune** along with opportunities for **sudden travel or long journeys**.

Moon 10th from Jupiter:
Indicates **changes in profession** and a **relocation for the father** after the native's birth. The **mother will find happiness at home**.

Moon in 11th from Jupiter:
The native may have an **elder sister** and a **good-natured personality**. Likely to **change friends frequently**. The

mother may have a **younger brother** and might take **short religious trips**.

Moon in 12th from Jupiter (2-12 relationship):
This placement indicates **differences of opinion with the mother**. The native may **ignore the mother's advice** and could have **secret or undetected loans**. The mother is **truthful** but has **fast expenses with little savings**. The **mother's family is financially stable**.

Moon in Different Signs

Moon in Aries:

The **mother is courageous** and **stubborn**, with some sympathy for those in trouble, although she may not take action to help. The native tends to have **fast eating habits**, is **self-centered** and **cares deeply about appearance and personality**.

Moon in Taurus:

The **mother is money-minded** and may have an **artistic inclination**. The native has a high self-opinion but may fall into **low-level thinking** or trivial concerns.

Moon in Gemini:

Both the **mother and native are intelligent** with strong **communication skills**. The mother is **diplomatic and clever** at achieving her goals, while the native has a natural inclination toward **business-minded thinking**.

Moon in Cancer:

The **mother experiences many changes** throughout life and is **caring and nurturing**. The native is also **emotional and somewhat fickle-minded**, with a strong **love for the arts**.

Moon in Leo:

The **mother is authoritative** and **rules the family**. The native has **clear and determined thoughts** and aspires for **honor and recognition in life**.

Moon in Virgo:

The **mother shares traits with Gemini** but is more **organized**. She tries to **accumulate wealth** diligently. The native is **competitive and jealous** by nature, very **social** and prone to **overthinking and deliberation**.

Moon in Libra:

The **mother is beautiful** with traits similar to Taurus. The **native has high sexual drive** and attraction toward the opposite sex, as Libra governs sexual themes and relationships. There's a strong **ambition for financial success**.

Moon in Scorpio:

The **mother shares characteristics with Aries**, with a determined and sometimes intense personality. The **native has a mysterious mind** with interests in **history, mystery and the occult**. Scorpio's hidden qualities manifest as a **fickle nature** and a desire to **influence others subtly**.

Moon in Sagittarius:

The **mother is religious, social** and has **good public relations**. The **native is similarly social, values public recognition** and is **broad-minded** with a generally pious disposition.

Moon in Capricorn:

The **mother faces hurdles** in life and holds orthodox views. The **native also encounters obstacles**, particularly in professional life, with a strong sense of **justice and equality**. This can lead to **emotional decision-making** that causes regret.

Moon in Aquarius:
The **mother has similar traits to Capricorn** but with a more **unconventional (sanki) mindset**. The **native exhibits a unique, psychic quality**, with a **secretive, manipulative thought process**.

Moon in Pisces:
The **mother is like Sagittarius**, with a religious and spiritual nature. The **native is even more spiritual**, knowledgeable in **metaphysical subjects** and carries a deeper sense of wisdom.

Moon Combination (1,5,9)
Irrespective of Degrees

Moon + Sun:

After the native's birth, the **mother gains a royal, authoritative nature**. This combination suggests a need for **soul purification** and **enlightenment** since the Sun represents pure energy, balancing the subconscious.

Moon + Mars:

The **mother may have a younger brother** and there may be a **surgery, accident, or land purchase** following the native's birth. The native tends to have **anxiety and a strong, aggressive mindset**, often acting out of habit and driven by ego and Martian qualities. Physical activity can help balance the mind. The native's **brother's life will experience many changes** and the **husband will likely come from a distant place**.

Moon + Mercury:

The **mother has a younger sibling** following the native's birth and a sibling may be born within 1.5 years of the native. If this combination is in an odd sign, it suggests a male child; in an even sign, a female child. The native has **effortless learning abilities** and can train the subconscious by **continually learning and educating** themselves.

Moon + Jupiter:

The **native resembles the mother in looks** and has a **religious, spiritual mindset** with a liking for public activities and travel. There's a **flickering mind** that likes sweets and undergoes positive changes. The native will **gain luck by moving from their birthplace**. The mother serves as a **source of wisdom** and **subconscious training** may occur through knowledge or a guru's blessings.

Moon + Venus:

The **mother is beautiful, musical and enjoys luxury and cleanliness**. She is **money-minded**, with an exalted Moon due to Venus's influence. The native may need medication related to the body part associated with Venus's sign. **Wealth increases after the birth of a daughter**. However, there may be **conflict between the wife and mother-in-law** if they live together and **uncontrolled expenses can lead to financial losses**.

Moon + Saturn:

This combination brings **obstacles in the mother's life** after the native's birth. The **mother is a traditional, old-fashioned woman**. The native may experience **frequent changes in profession** or will travel often for work. If there is no change, the native may feel **unsatisfied** and think about changing jobs. A tendency towards **renouncing materialism** is common, as many with this combination have saintly traits. **Subconscious training** is aided by **accepting responsibilities, managing time and being disciplined**.

Moon + Rahu:

The **mother experiences obstacles** but also a **new beginning in life** after the native's birth. She may have **opulence and enjoys luxuries**, with Rahu bringing Venus-like qualities but with a slightly malefic twist. The native is similarly **opulent** and may be **spendthrift** yet receives enough income. There's a **fear of the unknown** in the native's mind, along with a talent for **keen observation**. **Subconscious training** is achieved by **observing and focusing on positive influences**, as "what you see, you become."

Moon + Ketu:

The **mother resembles her parents**, has a **spiritual disposition** and may be the **youngest child** in her family. She may carry **lifelong tension** after the native's birth. The native often has a **disturbed mind**. **Subconscious training** is most effective through **writing positive thoughts and practices** to embody them. This combination emphasizes that **"what you write and feel, you become."**

Moon's Secrets

- **Moon + Venus (Conjunction)**: The native may have a **strong desire for romantic relationships** and enjoys the company of multiple partners.
- **Moon + Ketu + Mars in 7th House**:There may be **difficulties with pregnancy**.
- **Moon Behind Venus**:The native may experience **unhappiness in married life**, with the **wife dominating the mother-in-law**.
- **Venus Behind Moon**: Here, the **mother-in-law tends to dominate** the family dynamic.
- **Rahu in 12th and Mars in 11th from Moon**: The native may be **vulnerable to possession, black magic and the evil eye (nazar lagna)**.
- **Saturn in 2nd from Moon and Ketu in 3rd from Moon**:
  The native's life resembles that of a **sanyasi (ascetic)**, with a detached or spiritual lifestyle.
- **Saturn + Moon + Ketu (Chandra Maneshwar Yog)**:
  Symbolic of the **Moon on Shiva's head**, indicating a powerful spiritual connection.
- **Rahu in 2nd from Moon**: The native may struggle with **mental peace**.
- **Moon + Rahu**: The **mother may experience hardship** and tough times.
- **Venus in 7th and Ketu from Moon**: The native may lack **happiness in relationships**.
- **Debilitated Moon**: Indicates **lack of happiness for the mother**.
- **Debilitated Moon 3rd from Jupiter**: The native may be **frequently deceived by friends and others**.
- **Moon + Mars + Rahu**: Causes **disturbances and lack of mental peace** for the native.
- **Moon in Leo**: The **mother feels a sense of regality** and behaves as though she is a queen, possessing pride and authority in the family.

- **Moon + Rahu / Ketu**: This combination often leads to **mental depression** for the native due to the destabilizing influence of Rahu or the detachment of Ketu.
- **Moon and Mercury Exchange**: The native may experience **ill fate and humiliation** as a result of this exchange, affecting reputation and luck.
- **Moon and Ketu in Capricorn + Jupiter in Leo**:
  This combination can indicate a **risk for bypass surgery** for the native, as the placement brings health challenges related to circulation and the heart.
- **Moon in 2nd to Jupiter and Mars in 4th from Jupiter**:
  The native may inherit **landed property from the mother**, suggesting maternal wealth in the form of real estate.
- **Moon + Jupiter in Scorpio + Mars in Cancer**:
  This combination may lead the native to **form relationships with individuals from lower social backgrounds**, reflecting influences of intense emotions and desires.
- **Moon and Mars Exchange**: This exchange brings a mix of **emotional intensity and impulsive behavior**, with possible challenges in managing anger and desires, though specifics would depend on the houses and signs involved.

Conjunction

Moon conjuncts a malefic while that malefic has exchanged places with another planet - Affects mother's health.

House Placement from Jupiter

- **2nd House**: Moon placed here - Friends involved in chemical-related work.
- **5th House (Female)**: Indicates one child settled abroad.
- **6th House**: Suggests the birth of a female child.

- **6th House (Female Horoscope)**: Likelihood of multiple female children.
- **8th House**: Possession of foreign currency.
- **12th House**: Indicates mother's long life.
- **4th House**: Nearby water source or locality name related to water.

Understanding Mars :The Warrior Spirit

Mars in Different Houses from Jupiter

1st House:

The native is likely to experience an **accident or surgery** at some point, especially when Saturn or Jupiter transits this sign. There is **good relationship and resemblance with the brother**; in female charts, compatibility with the husband is strong. The **brother or husband may be a public figure** and could own **three properties or a spacious home**. The native's property may be located **near a religious site**.

2nd House:

Mars here can lead to **delays in marriage** and **obstructions in family matters**. The native may have a **harsh tone**. If Venus aspects this position, these issues lessen, particularly in finances, which improve if Mars-related professions (such as uniformed services) are pursued. Otherwise, **financial problems may arise**. **Accidents or surgeries** could impact the family and there may be **differences with the husband or brother**. If Jupiter is in the 12th from Mars, expect **expenses related to religious activities**.

3rd House:

This position may bring **accidents or surgeries to siblings**. The native's **siblings benefit from them**, though the native may face **obstructed short travels**. If Jupiter is in the 11th from Mars, the **husband has an elder brother** and both **brother and husband enjoy supportive friendships**.

4th House:

The **mother may exhibit a rough, aggressive nature**. The native might **lack full domestic happiness**. If Jupiter is in the 10th from Mars, the **brother or husband may work as a teacher or be involved in religious activities**. The native may also hear **nighttime noises related to machinery or manual work**, indicating proximity to a **workshop or factory**.

5th House:

There may be **difficulties in having children**, with **childbirth likely via C-section**. If Jupiter is in the 9th from Mars, the **husband or brother may receive blessings from a guru** and experience **good luck**, with a higher chance of having **sons as second and third children**.

6th House:

The native's **relationship with their brother is strained** due to the 6/8 axis and there may be **property disputes**. Relationships with the **husband are also challenging**.

7th House:

Business partners are likely to be stubborn. The **partners of the native's husband or brother are reliable and good-natured**. The native's **day-to-day activities are marked by hastiness and anxiety**.

8th House:

The **6/8 axis** brings **relationship issues with the brother or husband**. The native may face **problems with**

inherited property, possibly receiving less than expected or deserved.

9th House:

The **brother or husband has good habits, ethics and a moral nature** if Jupiter is in the 5th from Mars. The native may face **obstacles in higher education** and **challenges with long-distance travel**.

10th House:

In a **female's chart**, the **mother-in-law will be supportive**, especially if Jupiter is in the 4th from Mars. The **husband or brother enjoys home happiness and good property**. The native's **profession may involve Mars-related fields**, with potential struggles if these energies are not channeled appropriately.

11th House:

Elder siblings and friends are likely to be aggressive or bullying. The **husband may have a younger brother**. Short travels to religious places are common.

12th House:

Relations with the **brother are strained** and there may be **differences of opinion with the husband**. The native experiences **lack of pleasure in marital intimacy** and **limited enjoyment of honeymoon or bed pleasures**, although **brother and husband's finances are stable**.

Mars in Different Signs

Aries:

Brother/Husband: Exhibits **athletic skills** and may be a **public figure**, displaying courage and stubbornness. The husband may come from the **east direction**.
Native: Prone to **head injuries or surgeries**; **land is located in the east**. Has an **aggressive and daring nature**, relying on their talents.

Taurus:

Land: Situated in the **south**.
Husband: Likely to be from the **south direction** with **good financial standing** and attractive looks.
Native: Prone to **accidents or surgeries in the throat area**. Patient and adaptable, with a preference for **attractive things** and an ability to earn with ease.

Gemini:

Land: Located in the **west**.
Husband: Likely from the **west direction**, with a talent for **communication, medium height and good looks**.
Native: Likely to experience **shoulder or hand injuries** and is generally **intelligent**.

Cancer:

Land: Found in the **north**.
Husband: From the **north direction**; **round-faced, dark complexion, tall**; may work in **food, travel, or hotel industry**.
Native: Prone to **back or chest injuries**; may face accusations, lacks courage and tends to be **henpecked**. Often feels **deceived or cheated**.

Leo:

Property/Land: Located in the **east, usually in a prime area**.
Husband: From the **east direction**, possibly in a **government-related profession** and physically attractive.
Brother/Husband: Dominating personality; **accident-prone in the stomach area**.
Native: Hot-tempered, proud and stubborn; **expects respect from others**.

Virgo:

Property/Land: Located in the **south, often vacant or commercial**.
Husband: From the **south direction, intelligent and competitive** with a tendency to be **jealous and talkative**.
Native: May suffer **intestinal issues or surgeries** and is prone to having a **commercial or vacant property**.

Libra:

Land: Located in the **west direction**.
Husband: Likely from the **west**, medium height, well-spoken and fortunate. **Husband/Brother** is typically **good-looking**.
Native: May face **issues in the private parts**. Driven by money, faithful and trustworthy.

Scorpio:

Land: Found in the **north direction**.
Husband: Likely from the **north; stubborn and secretive**.
Brother/Husband: Shows similar **stubbornness and secretive nature**.
Native: Prone to **surgery or accidents in internal private parts**; has a **self-centered and troublesome personality**.

Sagittarius:

Land: Located in the **east direction**.
Husband: Likely from the **east**, tall, honest, intelligent and may achieve **fame after marriage**.
Brother/Husband: Religious, involved in **spiritual or religious activities**, introverted.
Native: May experience **injuries or surgery on the thighs**; has a **kind-hearted and contemplative nature**.

Capricorn:

Land: Situated in the **south direction**.
Husband: Likely from the **south**, may have a **lazy nature**.
Brother/Husband: Similar lazy disposition; accident-prone in the **knee area**.
Native: Self-assertive, holds firm opinions, speaks harshly, goes out of their way to help others yet often receives **blame and criticism in return**.

Aquarius:

Land: Located in the **west direction**.
Husband: Likely from the **west**, of **vocal and expressive nature** (vahmi).
Brother/Husband: May experience accidents or surgery in the **calf area**.
Native: Mild-mannered and gentle.

Pisces:

Land: Found in the **north direction**.
Husband: Likely from the **north**, tall, knowledgeable and often recites **Vedic mantras**.
Brother/Husband: Public figure, family-oriented.
Native: Prone to **foot injuries**; of **helpful and pious nature**.

When **Mars is in the 3rd, 6th, 9th, or 12th signs**, the native is likely to:

Own multiple properties, with at least **two properties minimum**.

Enter into joint ownership for purchasing property, partnering with someone else to hold the property in **both names**.

Quickly acquire additional properties soon after the initial purchase, showing a propensity for **rapid property investment**.

Key Aspects of Mars as Energy

Energy as Life Force: Mars represents the life force necessary for all activities. Proper energy use leads to constructive outcomes, while improper use may lead to destructive results.

Mars and Sexuality: One of Mars's primary expressions is through sexuality, which directly links to procreation. An afflicted Mars can interfere with sexual performance, potentially leading to challenges in fulfilling progeny-related goals in marriage.

Mars Dispositor: The ruler of the sign Mars occupies (dispositor) profoundly affects how Mars's energy manifests. A well-placed dispositor can balance Mars's energy, while an afflicted dispositor may intensify its negative aspects.

Manglik Dosha and Rashi Placement: Manglik dosha traditionally considers Mars's placement by Rashi rather than by house. If Mars is positioned unfavorably in either a male or female chart, it can create difficulties in sexual harmony within relationships.

Mars in Female Chart: **Mercury Signs (Gemini, Virgo)**: When Mars is in Mercury's signs, a female may feel an attraction towards individuals who might be seen as 'roadside Romeos' or those of lower social or financial standing. **Protection by Jupiter or Sun**: If Jupiter or the Sun aspects Mars, it can act as a protective influence, potentially steering the native away from inappropriate associations.

Mars in Male Chart and Sexuality: An afflicted Mars may indicate homosexual tendencies, especially if supported by certain placements or aspects that suppress Mars's typical outward expression of sexuality toward the opposite sex.

Mars Combination (1,5,9) Irrespective of Degrees

Mars + Sun:

- **Brother**: Resembles **father** in appearance and behavior; **good compatibility** with the father, possibly a **government employee** or VIP with **high status**. He will **assume family leadership after the father**.
- **Husband**: From a **reputable and famous family**, possibly a VIP.
- **Native**: Likely to own **land near a VIP area**. Accidents or surgery may impact the **father**, who will own property. **Deity** is likely **Hanuman or Kartikey**.

Mars + Moon:

- **Brother**: Resembles **mother** in looks and character. Likely to have **good intentions** and may **travel abroad**.
- **Husband**: Could be from a **distant place or abroad**, of a good caste.
- **Native**: Land might be near **water**. **Mother** may face an **accident or surgery**.

Mars + Mercury:

- **Native**: Has a **highly calculative mind**; experiences **conflicts with relatives or neighbors** and **hurdles in business and education**. Disruptions in education are likely, especially if Mars has a higher degree.
- **Brother/Husband**: Educated, intelligent, possibly in **business**.

Mars + Jupiter:

- **Brother/Husband**: Religious, a **public figure**, or involved in social activities.
- **Native**: Property may be near a **religious or social gathering place**. **Accidents or surgery** are likely for the native. **Brother and native resemble each other**.

Mars + Venus:

- **Brother/Husband**: Good-looking, financially secure, interested in fine arts and fond of vehicles.
- **Native**: Likely to own **property near luxury establishments**, such as a bank or medical shop. The **wife may face surgery or an accident** and is likely to own property.

Mars + Saturn (Yantra Yoga):

- **Native**: Saturn acts as a **speed breaker**, creating delays and obstructions. Success in **Mars-related professions** (e.g., technical, engineering, mechanical) will minimize issues. Will need to exert more effort for smaller returns.
- **Brother/Husband**: Likely to face **obstacles and delays in their career**, especially in land-related matters.

Mars + Rahu:

- **Native: Land ownership may involve challenges** and **grandparents may have experienced surgery or an accident** related to their land. Rahu begins to act like Venus after age 30.
- **Brother**: Initially faces challenges but later improves in life; may look like a grandparent and might relocate to a distant land.
- **Husband**: May be from a different caste; an intercaste or foreign marriage could reduce marital issues.

Mars + Ketu:

- **Native**: Experiences **persistent tension related to property**, with land likely situated at the edge of a city or colony.
- **Brother/Husband**: Life-long tension and possibly an interest in occult matters.
- **Maternal Grandparent**: May own land and have a history of surgery or accidents.

Mars Secret Combinations

- **8th from Mars – Rahu/Ketu**: Longevity of the **husband is compromised**.
- **10th from Mars – Rahu/Ketu**: **Husband's profession** faces challenges, absence of **peace and home happiness**. Benefic aspects can improve the situation.
- **Mars + Rahu**: The **native may have negative traits**.
- **Mars debilitated + Ketu**: The **brother's life is compromised**.
- **Mars 7th from Jupiter with Saturn conjunct**: Creates **enmity between the native and brother**.
- **Mars 2nd from Jupiter with Saturn aspect**: Indicates an **unhappy married life** for the native.
- **Mars aspect on 4th House**: The native is likely to have **landed property**.
- **Mars aspecting Moon with Moon between Jupiter and Ketu**: **Mother's lifespan may be short**.
- **Mars in 7th from Saturn**: **Unsuccessful professional life**; a career related to **Mars (e.g., technical or mechanical work)** is recommended.
- **Mars aspecting 4th house from Jupiter**: **Native's mother may show less affection** towards the native.
- **Mars in Taurus**: The native may have a **mark or scar on their face**.
- **Mars + Ketu behind Jupiter**: The native may **suffer from piles**.
- **Mars + Saturn**: Native will have a **quarrelsome nature**.
- **Mars 7th from Mercury**: Indicates **limited educational attainment** for the native.
- **Mars + Sun in Cancer**: Native may be prone to **diabetes**.
- **Mars + Rahu behind Jupiter**: This placement can lead to **interruptions in education**.

- **Venus in 2nd from Mars**: The **brother of the native may deceive one of his sisters**.
- **Mars and Venus Exchange**: The native will be **highly attractive**, easily drawing the attention of the opposite sex, though it may come at the cost of **reputation or financial loss**.
- **Mars + Sun**: Native may have **reddish eyes**.
- **Mars + Ketu + Saturn**: This combination suggests the native might be a **tailor**.
- **Mars positioned between Sun and Jupiter**: Indicates that the **father of the native may pass away at an early age**.
- **Mars with Jupiter in Libra and Venus exchanging with Jupiter**: This combination suggests the native may have **multiple romantic affairs**.
- **Mars in Leo and opposed by Sun or Mercury**: **Father may have a priestly role** or religious inclination.
- **Mars positioned between Jupiter and Mercury**: Indicates **interruptions or breaks in the native's education**.
- **Mars aspecting 2nd house from Jupiter**: The native faces **financial and family issues**.
- **Mars in Leo or aspecting Leo**: Indicates **financial challenges for the father** of the native.
- **Debilitated Mars**: Indicates **low energy levels** for the native.
- **Mars next to Venus**: Suggests the **possibility of miscarriages or abortions** for the native's wife.
- **Mars in 10th to Mercury**: This alignment can result in **interruptions or breaks in education**.
- **Mars + Rahu + Saturn**: Indicates that the **brother of the native may be troublesome** or cause difficulties.
- **Mars in the next house from Moon, with Venus in the following house** (Female Horoscope): This combination suggests that the **female native may be a second wife** to her husband.

- **Mars in 7th from Jupiter**: Indicates that the **native's husband will have good character** and integrity.
- **Mars in 2nd from Jupiter**: Can cause **challenges in earning money** or sustaining finances.
- **Mars + Moon in a Venus-ruled sign**: Can lead to **disturbing desires or tendencies**, including unhealthy attractions.
- **Mars + Mercury + Rahu in the 4th or 10th House**: The native may have a tendency toward **gambling or financial losses**.
- **Jupiter in 2nd from Mars**: Signifies that the **native is adaptable and capable of handling a variety of work or responsibilities**.
- **Mars conjunct Rahu** - Disturbances in education, persistent nature.
- **Mars in Pisces for Female** - Educated husband.

House Placement from Jupiter

- **10th House**: Help from brothers.
- **2nd House to Sun**: Acts hastily.
- **8th House**: Sudden death.
- **12th House**: Issues with brother.
- **8th House from Lagna**: Maha Mrityunjay Jaap advised.
- **10th House**: Gains from the government.
- **11th House**: Land purchases bring profit.
- **12th House**: Likelihood of foot injury.
- **3rd House**: Caution needed in short travel.
- **6th House**: Avoid proximity to tools.

Position of Jupiter from Mars & Age of Buying Property

Jupiter Position from Mars	Age for Property Acquisition
1st House	24 or 39
2nd House	36 or 48
3rd House	35 or 47
4th House	34 or 36
5th House	33 or 45
6th House	32 or 44
7th House	31 or 43
8th House	30 or 42
9th House	29 or 41
10th House	28 or 40
11th House	27 or 39
12th House	24 or 39

This table provides a guide to the probable ages for property acquisition based on the positioning of Jupiter in relation to Mars in the chart.

Understanding Venus: A Journey into Love, Wealth and Comforts

Venus in Different Signs

Venus placement in whichever sign and its 7th aspect - nativemay have to take medicine of that part (signs as represented in Kaal Purush Kundli)

Venus in Aries

- **Wife's Appearance**: The spouse will have a unique charm, likely attractive and engaging, though not necessarily fair-skinned.
- **Finance and Money**: Native has a strong habit of saving money and may have a tendency to look at others' resources or wealth. The person is inclined to amass wealth, even being interested in the possessions of others.
- **Vehicles and Luxury**: The native will own a well-maintained and stylish vehicle, often having a taste for high-quality models.
- **Medicine**: Venus in Aries allows the native to adapt well to various medicines, with a particular focus on remedies for head-related concerns due to Aries' association with the head.
- **Social and Romantic Life**: Being in a Mars-ruled sign, Venus here increases the native's attraction to the opposite sex and makes them inclined to enjoy companionship.

Venus in Taurus

- **Wealth and Financial Flow**: Taurus is a very favorable placement for Venus, indicating a consistent flow of wealth and financial prosperity.
- **Spouse's Appearance**: The spouse will likely have a beautiful appearance and possess refined tastes.
- **Luxury and Comforts**: Native is attracted to high-end brands and may favor premium vehicles, showing a taste for luxury and quality.
- **Medicine**: Allopathic treatments are effective for this placement, especially concerning throat health (Taurus rules the throat area).
- **Fine Arts and Hobbies**: Native may have an inclination towards the arts, such as music or singing and likely has a soothing or melodious voice, barring any disruptive planetary aspects like Mars, which could make the voice more forceful or intense.

Venus in Gemini

- **Career and Finances**: Native may pursue a career in media, with potential for journalism, especially if Saturn aspects Venus, adding discipline and seriousness. There will likely be two sources of income and two vehicles.
- **Medicine**: Ayurvedic medicine will be beneficial, particularly for ailments related to shoulders and arms.
- **Spouse**: In a male chart, the wife may exhibit dual characteristics or personalities, reflecting adaptability and versatility in her nature.

Venus in Cancer

- **Spouse**: The wife is likely nurturing, motherly and attractive.
- **Finances**: Money flow is high but unpredictable, coming and going like water.
- **Vehicles**: Purchases are often impulsive, with minimal consideration beforehand.
- **Medicine**: Homeopathic treatments work well and there may be a need for heart, lung, or breast-related care.

Venus in Leo

- **Spouse and Relationship Dynamics**: The wife tends to dominate household matters, often taking charge of finances and household rules. In a female chart, this placement indicates a beautiful, authoritative presence.
- **Finances and Spending**: Money management is a challenge as Leo often brings a spendthrift tendency. Despite material comfort, there is often dissatisfaction or a sense of unfulfilled desires.
- **Vehicles**: Vehicles are luxurious, often high-end or royal in style.
- **Medicine**: Allopathic treatment is generally effective, particularly for spine or stomach-related issues.

Venus in Virgo

- **Spouse**: In a male chart, the wife is likely stubborn and strong-willed, following her own inclinations despite others' advice.
- **Finances**: Native handles finances well, demonstrating careful, organized money management and a steady income.
- **Vehicles**: The native buys two vehicles, often purchasing the second immediately after the first.

- **Health and Medicine**: Herbal medicine is suitable, with a potential need for treatments related to the small intestine, liver, or pancreas.

Venus in Libra

- **Health**: For males, potential issues with external sexual organs; for females, possible menstrual cycle irregularities.
- **Spouse**: In a male chart, the wife will be attractive and marriage will bring positive growth and development to the native's life.
- **Desires and Lifestyle**: Strong inclination toward the arts, especially music and a notable attraction to younger partners.
- **Medicine**: Generally adaptable to any form of medicine, without adverse effects.

Venus in Scorpio

- **Spouse**: The wife is beautiful and although she may be stubborn, she is also flexible and understanding.
- **Health**: Males may face kidney issues, while females could have uterus-related health concerns.
- **Character**: The native may have a tendency toward financial manipulation or fraud, potentially taking advantage of others' money.
- **Medicine**: Medical needs could include treatments related to the kidney or uterus, as well as those involving reproductive health.

Venus in Sagittarius

- **Spouse**: The wife is kind and possesses good character.
- **Finance and Vehicles**: Financial flow may be limited and the native might have fewer or no vehicles.

- **Health and Medicine**: Ayurvedic medicine is beneficial. Possible health issues include those related to the eyes or thigh area.

Venus in Capricorn

- **Spouse**: The wife holds importance within a smaller social circle and is influential, although she may not be notably attractive, with duller looks or irregular teeth.
- **Finances and Vehicles**: Good financial flow and the native often uses others' vehicles, such as company or government-provided ones.
- **Health and Medicine**: Any type of medicine is suitable. Knee cap issues may require specific treatment.

Venus in Aquarius

- **Spouse**: The wife may have psychological tendencies or mood swings and may experience trust issues with her husband. She might have friends who negatively influence her.
- **Finance and Vehicles**: Money and vehicles come quickly to the native.
- **Health and Medicine**: Homeopathic or Ayurvedic medicine works best, with possible health issues related to the calves or nerves.

Venus in Pisces

- **Spouse**: Being an exalted placement, the wife is of good character and inclined towards service.
- **Development and Finance**: The native progresses rapidly after marriage, possibly traveling abroad in luxury. There's an abundant inflow of money.
- **Health and Medicine**: All medicines are suitable, though potential health concerns might involve the feet or arteries, requiring specific attention.

Venus Combination with Other Planets Irrespective of Degrees (1,5,9)

Venus + Sun

- **Spouse and Family**: In a male chart, the **wife is strong, practical** and often **rules the family**. The native's **sister is also powerful** and the **father is attractive, well-organized**, with a keen sense of appearance.
- **Finances and Luxuries**: The native has a **habit of gathering wealth and luxuries**, favoring **top-class items**, including **high-end vehicles** and **luxurious travel**.
- **Health**: Prone to **bile-related issues** (*Pitta*).
- **Mentality: Overlooks others' mistakes** and has a strong attraction to **luxury and organization**.

Venus + Moon

- **Spouse and Family**: The **wife is from a distant place**, with potential **misunderstandings with in-laws**. She is **open-hearted and good-natured**. The native's **sister may look like the mother**, who is **beautiful, open-minded and financially astute**.
- **Finances and Luxuries**: Money flows easily, often **coming unexpectedly when needed**. The native makes **quick luxury purchases** (vehicles and high-end items) and enjoys **luxurious travel**.
- **Health**: May face **cold, cough and respiratory issues**.

- **Mentality**: **Constant desire for luxury** and indulging in life's comforts with a spontaneous, **spend-thrift mindset**.

Venus + Mars

- **Spouse and Family**:
    - **Male Chart**: **Wife is assertive, prideful** and **won't easily back down** in conflicts, even if she acknowledges mistakes. She is **straightforward and good-looking**.
    - **Female Chart**: The native may **enjoy flattery** and have **income from rental properties** or **government-provided vehicles**. The **sister may have a strong, athletic nature**.
- **Finances and Luxuries**: Income may come from **landed property** or **government associations**. Vehicles may experience **frequent issues**.
- **Health**: Prone to **cardiac problems**.
- **Mentality**: Practical in utilizing resources, with an inclination for **sports and fine arts**. The husband/brother might be **good-looking, wealthy and focused on financial gains**.

Venus + Mercury

- **Spouse and Family**:
    - **Wife is intelligent and wise**, may not be formally highly educated but has excellent communication skills. She is **socially adept** and **handles various challenges** well.
    - **Sister is intelligent** and **inclined towards practical problem-solving**.
- **Finances and Luxuries**: The native enjoys **multiple sources of income** and tends to **buy family-oriented vehicles** (such as a 7-seater) after

careful consideration. **Luxuries are shown off strategically**.
- **Health**: May develop **skin issues later in life**.
- **Mentality**: **Prudent with expenses**, avoids unnecessary spending and finds **purpose in showcasing expenses** when appropriate. The native also **appreciates recognition** for saving and financial management.

Venus + Jupiter

- **Spouse and Family**:
  - **Wife is pious, polite and highly respected**, often serving as a **guide and moral compass**. She **enjoys a position of honor** and brings **esteem to her family**. Known for being talkative, she earns admiration for her **maternal family**.
- **Finances and Luxuries**: Steady **cash flow** whenever needed, **good bank balance** and a preference for **moderate luxuries**. Vehicles kept are practical and balanced, not overly extravagant.
- **Health**: The wife or other female family members may face **weight-related issues**, particularly from a diet rich in dairy.
- **Mentality**: Native is **good-looking** and may **earn well in teaching professions**.

Venus + Saturn

- **Spouse and Family**:
  - **Wife is professional and authoritative**, often in a **working role**. Her **strength is forged by past hardships**, making her resilient. The **sister may be strong but could bring negative attention** to the family.

- **Finances and Luxuries**: The native might own **high-end second-hand vehicles** and **indulge in long-distance travel and luxurious experiences**.
- **Mentality**: Grounded by experience, these natives **value perseverance** and are **resourceful in financial and material pursuits**.

Venus + Rahu

- **Spouse and Family**:
    - **Wife is highly attractive and beautiful** but has a **secretive and independent nature**, often gathering money for her own use. The **sister is also good-looking but faces numerous challenges** in life.
- **Finances and Luxuries**: Native **prefers living in high-rise apartments** and has a **flair for spotting financial opportunities, including other people's money**. Vehicles are typically beneficial for the native, while **flirtatious tendencies** are pronounced, seizing any chance to charm.
- **Female Chart Specific**: **Husband may earn money through vehicles**, possibly in the vehicle trading business.
- **Health**: Native may experience **gastric issues and excessive body heat**.

Venus + Ketu

- **Spouse and Family**:
    - **Wife is frequently anxious, sometimes without apparent reason** and is interested in **saving money** but can be **domineering with a dual personality**. The **sister may also carry tension and could cause troubles** within the family.
- **Finances and Luxuries**: Native's **money tends to drain quickly** and may **enjoy luxuries that are**

donated or gifted by others, rather than those purchased personally.
- **Health**: Tendency to **spend money impulsively**, which can lead to financial strain.

Venus Secrets

- **Venus (Retrograde) : Financially Favorable**: Signifies strong finances and prosperity.
- **Venus + Mercury: Smooth Life**: Promises a smooth, less problematic life if malefics are absent.
- **Affair Potential**: Exchange in a male chart can indicate extramarital affairs or a mistress.
- **Well-Placed Venus**: Indicates happiness, wealth, health and luxury.
- **Venus + Jupiter: Harmonious Marriage**: Spouse likely from the same town; prosperity improves after marriage if Venus is next to Jupiter.
- **Exchange of Venus and Jupiter**: Benefits the native in phases due to Jupiter's influence, promoting prosperity.
- **Venus + Rahu :Secret Affairs**: Tendency for hidden relationships and attraction to luxury.
- Challenging Venus Placements in Relationships
- **Venus in 6th, 8th, or 12th from Mars (female chart)**: Marital challenges.
- **2nd Lord in 3rd from Venus**: Unhappiness in marriage; retrograde Jupiter shows initial marital issues but gradual adjustment.
- **Mercury and Saturn between Venus and Mars**: Indicates marital issues, lack of physical intimacy; improves if a benefic follows Mars.
- **Ketu after Venus**: Potential for separation, especially if no benefic follows or aspects.
- **Mars after Venus**: Indicates risk of miscarriage.
- **Jupiter next to Venus + Mars**: Promises a harmonious married life.
- **Venus + Moon + Ketu**: Mother may cause marital troubles leading to potential separation.
- **Venus + Moon**: Not ideal for finances; can lead to financial drain and relocation after marriage.
- **Moon behind Venus**: Problems may arise from the mother-in-law.

- **Saturn or Ketu following Venus + Moon**: Indicates risk of extramarital affairs and possible separation.
- **Housewife Indicator (Female chart)**: No planet in 7th, 2nd and 12th from - Saturn is weak and may not support profession, suggests the woman may be a housewife.
- **Saturn in Own House**: Signifies ownership of at least two properties.
- **Mars + Rahu**: Intercaste marriage indicated; marriage is more likely to succeed if intercaste.
- **Planet in second house to Venus : Wife's Profession or Source of Income: Sun**: Government job or work involving chemicals.
  - **Moon**: Hotel, café, or dairy industry.
  - **Mars**: Rental income, land dealings, or government-related work.
  - **Mercury**: Multiple sources of income.
  - **Jupiter**: Teaching, HR, administration, or media.
  - **Rahu**: Chemicals or photography.
- **Venus in Aries or Scorpio**: Marriage within a known family.
- **Sun + Venus + Moon**: Indicates the native might be a child of the father's second marriage.
- **Venus + Ketu**: In males, may cause constipation or piles; in females, vaginal issues.
- **Venus + Moon**: Tendency toward addiction; Jupiter's aspect can nullify adverse effects.
- **Mars + Saturn + Venus**: In a female chart, risk of molestation by an older person; can also apply in male charts.
- **Saturn aspecting the 2nd house from Jupiter**: Delays marriage for both males and females.
- **Saturn aspecting Venus in Male Chart (1,3,5,7,9,10)**: Causes delay in marriage.
- **Saturn aspecting Mars in Female Chart (1,3,5,7,9,10)**: Causes delay in marriage.

- **Denial of Marriage**: If the 2nd and 4th houses from Jupiter have malefic aspects and no benefic aspect, it may indicate denial of marriage.
- **Early Marriage**: Jupiter + Mars in a female chart or Jupiter + Venus in a male chart in the 1st, 3rd, 5th, 6th, or 9th houses suggests early marriage.
- **Venus in Aries**: Potential for accidents.
- **Moon behind Venus**: Likely to experience an unhappy married life.
- **Venus and Mars Exchange (Male chart)**: Indicates multiple sexual relationships.
- **Venus in Mars signs**: Marriage within a known family.
- **Venus in Leo or Cancer, or Ketu next to Venus**: Possible vaginal issues for the wife.
- **Venus + Moon, or Venus in Cancer**: Tendency toward an unstable mind.
- **Venus aspected by Mars**: May result in an unhappy married life.
- **Venus + Rahu + Mars**: Native may elope with someone else's spouse.
- **Jupiter in 2nd from Venus**: Brings prosperity after marriage.
- **Venus + Moon + Ketu**: Wife may be argumentative.
- **Venus in debilitation**: Unhappiness in married life.
- **Venus + Saturn in Taurus**: Native is likely to become very wealthy.
- **Venus and Jupiter exchange**: Indicates good fortune and luck for the native.
- **Venus in Libra and Jupiter in Taurus**: Native likely to be born wealthy.
- **Venus in 3rd House from Jupiter**: Indicates average financial status.
- **Venus aspected by Mars**: Suggests average financial circumstances.
- **Venus in trine to Ketu**: Wife may suffer from piles.

- **4th House Lord from Venus in an inimical sign**: Wife may not be highly educated.
- **Venus in 6th from Jupiter**: Unhappy married life.
- **Mars in 2nd from Venus**: Also indicates potential for an unhappy marriage.
- **Venus – Mars – Jupiter**: Younger brother may marry before the native.
- **2nd House Lord from Venus aspected by Jupiter**: Wife may work in teaching.
- **Venus + Moon**: Native has heightened sexual drive.
- **Venus + Mercury**: Good educational prospects.
- **Venus in Cancer**: Wife may experience mental stress or depression.
- **Venus + Mercury in Leo**: Native is likely to be exceptionally intelligent.
- **Venus hemmed between Sun and Moon**: Native may not experience marital happiness or pleasure.
- **Venus and Sun exchange**: Financial gains and career promotions, especially during Jupiter and Saturn transits.
- **Venus + Saturn**: Indicates a working or employed spouse.
- **Venus + Sun + Mars + Jupiter**: Native likely to marry a relative.
- **Venus in 6th from Jupiter**: Unfavorable luck for the native.
- **Venus in Gemini**: Possible extramarital relationships.
- **Venus in 3rd from Jupiter**: Likely delay in marriage.
- **Venus + Mercury + Ketu**: Indicates potential addiction to alcohol.
- **Mercury next to Venus**: Native may marry someone who was previously in love with another person.
- **Venus in Taurus and Sun in Aries**: Native's mother is of excellent character, with Venus exalted in the Moon's house.

- **Venus + Jupiter in Cancer**: Native may marry a very beautiful spouse.
- **Venus + Rahu behind Jupiter**: Indicates the possibility of two marriages.
- **Rahu next to Venus**: Suggests potential for extramarital relationships involving the wife.
- **Venus aspected by Mars with Mars in the 3rd from Jupiter**: Native's wife may engage in extramarital affairs.
- **Venus with Moon in the 7th house**: Native may have a tendency toward drinking.
- **Venus, Moon and Saturn in own signs; Jupiter in Leo with Mars**: When planets are well-placed in comfortable signs, the native is likely to be born wealthy.
- **Venus and Mars in Cancer**: Wife may experience depression combined with aggression.
- **Venus and Mars in Virgo**: Wife may exhibit aggressive or negative traits, possibly with unwarranted ego.
- **Financial gains when Jupiter transits Venus**: Depending on the native's age and Jupiter's cycle, the native may experience financial gains.
- **Professional income increase with Saturn's aspects on Venus**: Income from profession grows significantly when Saturn aspects Venus from the 1st, 3rd, 7th, or 10th houses.
- **Venus alone in its own house** - Noble and good-charactered wife.
- **Venus conjunct Mercury** - Pleasure from girlfriend.
- **Venus conjunct Ketu** - Mantra Siddhi, medicinal dealings, wife may have mental issues.
- **Venus in Cancer** - Humiliation through a woman during Jupiter's transit.
- **Venus in Taurus with Saturn** - Wealth and prominence.

- **Venus opposite Moon** - Loss or illness of mother before marriage.

House Placement from Jupiter

- **6th House from Mars**: Delay and legal issues in marriage.
- **12th House to Jupiter**: Unhappy married life, issues from female.

Understanding Mercury: The Path of Knowledge and Learning

Mercury's Influence on Education and how different factors shape it:

- **Mercury's Primary Traits**: Mercury signifies **intelligence, education, business, languages, positive outcomes, communication, trade and business** activities. Education stands out as its most crucial influence.
- **Type of Education**: Determined by the **Rashi (sign) of Mercury** in the chart.
- **Language Skills**: The **number of languages** a person may know is indicated by the **number of planets conjunct with Mercury** in the same sign.
- **Nature of Education**: Influenced by **planets in adjacent houses** to Mercury.
- **Retrograde Mercury**: If Mercury is retrograde, there is a chance of **changing the field of education** (e.g., science to commerce).
- **Retrograde Mercury in Dual Signs (3, 6, 9, 12)**: Amplifies the likelihood of **shifting educational direction** and this shift often becomes more prominent.
- **Saturn Between Jupiter and Mercury** (when moving from Jupiter): Indicates **disturbances in education**.
- **From Mercury to Jupiter with Lower Mercury Degree**: When Mercury's degree is lower than Jupiter's, the native may study **commerce, accounting, or spiritual fields**.
- **Malefic Influence (Ra/Ke/Sa/Ma) Between Mercury and Jupiter**: Any malefic planets between Mercury and Jupiter can cause **disruptions in education**.

- **Jupiter in the 12th from Mercury**: Suggests education related to **banking, law, labor law, or public law**.
- **Rahu/Saturn/Mars Ahead of Mercury** (or in conjunction with higher degrees):Native is inclined toward studying **Mantra Vidya** (spiritual or mystic knowledge).
- **Mars and Saturn Ahead of Mercury**:Indicates an interest in learning instruments like **drums, dholak, or tabla**, provided they are in the same sign with degrees higher than Mercury.
- **Venus Ahead of Mercury** (or higher degree in conjunction): **Interest in music and arts**, particularly artistic pursuits, if Venus is in the same sign with a higher degree than Mercury.
- **Venus and Mercury Ahead of the Sun** (higher degrees in one sign): Father is likely to be a **wealthy businessman**, provided no malefic planets are positioned between or aspecting this combination.
- **Mercury and Venus Next to Jupiter**: Signifies **two marriages** or multiple romantic relationships and **diverse income sources** for the native.
- **Mercury and Saturn in the 10th House from Jupiter** (or in trine): Indicates an **interest or involvement in education-related businesses**, small institutes, or tutorial services.
- **Mercury + Mars in Gemini**: Suggests a career in **media, writing, or mass communication** fields.
- **Jupiter + Mercury + Sun Combination**: Known as the **best combination for education** if not impacted by malefics, supporting academic and intellectual excellence.

Mercury in Different Signs & Education

Aries : Lord – Mars Influence:

- **Fields of Study**: With Mercury in Aries, the native is inclined toward studies in **archeology** (surface studies), **technical fields** and **mechanical engineering** specifically, as Mars, Aries' lord, is linked with machinery and tools.
- **Additional Fields**: **Hotel management** or **culinary arts** are also possible due to Mars' connection with food and cooking. **Agriculture-related education** may also attract the native, as Mars governs land.
- **Medical Interest**: Mars represents blood, cutting and skills, which align with surgical and medical skills. **Sun + Mars** together can make a good combination for a surgeon, while **Sun + Ketu** can also support medical studies, particularly for those inclined toward becoming doctors.

Mercury's Influence as Knowledge Bearer:

- **Books and Paper**: Mercury in Aries emphasizes a practical, skill-based education involving technical manuals, blueprints and possibly the handling of **instruments or machinery**.

Effects of Specific Planetary Combinations:

- **Mercury + Mars**: This combination enhances **technical skills** and leans toward **land-based education** (e.g., surveying, land registration) or **instrumental music education**, where precise skill is required.
- **Moon + Mercury**: This can lead to indecisiveness in education as the mind (Moon) might create distractions or a sense of dissatisfaction, leading

the native to often want what they do not have. This can result in **distraction from current pursuits** and an ongoing desire to chase new interests, rather than focusing on the present.

Mercury in Taurus (Lord is Venus):

- **Fields of Study**: The native is drawn toward fields associated with **finance, medicine, beauty, fine arts** and **nature-related studies** due to Venus' influence. This position encourages a love for aesthetics, finance and wellness.
- **Mercury Conjunct with Venus (1-5-9, 7, 2-12)**: Such natives are often resourceful and adaptable (sometimes known as *jugaad baaz*), inclined toward finding unconventional solutions and sometimes engaging in *grey market* or *black money* activities. Their education may also cover areas connected to finance and business management with an emphasis on earning.

Mercury in Gemini (Lord is Mercury):

- **Fields of Study**: Mercury's own sign heightens the native's interest in **communication fields** like **media, radio jockeying (RJ/DJ), film hosting, marketing, sales, travel and tourism** and **accounting** due to Gemini's association with communication and travel.
- **Strengths**: The native's education is often focused on building strong verbal and written skills, making this placement ideal for careers requiring networking, public speaking and content creation.

Mercury in Cancer (Lord is Moon):

- **Fields of Study**: With Mercury in Cancer, the native's educational interests lean toward **psychology** (understanding the mind), **social service, hospitality** and **hotel management**.

Moon's influence brings in **service-oriented education** and involvement with **liquids or water-related industries**.

- **Mercury Conjunct with Moon (1-5-9, 7, 2-12)**: This combination can bring about *changes in education*, possible education abroad, or fluctuations in the native's commitment to studies. The mind (Moon) can lead to frequent shifts in academic focus, but there is also strong potential for education in **hospitality, service**, or **water-related fields**.

Mercury in Leo (Lord is Sun):

- **Fields of Study**: This placement inclines the native toward **administrative roles** or **government-related fields** such as IAS or IRS (IPS would require Mars' influence). Politics, public administration and **arts-related studies** are also supported. Additionally, the native may pursue **medicine** specializing in general health or bones.
- **Special Combinations**: **Mercury Conjunct with Sun** (in houses 1, 5, 9, 7, 2, or 12): The native could excel in **political science, government** studies, or pursue **general medicine** (rather than surgery).

Mercury in Virgo (Lord is Mercury):

- **Fields of Study**: Virgo represents **law** and natives are often inclined toward **agriculture**, **botany** (specifically **Ayurvedic** studies), **law** (becoming a lawyer or advocate) and **finance** fields such as chartered accountancy or company secretary roles.
- **Special Notes**: With Virgo being Mercury's own sign, natives may excel in **logical and analytical studies**, making them suited for careers requiring precision and structure.

Mercury in Libra (Lord is Venus):

- **Fields of Study**: Libra encourages natives toward fields that require **public interaction**, such as **HR, public relations** and **diplomacy**. **Medicine** (like pharmacy or public health), **finance, insurance (e.g., LIC)** and positions requiring **aesthetic knowledge** are also common.
- **Special Combinations**: **Mercury Conjunct with Venus** (in houses 1, 5, 9, 7, 2, or 12): Increases inclinations toward **finance, fine arts, beautification** fields, or **cosmetic** services.

Mercury is in Scorpio (Lord is Mars):

- **Fields of Study**: This placement indicates an affinity for studies that explore **depth, mystery and hidden knowledge**. Some suitable fields include:
- **Navy or Marine Engineering** (if Moon is also supportive, as Moon represents water-related pursuits)
- **Occult or mystical studies** involving hidden or spiritual knowledge
- **Detective or forensic studies** focused on uncovering secrets or details
- **Irrigation engineering, water management**, or **studies involving the water element**
- **Post-mortem or pathology** for careers in forensic science
- **Weaponry knowledge with a focus on secrecy or covert operations**
- **Mines and excavation** (like archaeology under the earth)
- **Special Combinations**:
- **Mercury Conjunct with Venus**: The native's education will be of **high quality** or conducted at a high-standard institution. This adds a layer of refinement and a preference for quality in their educational journey.

- **Water Element** in the chart shows specific inclinations:
- **4th Sign** – Lake-related fields or calm water bodies
- **8th Sign** – Rivers or flowing water bodies, ideal for irrigation or marine studies
- **12th Sign**– Oceans, indicating a connection to marine sciences, long-distance travel by sea, or international waters
- **Other Planetary Influences**:
- **Jupiter**: As a guide, Jupiter supports **law** and **higher education**. Jupiter's influence with Mercury can drive natives toward **spiritual, philosophical, or legal studies**.
- **Rahu**: Known for **unconventional education** paths, especially in **electronics** or secretive subjects, Rahu supports non-traditional educational fields.
- **Ketu**: Linked to **electrical** knowledge and studies that involve hidden, mystical, or detached approaches, Ketu can incline natives toward **technical or metaphysical** studies.

Mercury Is in Sagittarius (Lord is Jupiter):

- **Fields of Study**: Teaching, Religious Studies, Public Relations, Social Relations, General Education.
- **Traits**: Native may pursue education up to post-graduation. However, there may be a lack of focus in studies.
- **Mercury Conjunct with Jupiter**: Leads to interests in Public Welfare, Education (Teaching), Bachelor of Education (B.Ed), Religious Law.

Mercury Is in Capricorn (Lord is Saturn):

- **Fields of Study**: Law (especially Judiciary), Labour Law, Mining, Stonework, Iron, ITI Diplomas (focused on lower-paid or technical professions).

- **Mercury Conjunct with Saturn**: Focus on Machinery, Skilled Labour, Archaeology, Mining.

Mercury Is in Aquarius (Lord is Saturn):

- **Fields of Study**: Psychology, Neurology, Philosophy, Aviation and possibly more practical or low-grade education.
- **Traits**: Interests may focus on unconventional or mind-related topics.

Mercury Is in Pisces (Lord is Jupiter):

- **Fields of Study**: Spirituality, Public Welfare, Social Development, Law.
- **Traits**: Focus on philosophical and spiritual studies, with an inclination toward community service and social upliftment.

Mercury in Different Houses from Jupiter

1st House: Native **Highly intelligent**, **dual personality** (inner self differs from outer presentation), education in **public-related subjects**; brings **fame and recognition**. **Good and religious relatives** and neighbors; born in a supportive environment.

2nd House: **Education in finance**, poetic, quick-flowing speech. **Multiple income sources**, minimal expenses and **sudden financial gains**. **Religious and prosperous family**. Malefic aspect may lead to **quick financial drain**.

3rd House: Skilled in **communication and public speaking**; **extensive travel** for business but **lacks boldness in education** and strong academic interest.

4th House: Interest in **learning about different cultures**. Home may be **rectangular in shape**; **mother is noble**. **Neighbors may be migrants** from other cities or countries.

5th House: Education likely in **hospital or medical field**. **Powerful neighbors**, possibly influential but potentially negative. Relatives are **wealthy and strong**.

6th House: **Highly intelligent**, owns land with **plantation or vegetation**. Education may focus on **ayurveda or botany**. **Relations with neighbors and relatives** are challenging due to their **dominating nature**.

7th House: **Low income**, with **high expenses**; may have **sexual orientation variations** (homosexuality or transgender associations). **Wealthy neighbors**; education may be **finance-related**, with **money-minded relatives**.

8th House: **Technical, industrial, or culinary education**; may study **archaeology** or **Navy-related fields**. Has a

fondness for cooking. Relatives or neighbors might be in **government jobs, military, or police**.

9th House: **Education in finance or banking**; native may encounter **educational disturbances** and experience **duality in decision-making**. **Distant relatives** may visit frequently.

10th House: Education likely in **accountancy** or **research fields** (e.g., CA, trading). Becomes an **important social figure**. Relatives and neighbors may also be **socially prominent**.

11th House: Education focused on **psychology, neurology, or petroleum**, possibly in **foreign countries**. Relatives or neighbors may have **international connections**.

12th House: **Foreign study** or education in **aviation-related fields**. Potential for a career in **aviation or international areas**.

Mercury Combinations with Planets (1,5,9 positions irrespective of degrees):

Mercury-Sun: **Intelligent and sharp**; forms **Budh-Aditya Yoga**, supporting **spiritual education and knowledge**. Native excels in studies unless impacted by malefic aspects.

Mercury-Moon: Likely to pursue **education in a different location**; has **sharp memory**. Fields may include **Navy or psychology**; mother is also intelligent.

Mercury-Mars: Associated with **technical education**. Indicates an **intelligent brother or husband**, though may bring **challenges in education**.

Mercury-Jupiter: Education related to **public relations** and communication; **learned neighbors**, an educated and well-informed native.

Mercury-Venus: Often connected with **medical education**; **intelligent spouse**, **beautiful sister** and multiple income sources. This combination brings **comfort, luxury and ease** in education and life.

Mercury-Saturn: Academics in fields like **mining, metals, minerals** and underground sciences. **Problematic relationships with neighbors and relatives**; can cause lethargy in education and a career in **education-related fields**.

Mercury-Rahu: Leads to **research-oriented studies**; fewer relatives and **dry relationships with neighbors**.

Mercury-Ketu: Studies in **chemical, electronics, electrical, or railway fields**; interest in **occult** and afterlife topics. Few relatives and neighbors tend to be few and challenging.

Mercury Secrets

- **Mercury in Virgo (Exalted) with Venus**: The native is **extraordinarily intelligent** and will **excel in academics or business**.
- **Jupiter and Sun in 2nd to Mercury**: The native is an **expert in legal knowledge** and may excel in law or legal professions.
- **Mercury with Venus in 2nd to Sun**: **Father is a wealthy businessman** involved in **high-value or luxury items**.
- **Mercury + Venus in Libra**: **Intelligent native** with a logical mind. **Wife may have memory-related issues**.
- **Ketu next to Mercury**: The native will have **high regard for elders** and shows respect for traditional values.
- **Mercury + Venus between Sun and Saturn (in a Female Chart)**: Indicates that the **female native may experience struggles** or **hardships after marriage**.
- **Saturn + Ketu 2nd to Mercury**: **Educational obstacles** are likely, creating **challenges in academic pursuits**.
- **Mercury + Venus aspecting Jupiter**: The native is inclined towards **business** and may have strong **entrepreneurial skills**.
- **Mercury with Debilitated Sun and Ketu**: Indicates **limited educational attainment** due to challenges in focus or support.
- **Mercury + Ketu**: The native has a **noble character** and is seen as **principled and good-natured**.
- **Saturn + Moon in 2nd house to Mercury**: The native may **lose interest in education** or face obstacles in maintaining their educational pursuits.

- **Mercury exalted with Ketu**: Native is highly intelligent.
- **Mercury in Enemy Sign with Mars and Rahu next**: Struggles in education and career.
- **Mercury + Ketu + Saturn aspected by Jupiter**: Native will be well-educated and attain a high position in life.
- **Mercury + Venus**: Indicates extraordinary intelligence and beautiful handwriting.
- **Mercury in Mars sign with no adjacent planets**: Poor educational progress.
- **Mercury exalted with Jupiter + Saturn**: Smooth educational journey.
- **Mercury in Taurus with Ketu**: Native likely studies law and accountancy.
- **Moon 2nd from Mercury and Ketu 5th from Moon**: Strong knowledge in Vedic astrology.
- **Moon 2nd from Mercury**: Broad knowledge across different subjects.
- **Mercury + Sun in Virgo**: Potential for expertise in accountancy.
- **Mercury as 12th Lord from Jupiter, aspected by Mars and Sun**: Indicates the native may have multiple romantic or sexual relationships.
- **Mercury in Sagittarius**: Suggests a tendency for dullness or a less focused intellect.
- **Mercury + Venus in 12th from Sun**: Signifies a person with strong moral character.
- **Mercury + Moon**: Denotes intelligence and a sharp, adaptable mind.
- **Venus in the 2nd House from Mercury**: Indicates a love for art and creative pursuits.
- **Mercury in a Jupiter sign and aspected by Jupiter**: Enhances fluency in the native's mother tongue.
- Mercury conjunct Ketu - Overthinking.
- Mercury conjunct Mars or Moon - Thyroid issues in family.
- **Exchange with Mars** : Educational hurdles, financial gains from brothers.

House Placement from Jupiter

- **Lagna**: Pilgrimage at age 27.
- **7th House**: Disturbed marriage, likely two marriages.
- **6th, 8th, or 12th House**: Challenges in education and business.
- **2nd House (with Rahu)**: Younger sibling may settle abroad.

Steps to Analyze Education:

1. **Identify Mercury's Sign**: This shows core tendencies and preferences in education.
2. **Examine Mercury's Conjunctions**:
   - Defines the field of study and whether the educational journey is smooth or challenging.
   - Indicates intelligence level, potential for foreign education and alignment between education and career.

Jupiter's Influence: Understanding the Jeev Lagna

Jupiter in Different Signs

Aries: Personality and Characteristics

- **Build**: Typically shorter structure unless benefic aspects are present.
- **Nature**: Struggles hard in life, with a love for sports (indoor and outdoor), adventurous and daring.
- **Health**: Prone to heat-related issues.
- **Interests**: Likely to engage in work or business, enjoy adventure sports and may be drawn to subjects like archaeology, geology, history, or earth sciences.

Taurus: Personality and Characteristics

- **Appearance**: Solid body structure, attractive, with a smile showing upper gums.
- **Nature**: Money-minded, calculating and keeps a close watch on expenses. Enjoys a comfortable, luxurious lifestyle and speaks softly unless malefic influences are present.
- **Interests**: Fine arts, neat and fashionable dressing, often drawn to the opposite sex and dedicated in relationships.

Gemini: Personality and Characteristics

- **Appearance**: Good height and attractive features, with a dual nature that's difficult to understand.
- **Nature**: Intelligent, affectionate, sociable, skilled in advising on commercial matters, with an engaging personality.
- **Interests**: Media, writing, filmmaking, public speaking and traveling. Known for diplomatic and persuasive speech and may have a mark on the face. Family history may include twins.

Cancer: Personality and Characteristics

- **Appearance**: Semi-crescent-shaped nose; heart line extending below the three fingers on the palm.
- **Nature**: Open-hearted, good-natured, dislikes lies and is respectful and soft-spoken. They tend to settle in different places, often in foreign lands. In female charts, while Jupiter exalted brings similar qualities, it also introduces lifelong worries - valid or not. Despite efforts, these women may face humiliation and are prone to feeling insulted, often staying with their mother or inviting her to stay.
- **Interests**: Side pursuits in art or medicine; casual remarks by these natives often come true, showing a unique intuition. They may experience throat ailments or frequent colds.
- **Other**: Gains honor and prestige later in life.

Leo: Personality and Characteristics

- **Appearance**: Strong, well-built with broad shoulders, a good height, prominent face and commanding voice. Known for a powerful presence, with intense eyes that can instill fear or respect.
- **Nature**: Dominant and practical, these natives enjoy a strong, ruling personality and are respected by others. They tend to be straightforward and

dislike flattery. In female charts, Jupiter in Leo indicates a woman who often takes charge within the family, leading with confidence and authority.
- **Interests**: Close associations with powerful friends or local leaders; enjoys support from influential people and elderly figures in society.
- **Other**: Settles comfortably in life with a stable marriage, often benefiting from cooperation and patronage within the community.

Virgo: Personality and Characteristics

- **Appearance**: Medium height, well-built body, good facial features and slightly short in height but with overall good health.
- **Nature**: Soft-spoken but exceptionally stubborn, Virgo natives listen to others but ultimately follow their own plans. They think highly of their intelligence and often underestimate others, showing a subtle yet dominant personality. Male and female natives share similar characteristics, especially in their confident approach and argumentative abilities.
- **Interests**: Skilled in fine arts, with a potential to excel in media or arts at any stage in life. They are naturally good at planning and can achieve their goals through careful strategy.
- **Other**: Family often has twins and they generally earn well, often shining in life through their artistic talents.

Libra: Personality and Characteristics

- **Appearance**: Good-looking, with soft, tender speech and attractive eyes.
- **Nature**: Social, with a tendency towards relationships and interactions with the opposite sex. Male natives may have numerous female friends and strong sexual drives. Female natives attract the

opposite sex and are generally money-minded with a gentle demeanor, often mediating disputes and helping to resolve issues through kind words. They are pleasure-loving and enjoy accumulating wealth.

- **Interests**: Fond of fine arts, such as singing or painting and may have poetic or artistic abilities. Both male and female natives tend to enjoy good food and are drawn to financial stability and comfort.
- **Other**: Talented mediators, these natives have a natural flair for resolving conflicts, especially in family or relationship matters.

Scorpio: Personality and Characteristics

- **Appearance**: Intense and somewhat mysterious, reflecting the inner spiritual and emotional struggles of this placement.
- **Nature**: Natives in Scorpio face an inner conflict between spiritual aspirations and material desires, often feeling unsettled or as though something is missing. They are empathetic, stepping into others' shoes to understand their suffering and avoid blaming others for their own struggles. Hardworking yet narrow-minded, they deal with significant challenges in life but remain resilient and compassionate.
- **Interests**: Drawn to mystical sciences and spirituality, especially as they grow older. This journey often involves helping others and striving to make sense of both material and spiritual worlds.
- **Other**: Life is often difficult with many family issues and internal struggles, but they fight persistently. As they age, they tend to achieve a peaceful, meaningful life focused on spirituality and compassion.

Sagittarius: Personality and Characteristics

- **Appearance**: Open and expressive, with a personality that conveys wisdom and experience.
- **Nature**: These natives are often independent, displaying a self-made personality and a wanderer's spirit. Although they are affectionate and intelligent, they tend to be distant from family life and may not invest much time with family, home, or children. With age, they realize the limitations of material life and increasingly seek spirituality, eventually recognizing and respecting cosmic energy and supreme knowledge.
- **Interests**: Knowledge-sharing is a key trait; they are inclined to teach, mentor and guide others. They have an intrinsic drive to gain wisdom and impart it to the world.
- **Other**: They may enjoy a prosperous life after a certain age, often finding a path toward spiritual growth as they advance in life.

Capricorn: (Debilitated): Personality and Characteristics

- **Appearance**: Commands respect, with a demeanor that reflects authority and wisdom.
- **Nature**: Known for their balance between materialism and spirituality, Capricorn natives approach life with a practical outlook. Although Jupiter is debilitated here, it still brings a strong sense of duty and wisdom, making them popular within their circle. They often see themselves as wiser than others and are unafraid to voice their opinions, even at the risk of disrupting relationships.
- **Interests**: They value authority, wisdom and teaching, often enjoying opportunities to impart their knowledge and influence others in their close community.
- **Other**: Capable of blending material and spiritual pursuits, they come from good families and believe

in making the best of both worlds, even if it's challenging.

Aquarius: Personality and Characteristics

- **Appearance**: Slightly eccentric with a distinct, enigmatic presence.
- **Nature**: Aquarius is a challenging sign for Jupiter, as it brings out a psychic, unpredictable side in these natives. They are fast thinkers, often difficult to understand or predict, with a "sanki" (whimsical) personality that leads them to harm themselves before causing harm to others. Non-judgmental and deeply experimental, they explore life's philosophies and guard their honor zealously. Although they come from a good family, they tend to face family life issues due to their fluctuating moods and unconventional mindset.
- **Interests**: With a strong drive for experimentation and a desire for leadership, they are naturally drawn to fields that allow for innovation and exploration, particularly if it involves foreign travel or a progressive, modern outlook.
- **Other**: While family life may not be ideal, they achieve distinction in their social circles and work tirelessly to uphold their self-esteem and honor.

Pisces: Personality and Characteristics

- **Appearance**: Soft-spoken and gentle, with a presence that exudes warmth and compassion.
- **Nature**: This is an ideal placement for Jupiter, bringing out the best qualities in the native. They are self-made individuals with a golden heart, often driven by a deep sense of compassion and service. Generous and spiritually inclined, they readily help the poor, elderly and those in need without expecting anything in return. As they progress in life, they naturally detach from materialistic desires,

leaning toward spiritual and philosophical pursuits. They are often ready for liberation, aiming to rise above worldly attachments.

- **Interests**: Highly drawn to Vedic literature, spiritual teachings and divine contemplation. They frequently contribute to temples, old age homes, orphanages and other charitable causes.
- **Other**: Known for their selflessness and readiness for liberation, these natives are celebrated for their contributions to society, reflecting the compassionate and wise nature of Jupiter in Pisces.

Planets in Different Houses from Jupiter

2nd House : Family, Finance, Speech

Family

- **Saturn**: Native aims for marriage by choice, often with someone from a known or familiar family.
- **Any Malefic (including Sun)**: Strains family relationships; creates a challenging environment within the family.
- **Rahu**: Brings dryness and detachment in family ties.
- **Ketu**: Can lead to unnecessary arguments within the family.
- **Jupiter to the 4th House with Malefics in Between**: Native may not feel comfort or harmony within the home and family if malefics lie between Jupiter and the 4th House. However, **Mercury** in between these houses can help maintain a happy family atmosphere.

Finance

- **Any Malefic (including Sun)**: Financial struggles with high expenses.
- **Rahu**: Losses in finances, creating difficulty in savings.
- **Ketu**: Leads to unpredictable expenses or depletion of resources.
- **Mercury**: Facilitates a spontaneous flow of money - money comes and goes easily.

- **Venus**: Ensures regular income, often with access to money whenever needed.
- **Venus + Mercury**: Increases financial inflow, often from multiple sources, leading to more consistent income.
- **Venus + Malefic**: Income increases but accompanied by unnecessary expenses.
- **Venus in Cancer**: Fast inflow and outflow of money.
- **Venus in Sagittarius**: Lower than average income or financial inflow.
- **Venus in Pisces (Exalted)**: Native accumulates a significant amount of wealth.
- **Very Rich People's Chart**: If **Jupiter** is in any sign with **Venus in the 4th House** and there are no malefics between the 2nd and 3rd House (and **Venus** is not aspected by malefics), this setup points to abundant wealth.

Speech

- **Saturn + Mars**: Native speaks harshly or roughly.
- **Sun**: Practical, straightforward and often blunt speech.
- **Ketu**: Tends to provoke unnecessary arguments.
- **Rahu**: Makes speech dry and detached; can also lead to strained family relations.

3rd House : Siblings, Short Travels, Inner Strength, Losses

Siblings

- **Sun**: Suggests a younger sibling, usually a brother. Financial losses may come through connections with the father or government.
- **Moon**: Sibling relationships are marked by potential misunderstandings or blames.
- **Mars**: Points to a younger brother and a bold personality; strong communication style.
- **Mercury**: May have siblings involved in academics or education, though there could be struggles in the educational journey.
- **Venus**: Relationships with siblings might be focused on financial or luxury matters.
- **Saturn**: Indicates strong, serious sibling relationships with potential for obstacles.
- **Rahu**: May feel disconnected from siblings or have weak ties.
- **Ketu**: Siblings may be involved in religious or spiritual practices.

Short Travels

- **Sun**: Short travels for religious purposes or pilgrimages.
- **Moon**: Frequent travels but often with some anxiety or reluctance.
- **Mars**: Travel is often for leisure and adventure, but it may include risks or accidents.
- **Mercury**: Travels primarily for educational purposes, possibly to different states or regions.
- **Venus**: Luxurious travel modes, focusing on comfort and style.

- **Saturn**: Travel is often lengthy or demanding, with potential cross-country adventures or challenging journeys.
- **Rahu**: Engages in travel without a clear purpose; travel may bring unexpected fears.
- **Ketu**: Travel related to pilgrimages or religious places and often visits places of mourning.

Inner Strength

- **Sun**: Inner strength is strong, often marked by a sense of purpose.
- **Moon**: Lacks boldness; native may be prone to internal fears.
- **Mars**: Possesses boldness and a strong inner resolve.
- **Mercury**: Inner strength is derived from intelligence, but there may be introversion.
- **Venus**: Strength is more passive, relying on communication charm.
- **Saturn**: Bold, determined strength, often unyielding; may act with little regard for consequences.
- **Rahu**: Lacks inner strength, prone to fears and insecurities.
- **Ketu**: Calm, detached strength often linked to spiritual resilience.

Losses

- **Sun**: Financial losses due to father, government, or authority figures.
- **Moon**: Losses from travel, mental peace is often disturbed due to depressive thoughts.
- **Mars**: Potential losses or accidents during travel.
- **Mercury**: Losses related to neighbors or relatives, particularly in educational matters.
- **Venus**: Money loss, often related to luxuries or extravagant travel.

- **Saturn**: Losses may occur due to obstacles in travel or personal ventures.
- **Rahu**: Losses may arise due to misunderstandings or fear-driven decisions.
- **Ketu**: Losses could relate to religious or spiritual activities, possibly from excessive giving or detachment from material interests

4th House: House, Mother, Happiness, Academics

House Shape and Location

- **Sun**: A spiritually inclined environment with a unique energy presence, possibly a super soul in the house. This could bring prosperity and spiritual ambiance.
- **Moon**: Likely near a temple, main road, or a water source; father's origin might be from a different area.
- **Mars**: Potential for fire incidents in the kitchen; challenges may arise in constructing or securing the house.
- **Mercury**: House is rectangular, organized, with a clear layout and uncluttered environment.
- **Venus**: Small exterior but beautiful inside with a duplex design, organized and aesthetically pleasing.
- **Saturn**: An old house with low ventilation, possibly near a garbage or dump yard.
- **Rahu**: L-shaped structure, could be located abroad or far from birthplace, often with a focus on digital or photography-related setups.
- **Ketu**: Resembles a train coach, located at a dead-end or last lane, likely near an electric pole.

Mother's Characteristics and Family Dynamics

- **Sun**: Mother is dominant, with a strong, ruling nature over household affairs.
- **Moon**: Mother is kind and caring, with family origins possibly distant from the birth location.
- **Mars**: Mother may have a rough demeanor, potentially facing dissatisfaction or unhappiness.
- **Mercury**: Intelligent, balanced, clear-minded, fostering a peaceful home environment.

- **Venus**: Beautiful appearance, contributes to an opulent, well-decorated home environment.
- **Saturn**: Mother is a family pillar, enduring struggles; likely rules with a focus on responsibility.
- **Rahu**: Homemaker focused mainly on her immediate family without much outside influence.
- **Ketu**: Melancholy or sadness often surrounds her, marked by a lasting somber tone.

Happiness and Comfort of Home

- **Sun**: Spiritual prosperity, blessed by a guiding presence; potential for harmonious, growth-oriented home life if free from malefics.
- **Moon**: Peaceful and happy if not impacted by malefics, though some psychological struggles may appear.
- **Mars**: Limited satisfaction and comfort, with tension around family unity, especially after the father's time.
- **Mercury**: High levels of happiness, clarity and a calm, organized environment.
- **Venus**: Wealth and luxury bring consistent comfort; abundant happiness if not afflicted by malefics.
- **Saturn**: Comforts may be limited, with sacrifices or struggles often required for family welfare.
- **Rahu**: Illusory happiness, often daydreaming about comforts rather than truly feeling content.
- **Ketu**: Enduring sadness or discontent, with childhood struggles affecting long-term peace.

Academics and Education

- **Sun**: Administration, medicine, or chemistry-related studies; education typically smooth if free of malefics.
- **Moon**: Psychology, neurology, or counseling fields; likely involves travel or changing locations for studies.

- **Mars**: Challenges in securing or completing academic pursuits, particularly if pursuing technical or manual work.
- **Mercury**: Smooth educational path, especially in analytical subjects; no interruptions if free of malefic interference.
- **Venus**: Finance, fine arts, or electronics, with a strong artistic inclination; a stable educational journey.
- **Saturn**: Technical fields, with a focus on practical skills; may face delays but often gain ancestral support.
- **Rahu**: Digital, photography, or computer studies; might be drawn to unconventional or foreign academic pursuits.
- **Ketu**: Studies in chemistry or medicine; struggles often emerge from an early age, leading to difficult academic paths.

5th House - Purva Punya Bhava (House of Past Life Merits)

The 5th House signifies the **outcomes of past life karma** through progeny, creativity and personal joy. Jupiter's transits around the zodiac mark different phases of experiencing and exhausting past life karma, especially through one's children and the fruits of past actions.

Jupiter's Transits (Cycle of Purva Punya Karma)

- **1st Round (0-12 years):** Early years marked by innocence, foundational growth and learning experiences.
- **2nd Round (12-24 years):** Education, youthful ambitions and the start of independent actions. This phase often brings the first inklings of karma from past lives through education or personality development.
- **3rd Round (24-36 years):** Career establishment, family building and beginning to settle down; initial progeny or family responsibilities.
- **4th Round (36-48 years):** Maturity, responsibility and handling the outcomes of previous actions, often seeing one's children reach adolescence or adulthood.
- **5th Round (48-60 years):** Results of **Purva Punya** are evident here. Children's growth, settlement and liabilities manifest; fulfilling karmic responsibilities through them.
- **Positive Outcome**: Peaceful family life and settled children indicate positive past karma.
- **Negative Outcome**: Unsettled children or struggles indicate a karmic deficit or unresolved actions from past lives.

- **6th Round (60-72 years):** Completion of Jupiter's cycle, transitioning into a period governed by **Saturn**.
- **Pap (Negative) Phal:** Diseases, debts and other challenging conditions may emerge, indicating that any unresolved karmas are left for Saturn's judgment.
- **After 72:** Free will reduces as life transitions towards releasing karmic debts. A smooth or difficult phase here reflects one's past life balance, where **Saturn** decides the nature of one's end-of-life experience.

5th House Progeny Outcomes

The quality and experiences related to progeny are rooted in past life merits and are observed as follows:

1. **Planet in the 5th House from Jupiter:**
   - If there is a planet, its nature influences progeny outcomes.
2. **7th Aspect on the 5th House from Jupiter:**
   - Check if any planet aspects the 5th House for additional influences.
3. **If No Planet or Aspect on the 5th House:**
   - Evaluate the **Rashi lord** of the 5th House, examining its placement, conjunctions and aspects to predict progeny results.

Libra Sign - Progeny and Reproductive Health

- **Libra**, as the sign of balance and reproductive organs, plays a key role in progeny outcomes and reproductive health in both males and females.

Planets in Libra - Effects on Reproductive Health

- **Sun**:
  - *Male*: Low sperm count, reproductive challenges.
  - *Female*: Problems with egg cell viability; issues with white discharge.
- **Moon**:
  - *Male*: Early ejaculation or reduced sperm count.
  - *Female*: Menstrual irregularities, fast or irregular cycles.
- **Mars**:
  - *Male*: Strong reproductive health and vitality.
  - *Female*: C-section birth likelihood, potential for childbirth complications.
- **Mercury**:
  - *Both Genders*: Less inclination towards intimacy; however, no major reproductive issues.
- **Venus**:
  - *Male*: Low sperm count.
  - *Female*: Challenges due to white discharge.
- **Saturn**:
  - *Male*: Low sperm count.
  - *Female*: Issues with uterus health and strength.
- **Rahu**:
  - *Male*: Dryness and reduced viability in reproductive fluids.
  - *Female*: Complications in the ovaries.
- **Ketu**:
  - *Male*: Fertility challenges requiring medical intervention.
  - *Female*: White discharge challenges.
- **Jupiter**:

- *Both Genders*: No significant reproductive issues; supports progeny and healthy childbirth.

6th House - Health, Disease and Past Life Dosha

The **6th House** represents **disease and ailments** influenced by past life doshas (karmic afflictions). Planets positioned here reflect the **results of past karma** that impact health in this life, while planets in the 5th House indicate **past karma itself**.

Rules for Analyzing the 6th House for Health & Disease:

1. **Planet in 6th House**: Indicates the primary type of health issue.
2. **7th Aspect on 6th House**: If no planet is placed in the 6th, check for any 7th aspect.
3. **Rashi Lord and Conjunctions**: If neither a planet nor aspect is present, consider the Rashi Lord, conjunctions and any aspects on it.
- **Benefic Planet in 6th House**: If no malefic aspect is present, health issues will be easily recoverable.

Past Life Doshas (Afflictions) and Diseases by Planet in 5th House

1. **Sun - Pitra Dosha**:
   - *Disease*: Eye problems.
2. **Rahu - Sarpa Dosha**:
   - *Disease*: Skin allergies and related issues.
3. **Mars - Ancestral Untimely Death**:
   - *Result*: Financial and health issues for random family members due to an untimely death in the family lineage.
4. **Moon**:

- o *Result*: Miscarriage experienced by mother before the native's birth or loss of a sibling.
  - o *Disease*: Back pain at some life stage.
5. **Mercury - Curse of Improper Rituals (Puja Path)**:
  - o *Result*: Mental health challenges such as depression, fear psychosis and introversion.
  - o *If Linked by Rashi Lord*:
    - *Jupiter as Lord*: Curse of the guru.
    - *Venus as Lord*: Curse of a woman.
    - *Saturn as Lord*: Multiple past-life curses accumulating from many lifetimes.

Health Issues by Linked Planets:

Sun: Bone and eyesight problems.

Moon: Mental health challenges.

Mars: Blood-related issues, prone to accidents.

Venus: Chronic illnesses, difficulty with medicine efficacy.

Mercury: Skin allergies, nervousness.

Saturn: Chronic diseases requiring lifelong medication.

Rahu: Gastric issues, susceptibility to paranormal influences.

Ketu: Skin rashes.

6th Lord in 8th House or 6th and 8th House Exchange:

This combination suggests a death related to the same type of disease the native suffers from in life.

Jupiter and Marriage

- **Male Chart Marriage Timing**:
- *Second Round of Jupiter's Transit*: During the 2nd cycle of Jupiter's transit (starting around age 12 and repeating in subsequent cycles), the timing for marriage or a significant relationship may align with Jupiter transiting over natal Mars and then Venus, particularly if this occurs in the 1st or 7th house.
- *Effect of Ketu*: If Ketu follows Jupiter's transit during this cycle, there is a higher likelihood of breaks or challenges in the relationship or marriage.
- **Female Chart Marriage Timing**:
- In a female chart, the 2nd cycle of Jupiter's transit influences marriage prospects if Jupiter transits first over Venus (1st or 7th house) and then Mars in a single cycle.
- *Effect of Ketu*: As in the male chart, Ketu's involvement could lead to challenges or even breaks in relationships.

In current Scenario when marriage age is deferred and people are marrying late, we can check the same in 3rd round of Jupiter also & same applies for Male and Female Marriages both.

Multiple Marriages Indicators:

- **Second and Subsequent Marriages**:
- *Second Spouse*: Mercury signifies a second wife in male charts, while Jupiter signifies a second husband in female charts.
- *Third Spouse*: Saturn signifies a potential third spouse in female chart & Moon third wife in Male charts.
- *Likelihood of Remarriage*: If Jupiter or Saturn is positioned with planets of the opposite gender within the chart (for example, Jupiter or Saturn with

Mars in a female chart), it strengthens the possibility of remarriage.

Match Compatibility:

- Planets located in the 2nd or 12th house from Jupiter can offer insights into compatibility for marriage.
- *Male Chart*: Compatibility can be assessed based on Venus's position in male charts, as it represents the first wife.
- *Female Chart*: Mars's position holds significance for compatibility with the first husband in female charts.
- Compatibility assessment also includes analyzing the aspects and placements of these planets to determine marital harmony.

Other Influences of Jupiter's Placement:

- **Wanderer's Indicator**: When there are no planets in the four houses following Jupiter, the native may tend towards a wandering or unsettled lifestyle.
- **Sanyas Yoga (Detachment)**: If two malefic planets are placed in the four houses following Jupiter, this can indicate a Sanyas Yoga, leading to detachment from family responsibilities. However, benefic aspects can mitigate this influence, balancing the tendency toward renunciation.
- **3rd Lord from Jupiter in 2nd House**: When the 3rd lord is placed in the 2nd house from Jupiter, financial benefits may come through siblings.

Jupiter's Placement in Various Signs:

Jupiter in Cancer (Exalted):

- In a male chart, Jupiter in Cancer often indicates an inclination towards nobility, physical strength, or even settling in a different location.
- In a female chart, Jupiter in Cancer can result in hurdles and sorrowful experiences, often accompanied by a sense of blame or undue criticism.

Jupiter in Leo:

- Indicates a desire for authority and leadership; with positive aspects, this can create a "kingly" life, but negative aspects can hinder these qualities.

Jupiter in Virgo:

- Commonly associated with an interest in law and public arbitration, Jupiter in Virgo often creates a natural mediator with strong problem-solving skills.

Jupiter in Taurus or Libra:

- Natives may experience financial growth or gain following marriage due to the influence of these signs.

Jupiter in Aries or Scorpio:

- Generally, there is a lack of peace and a tendency to feel directionless, particularly in Scorpio, where Jupiter can create confusion between materialistic and spiritual ambitions.

Jupiter in the Sagittarius or Pisces:

- These natives may have a deep religious inclination, a propensity for travel and a love for their homeland even if they frequently visit foreign lands.

Retrograde Jupiter:

- A retrograde Jupiter often implies that the native will find success and growth more readily outside their place of birth, often experiencing progress or prosperity in a different location.

Additional Key Insights:

- **Mars in the 12th House from Jupiter**:
- The native is advised against taking on other people's responsibilities, such as offering legal guarantees or becoming a guarantor, as this position can lead them into others' difficulties or legal issues.
- **Exalted Jupiter or Strongly Positioned Jupiter**:
- This often grants natives a good balance of material and spiritual wealth and freedom of action (karma). However, Saturn's influence, which governs the outcome of actions, often affects how the karmic balance is ultimately realized, especially in later years.

Jupiter in different sign as per Exaltation and Debilitation of planets

Jupiter in Aries (Sun Exalted, Saturn Debilitated):

Impact on Father and Son: When Jupiter is in Aries, it strengthens the Sun, which represents the father. This is fortunate for the father's prosperity, bringing invisible and natural gains to him. The child (Jeeva) born with Jupiter in this position will bring fortune and support for the father's prosperity. During transits of Jupiter, Saturn, Rahu, or Ketu in Aries, these invisible gains and prosperity will be further activated for the father.

Impact on Servants and Elder Siblings: Since Saturn is debilitated in Aries, this position may bring challenges for servants or elder siblings, with potential issues during Jupiter, Saturn, Rahu, or Ketu transits in Aries.

Jupiter in Taurus (Moon Exalted):

Impact on Mother: With Jupiter in Taurus, the Moon's exaltation here benefits the native's mother. The native is naturally fortunate for the mother's prosperity, irrespective of malefic influences, which may actually turn favorable for the Moon's significations. Transits of Jupiter, Saturn, Rahu, or Ketu over Taurus are likely to bring gains or positive outcomes for the mother, including potential foreign travel, pilgrimage (especially influenced by Ketu), or beneficial changes.

Gemini : No planet is Exalted or Debilitated

Jupiter in Cancer (Jupiter Exalted, Mars Debilitated):

Impact on Native and Guru: Jupiter's exaltation here greatly benefits the native and brings positive support from the Guru (teacher, guide).

Impact on Father and Younger Sibling: However, Mars is debilitated in Cancer, affecting aspects related to land or property. This may cause hidden or visible losses for the father after the native's birth and may also strain the native's relationship with younger siblings. Transits of Jupiter, Saturn, Rahu, or Ketu in Cancer could further emphasize these issues, especially related to property or relationships with younger siblings.

Jupiter in Virgo (Mercury Exalted, Venus Debilitated):

Impact on Education and Family (Sister, Aunt): Jupiter in Virgo enhances educational gains and brings benefits to sisters and paternal aunts.

Impact on Father and Wife: Father may face financial losses after the native's birth and the native could experience issues related to the wife or marital life. Transits of Jupiter, Rahu, Saturn and Ketu in Virgo may further activate these effects.

Jupiter in Libra (Saturn Exalted, Sun Debilitated):

Impact on Servants and Elder Siblings: With Saturn exalted, Jupiter in Libra supports gains and prosperity for servants and elder siblings, especially during transits of Jupiter, Saturn, Rahu, or Ketu.

Impact on Father: Sun's debilitation may cause challenges for the father, possibly impacting his health, status, or financial stability after the native's birth.

Jupiter in Scorpio:

Impact on Mother: The mother may face health or other challenges after the native's birth, particularly during transits of Jupiter, Rahu, Ketu, or Saturn over Scorpio. This position may highlight emotional, mental, or familial issues related to the mother.

Jupiter in Capricorn (Mars Exalted, Jupiter Debilitated):

Impact on Father and Younger Sibling: Jupiter in Capricorn benefits the father through land or property gains, potentially bringing financial upliftment through real estate or assets. Younger siblings may also benefit from this placement.

Debilitation of Jupiter: Jupiter's debilitation may reduce some positive influences on the native's personal growth or fortune, though Mars's exaltation can bring strength in property-related matters.

Jupiter in Pisces (Venus Exalted, Mercury Debilitated):

Impact on Wife, Sister and Education: With Venus exalted, this placement supports harmony and prosperity in relationships, particularly with the wife and sister/aunt. However, Mercury's debilitation may indicate challenges in education or intellectual pursuits, potentially bringing obstacles in learning or communication.

Key Jupiter Combination (1,5,9)

Jupiter + Venus + Mercury

- **Relatives and Neighbors**: This combination indicates that the native has a supportive and respected social and family network. Relatives and neighbors are likely to be of good character and their presence positively impacts the native's life.
- **Academic and Language Skills**: With Jupiter, Venus and Mercury together, the native would excel in academics, often having a successful educational background. They will likely be proficient in *four languages*, as Jupiter's conjunction with each planet represents fluency in an additional language.
- **Dual Personality**: The native may exhibit dual tendencies, meaning they can adapt or present different sides of themselves in various situations.
- **Spiritual Inclination and Financial Gains**: There is a strong inclination towards spiritual knowledge, which may even become a source of income. Teaching can be a suitable profession and the native's intelligence and knowledge may relate to public or social affairs, enhancing their popularity.
- **Magnetism**: The native will have an attractive aura, naturally drawing others to them. However, if aspected by malefics, these positive attributes may fluctuate, leading to inconsistencies in how they're perceived by others.

Jupiter + Venus

- **Beauty and Charm**: This combination often bestows physical attractiveness, especially for the native's partner. In a male chart, the native's wife will be beautiful, while in a female chart, the native herself will likely have a pleasant appearance, often marked by *beautiful eyes*.

- **Vehicles and Material Comforts**: With Jupiter (3) and Venus (vehicles), the native may possess *three vehicles* over their lifetime, symbolizing a love for travel and comfort.
- **Financial Mindedness**: The native is financially savvy and is often driven by money management. While respectful of others, they can be selective with their hospitality, but when they do host, they are exceptional at it.
- **Family and Female Child**: The native may have a female child who is both popular and drawn to a luxurious lifestyle. This child will likely inherit the native's or the wife's love for comfort and beauty.
- **Marriage and Luck**: The native's wife is considered fortunate for the family, bringing positivity and possibly having a strong female influence or spiritual guide. She enjoys luxury and is respected by those around her.

Jupiter Secrets

- **Jupiter + Ketu and Saturn + Rahu in 7th House**: The native may work in a lower-grade job or face limitations in career growth due to restrictive influences from Saturn and Rahu.
- **Jupiter Contacts Rahu + Mars Before Mercury**: This suggests an interest in mystical or mantra-based studies, combining Mars' focus with Rahu's unconventional insights.
- **Sun in Leo in 7th from Jupiter**: Indicates possible government honors or recognition for the native's father.
- **Sun in 7th from Jupiter**: The native might receive government recognition or hold a respected position due to the Sun's influence.
- **Malefic in 7th from Jupiter**: Life challenges or personal difficulties may arise after the birth of a child.
- **Jupiter and Sun Exalted**: Signifies a religious or highly ethical person with strong moral values.
- **Jupiter + Saturn Conjunction Aspected by Mars**: Likely to cause tension or disputes between the native and their brother.
- **Jupiter + Mars + Mercury**: This combination can bring educational obstacles, possibly leading to limited formal education.
- **Jupiter + Saturn with Ketu in the Next House**: Symbolizes a birth with spiritual significance or divine blessings.
- **Jupiter Exalted with Sun in 7th**: The native is noble-minded and respected for their integrity.
- **Jupiter in the 9th or 12th, with Mercury and Saturn Aspecting Mercury's Signs**: Indicates a career in education or academics.
- **Mercury in 10th from Jupiter**: Further supports a profession in education, possibly as a teacher or in an academic setting.
- **Jupiter + Mercury in Cancer or Virgo**: The native is likely to be intelligent with a smooth educational

journey, as Mercury and Jupiter harmonize well in these signs.

- **Mars Aspecting 4th House from Jupiter**: Indicates ownership or acquisition of landed property.
- **Jupiter, Next House Venus, Next House Sun**: The native may have strained or challenging relations with their father.
- **Moon in 7th from Jupiter**: This placement gives the native an edge in overcoming opponents and competition.
- **2nd House from Jupiter Aspected by Venus**: Financial gains are likely through marriage or the spouse.
- **Jupiter Exalted**: The native possesses a well-proportioned body and a graceful presence.
- **Rahu + Mars Next to Jupiter**: The native has boldness and courage, with a brave outlook on life.
- **Jupiter in Libra, Sun in Scorpio and Mars Aspecting Jupiter**: Suggests gains or benefits from ancestral or parental property.
- **Mars/Saturn/Ketu Between Jupiter and Sun**: The native's father may have experienced a serious issue or crisis around the time of the native's birth.
- **Jupiter with Rahu + Saturn**: Indicates the native might inherit or take over their grandfather's line of business.
- **Jupiter + Venus + Ketu**: The native tends to be argumentative and may engage in debates or conflicts readily.
- **Venus in 12th or 6th from Jupiter (6/8 relationship with Jupiter)**: Indicates difficulties in marital life due to the challenging aspect between Venus and Jupiter.
- **Sun in 2nd to Jupiter Aspected by Saturn**: The native is likely to follow in their father's professional footsteps.
- **Jupiter + Saturn with Ketu in the Next House and Jupiter Aspected by Venus**: Indicates potential success in a medical or health-related profession.

- **2nd House Lord from Jupiter Aspected by Enemies**: The native may face significant struggles in maintaining livelihood due to adversarial influences.
- **Jupiter + Venus in Gemini or Scorpio**: Signifies possible involvement in multiple secret romantic relationships.
- **Sun and Saturn in 3rd from Jupiter**: Suggests the father may have experienced difficulties or challenges around the time of the native's birth.
- **Jupiter Aspected by Venus and Moon**: The native is likely to be of a pious and morally upright character.
- **Jupiter in Pisces and Ketu in Aries**: This combination inclines the native toward spiritual pursuits and a deep desire for liberation (moksha).
- **Jupiter in Taurus with Mercury + Mars in Gemini**: The native may possess legal knowledge, hold a respected position locally and often help others resolve conflicts.
- **Rahu in the Next House to Jupiter**: Indicates health issues that may arise in early childhood, typically between ages 2 and 4.
- **4th House from Jupiter Aspected by Venus and Moon**: The native is likely to possess knowledge and appreciation of fine arts.
- **Jupiter 2nd to Sun**: Signifies a person of good character and strong morals.
- **Jupiter in Pisces with Saturn + Ketu in the Next House**: This combination favors the native becoming a preacher or priest with a respected spiritual influence.
- **2nd Lord in 3rd from Jupiter with Saturn + Sun in 11th from Jupiter**: Indicates that the native may have a tendency to spend whatever they earn.
- **Jupiter + Mercury with Venus + Saturn + Mars in the Next House**: Suggests that the native might work as a money lender.
- **Saturn + Mars in 2nd to Jupiter**: There is a possibility of paralysis for the native.
- **6th Lord with Venus from Jupiter**: Points toward an unhappy married life.

- **Weak Jupiter if No Planet in 7th, 2nd, or 12th from It**: Suggests that the native may face limited support in life without planets in these key houses.
- **Saturn Aspects the 4th House from Jupiter**: The native's mother is likely to be the head or authority in the family.
- **Jupiter in Pisces or Sagittarius with Saturn**: Signifies potential for the native to achieve a prominent or high position.
- **Mars in 12th from Jupiter**: Indicates a lack of harmony or close relationship with the brother.
- **6th Lord from Jupiter with Ketu**: Suggests that health issues may be resolved through religious rituals like pooja or havan.
- **Jupiter + Rahu**: This combination may cause mental depression for the native.
- **Jupiter's Dispositor in 6th from Jupiter with 2nd Lord**: Indicates that the native's wife could bring ill fame or unfavorable reputation.
- **Mars + Moon in 3rd from Jupiter with 2nd House Aspected by Saturn**: Suggests the native may engage in an illicit relationship with a woman of lower status, potentially resulting in a child.
- **Jupiter in 2nd, Venus in 3rd, Rahu**: Points to the possibility of discovering hidden treasure or secret assets.
- **Jupiter + Mars in 6/8 Position**: In a female chart, this placement indicates understanding issues between the native and her spouse, particularly a lack of understanding of the male partner.
- **Venus in 2nd or 12th from Jupiter in Male Chart**: Implies challenges in mutual understanding with the wife, particularly around emotional and relational alignment.
- **Jupiter conjunct Mars in Capricorn** - Parental property.
- **Jupiter opposing Mars** - Unhappy married life.
- **Jupiter in trine to Ketu** - Spiritual inclination.
- **Jupiter trine Saturn and Ketu** - Fulfills spiritual ambitions.

Understanding Saturn: The Path of Profession & Karma

Saturn's Role as Karma Karaka: Saturn, the furthest and largest planet, represents karma or life's duties. Every person, seen as a soul with karmic obligations, manifests through various planetary influences that signify stages in life, starting from soul (Jupiter), body (Mars), mind (Moon) and desires (Rahu and Ketu), followed by enjoyment (Venus), intelligence (Mercury) and finally, the self (Sun).

Saturn's Transit – Fate Activation: Saturn's transit symbolizes the activation of fate. As Saturn moves across different natal planets, it unfolds karmic results related to each planet's domain, indicating unavoidable consequences of past actions.

Jupiter as Free Will: In contrast, Jupiter represents free will, the liberty to act and make choices. Jupiter's transit shows the timing of potential choices aligned with the natal planets, giving insight into personal initiatives and decision-making.

Harmonious Saturn-Jupiter Trines:

- When **transiting Jupiter** forms a trine with **natal Saturn**, it signifies a period when personal wishes and free will have the potential to be realized.
- Conversely, when **Saturn transits** in trine with **natal Jupiter**, fate takes precedence, indicating an outcome that must be accepted as the inevitable result of prior actions.

Distinction Between Saturn and Jupiter Events:

- Events **shown by Saturn** are fated and bound to occur.
- Events **shown by Jupiter** are driven by personal action and free will, providing an opportunity for

choice before the eventual outcome governed by Saturn.

Jupiter's Transit Over Natal Planets: Jupiter's transit impacts depend on how one utilizes the energies of the planet it transits. Proper, constructive use leads to positive Saturn results, while misuse results in Saturn manifesting negative consequences.

Rahu and Ketu – Karma Axis: Rahu and Ketu are key indicators of unavoidable karmic events:

- **Rahu** introduces sudden issues or rewards, creating problems that are challenging yet manageable.
- **Ketu** often obstructs or limits, making situations harder to navigate and live with, compared to Rahu.

Venus in Taurus with Rahu Transit: A Rahu transit over Venus in Taurus often brings unexpected financial gains or can open new income channels, exemplifying Rahu's potential for sudden, material benefits.

Jupiter and Saturn in 6/8 or 2/12 Positions:

- **6/8 Position**: When Jupiter and Saturn transit each other in the 6th and 8th houses from their natal positions, it can cause a major fall or loss, often following a scandal.
- **2/12 Position**: A 2nd and 12th house transit creates a fall as well, though the impact is usually less severe than the 6/8 transit.

Karak Planets in 6/8: Key planetary significators (karakas) should ideally avoid the 6/8 position from their natal counterparts to prevent disruptions. For example, transiting Mercury in 6/8 to natal Mercury may indicate document-related issues.

Moon and Mercury – Internal vs. External Mind: Moon represents the internal, emotional mind, while Mercury represents the logical, external mind, highlighting the different aspects of cognition and perception.

Saturn's Transit – Realization of Suffering: Saturn's transit acts as a guide to help one understand and accept the reasons behind their suffering, driving home lessons learned from past actions.

Saturn Position from Jupiter : Reason for Suffering

2nd House: Issues in family income, frequent financial hurdles; problems in spouse's life impact the native.

3rd House: Hidden or undeclared loans of a sibling, creating challenges for the native.

4th House: Mother's friendships or associations may be negative or problematic.

5th House: Professional challenges for children or issues in their career path.

6th House: Poor fortune related to servants; issues with or from hired help.

7th House: Partner and friends have long lifespans, indicating stability in relationships.

9th House: Health concerns related to the guru or for the native's second and third children.

10th House: Father's bad habits could lead to issues for the native.

11th House: Unreliable or troublesome friendships

12th House: Enemies lack courage or pose fewer challenges, though overconfidence might create issues.

Saturn in Different Signs : Profession

Professions Related to Mars:

- **Aries**: Law, Teaching, Sports, Police, Government Jobs, Military Service, Fire Services, Engineering, Land Development, Industrial work, Iron and Metal Factories, Boiler Plants, Brick-making, Pottery, Mining, Surgery, Arms Manufacturing, Cooking, Agriculture, Trade Union Leadership.
- **Scorpio**: Machinery, Financial Institutions, Metal and Iron Industries, Engineering, Mining, Agriculture, Electrical Departments, Instrument Manufacturing, Precision Development, Raw Materials, Priesthood, Astrology, Mantra and Tantra practices, Occult Sciences.

Professions Related to Venus:

- **Taurus**: Finance, Jewelry Business, Cattle Shed Management, Money Lending, Commission Agency, Financial Institutions, Handicrafts, Fancy Items, Perfumes and Scents, High-end Hotels, Flower Shops, Fruit Juice Shops, Drama, Cinema, Music, Poetry, Story Writing, Singing, Treasury Roles.
- **Libra**: Opportunities Abroad, Jewelry Shops, Fancy Stores, Handicrafts, Perfume Shops, Clothing Merchants, Money Lending, Commission Agents, Banking, Life Insurance, Law Departments, Hotel Management, Bars and Restaurants, Dance Halls, Beauty Parlors, Music, Dance and Cinema.

Professions Related to Moon:

- **Cancer**: Restaurant and Hotel Management, Liquid-related Industries, Dairy Products, Export and Import, Shipping, Transportation, Agriculture, Grocery Stores, Medical Shops, Milk Booths,

Vegetable Markets, Pearl Merchants, Distilleries, Mineral Water Sales.

Professions Related to Sun:

- **Leo**: Hospital Management, Government Jobs, Politics, Administrative Roles, Social Services, Charitable Institutions, Engineering Industry.

Professions Related to Jupiter:

- **Sagittarius**: Banking, Forestry, Saw Mills, Wood Merchants, Financial Institutions, Legal Departments, Temples, Educational Institutions, Military Training, Social Services, Charitable Organizations.
- **Pisces**: Banking, Education, Religious Institutions, Medicine, Financial Institutions, Legal Departments, External Affairs, Navy, Shipping, Temple Work, Priesthood.

Professions Related to Mercury:

- **Gemini**: Media, Documentation, Business, Press, Broadcasting, Space Department, Education, Telecommunications, Book Publishing, Mathematics, Accountancy, Auditing, Legal Counseling, Diplomacy.
- **Virgo**: Law, Judiciary, Agriculture, Trading, Auditing, Accounting, Teaching, Writing, Retail Shops.

Professions Related to Saturn:

- **Capricorn**: Chartered Accountancy, Professorship, Food Production, Manure and Pesticide Sales, Oil Merchants, Mining, Spare Parts and Hardware Shops, Leather Business, Construction, Stone and

Sand Business, Porters, Drivers, Shoe Polishing and Shoemaking.
- **Aquarius**: Wholesale Trade, Psychology, Astrology, Philosophy, Religion, Research and Development, Consultancy, Administration, Oil and Natural Gas, Aviation, Space, Defense Services, Fire Department, Jail Services, Bomb Manufacturing, Tourist Guide, Central Excise, Butchery, CBI Department.

Professions by Planet

- **Sun**: Politicians, Physicians, Goldsmiths
- **Moon**: Milkman, Farmer, Grass Vendor, Midwife, Nurse, Cook, Sailor, Travel Agent, Dry Cleaner, Waiter, Navigator, Pearl Maker
- **Mars**: Engineer, Butcher, Surgeon, Dentist, Constable, Mechanic, Blacksmith, Fireman, Soldier, Sculptor
- **Mercury**: Newspaper Vendor, Teacher, Novelist, Writer, Broker, Postman, Inspector, Publisher, Printer, Editor, Accountant, Public Speaker, Import/Export, Transportation
- **Jupiter**: Priest, Manager, Minister, Lawyer, Judge, Banker, Temple Worker
- **Venus**: Artist, Treasurer, Jeweler, Musician, Singer, Performer, Dancer, Perfume Seller, Call Girl
- **Saturn**: Watchman, Cleaner, Peon, Sweeper, Cobbler, Miner, Brick Layer
- **Rahu**: Shoemaker, Black Magician, Coolie, Driver, Drummer, Porter, Rag Picker, Wood Cutter, Robber, Scientist, Photographer, Actor, Gas Agent, Electronics Repair
- **Ketu**: Doctor, Priest, Fisherman, Weaver, Tailor, Astrologer, Snake Charmer, Faith Healer, Hunter, Beggar, Saint, Wireman, Herbalist, Pottery and Brick Maker

Saturn and Profession Guidelines:

1. **Saturn's Sign Placement**: Assess the sign Saturn occupies to understand the nature of the profession.
2. **Directional Chart**:
   - **Trine Houses (1, 5, 9)**: Indicates strengths or core directions of professional life.
   - **Aspect Directions (3, 7, 11)**: Shows influences on career success and modifications.
3. **2nd House from Saturn (Earnings and Career Progress)**:
   - **Venus/Jupiter**: Indicates a smooth path, with potential for stable income and positive growth.
   - **Mars/Ketu**: Indicates initial struggles or repeated obstacles. However, once past the initial challenges, stability is more likely.
4. **7th House from Saturn (Strongest Aspect)**:
   - **Malefics (Mars/Ketu)**: Creates significant challenges or setbacks in career.
   - **Benefics (Venus/Jupiter)**: Guarantees more favorable outcomes and ease in achieving success.
   - **Friendly/Enmical Aspects**: Friendly aspects support positive results; enmical aspects introduce difficulties.
5. **12th House from Saturn (Comfort in Profession)**:
   - **Mars/Ketu/Moon**: Signals discomfort in the work environment, including potential for workplace tensions, discomfort and politics.
   - **Other Benefic Planets**: Favor a harmonious work environment and a greater sense of satisfaction in professional surroundings.

6. **Saturn Transit**: Review Saturn's current transit to gauge the immediate status and shifts in career progression.

Key Saturn Aspects & Transits:

1. **Saturn's 3rd Aspect**:
   - **On Sun**: Indicates a strong professional foundation.
     - **Sun + Mercury**: Favors large-scale business ventures.
     - **Sun in 7th or 10th House**: Suggests a well-paid job.
2. **Destiny Makers**:
   - **Venus, Mercury, Jupiter, Sun**: When transiting Saturn connects with these planets, it brings positive professional results and the rewards of past good karma. Jupiter's transit over these planets yields similar benefits.
3. **Destiny Breakers**:
   - **Moon, Saturn, Mars, Rahu, Ketu**: Transiting Saturn over these planets creates obstacles and struggles, indicating consequences of past unfavorable karma.
4. **Destiny Modifiers**:
   - **Moon and Mars**: Modify fate, requiring adaptation and flexibility in response to challenges.
5. **Saturn's Return (Transit on Natal Saturn)**:
   - Considered beneficial for career growth but involves significant hard work and perseverance.

Saturn Transit over Natal Planets and its Impact on Profession

Saturn over Sun: New professional role for the son with hurdles; increased workload for the father. Brings recognition and fame to the native; potential support from government or influential sources.

Saturn over Moon: Changes in profession and emotional unrest; potential issues in the mother's and female relatives' lives. If benefic aspects are present, outcomes improve.

Saturn over Mars: Focus on property-related professions; potential disputes or accidents at work.

Saturn over Mercury: Initiation of new business, possible disturbances in education and the purchase of property. May cause issues with neighbors.

Saturn over Jupiter: Business expansion and health concerns, with possible lack of acknowledgment at work.

Saturn over Venus: *Karma Lakshmi Yoga* brings financial gain despite potential issues for the wife and daughter.

Saturn over Rahu/Ketu: *Karma Sankat Yog* can bring drastic status changes, particularly during the second Saturn cycle.

Saturn over Saturn: *Karma hi Karma* - an increase in workload and responsibilities.

Jupiter over Jupiter: Indicates growth and positive developments.

Jupiter over Rahu: Generally unfavorable.

Rahu over Jupiter: Brings challenges and problems to the native's life.

- **Rahu – Mars**: Health problems may arise.
- **Saturn + Ketu**: The native may feel compelled to learn astrology.
- **Jupiter + Ketu**: Astrology is learned by choice.

Saturn and Period of Struggles

Saturn, the planet of karma, administers the outcomes of past actions, affecting life's course based on our past deeds - positive or negative. The period of struggles in life can be seen through Saturn's influence, especially when Jupiter transits through Saturn's key aspects (3rd, 7th and 10th houses from Saturn), activating Saturn's karmic results.

Jupiter's transits interact with Saturn's karmic influence in cycles, each round revealing struggles in different areas:

1. **1st Round (0–12 years)**: Issues relate to health and education.
2. **2nd Round (12–24 years)**: Family and financial concerns emerge.
3. **3rd Round (24–36 years)**: Challenges with siblings, travels, or courage.
4. **4th Round (36–48 years)**: Problems tied to home happiness and property.
5. **5th Round (48–60 years)**: Children and their welfare are the focus.
6. **6th Round (60–72 years)**: Health issues become more prominent.

If Jupiter aspects benefic planets during these rounds, struggles may lessen; with malefics, they may intensify. Saturn's influence tends to delay results, making patience crucial. Each round's experiences vary as they reflect accumulated karma, not necessarily repeating exact issues but evolving with time.

Saturn and Jupiter transits have distinct effects based on the nature of the planets they interact with. When Jupiter transits over benefic planets or vice versa, the results are generally positive, regardless of Saturn's position. However, when Jupiter or malefic planets transit over each other, challenges may arise.

In particular, between the ages of **30–36 years**, during the **3rd round of Jupiter (24–36 years)** and **2nd round of Saturn (30–60 years)**, individuals enter a sensitive period marked by potential loss or financial challenges. This period is influenced by Saturn's 1st, 3rd, 7th, or 10th aspect on Venus, which can bring financial loss if it transits over Venus. This specific transit lasts about 2.5 years, during which financial setbacks are likely, although Saturn may yield positive outcomes in other areas of life.

Should Jupiter also aspect during this period, it can lessen the severity of losses, making them more manageable. This balance showcases how planetary transits interweave, shaping periods of growth and challenges based on past karma and planetary influences.

Saturn & Longevity

- **1st Round (0–30 years)**: Indicates possible death of a **grandparent**.
    - **Paternal Grandparent**: If Saturn aspects Rahu.
    - **Maternal Grandparent**: If Saturn aspects Ketu.
- **2nd Round (30–60 years)**: Indicates potential **death of a parent**.
    - **Father**: Saturn transits 8th house from the Sun or from the 8th lord, with 1st, 3rd, 7th, or 10th aspect involving Rahu.
    - **Mother**: Saturn transits 8th house from the Moon or 8th lord, with aspects involving Ketu.

Alternate Method:

- **D-9 Chart**: If Saturn transits in a trine from the 8th lord, it brings challenging, death-like situations for the father.
- **Self Longevity (3rd Round)**:
  - **8th House from Jupiter**: Presence of Rahu, Ketu, or Mars can compromise longevity. If Mars is in Aries or Scorpio, the risk is less severe; benefics nearby can mitigate the impact.
  - **Saturn in 8th from Jupiter or with an 8th house aspect**: Increases longevity.

Critical Situations:

- If **Saturn transits the 8th lord or 8th house**, with its 3rd aspect on Ketu, risks are heightened.
- **Jupiter transiting over Rahu** during this period can worsen the situation.
- In the **D-9 Chart**, if the 8th lord is aspected by Saturn or if Saturn transits in a trine from this position, it indicates severe, life-threatening conditions.

Saturn's 3rd Round (60–90 years): Death of Spouse Indicators

- **Male Chart (Death of Wife)**:
  - **Saturn Transiting 8th House from Venus or from the 8th Lord**: This transit can indicate the death of the wife.
  - **Saturn's Aspects (1st, 3rd, 7th, 10th) on Rahu/Ketu in Relation to Venus**: If Saturn aspects Rahu or Ketu through these aspects while transiting 8th from Venus or the 8th lord, the risk of the wife's death increases.
  - **Navamsa (D-9) Chart**: When Saturn transits in a trine from the 8th lord in the

D-9 chart, it brings life-threatening situations for the wife.

- **Female Chart (Death of Husband)**:
    - ○ **Saturn Transiting 8th House from Mars or from the 8th Lord**: This indicates the possibility of the husband's death.
    - ○ **Saturn's Aspects (1st, 3rd, 7th, 10th) on Rahu/Ketu in Relation to Mars**: The combination of these aspects and transit intensifies the risk.
    - ○ **Navamsa (D-9) Chart**: If Saturn transits in a trine from the 8th lord in the D-9 chart, it suggests critical, life-threatening conditions for the husband.

In both cases, if **benefic planets** are involved or provide aspects, they can help **mitigate** the severity of these indicators.

Disclaimer/Warning: Death or longevity is a very sensitive and important matter. This information is intended solely for academic purposes and should not be used to make predictions for oneself or others. As a practitioner, it is strongly advised not to reveal such predictions or examine them for personal insight. Matters of life and death should be left to divine will and delving into these areas can create significant negative karma. This should be avoided at all costs.

Saturn Secrets

- **Saturn Aspect on Sun and Ketu / Saturn in Leo / Sun in 12th from Saturn**: Government job likely.
- **Jupiter in 11th from Saturn**: Positive results whenever transiting Saturn touches Jupiter.
- **Scorpio Sign or Mars in 10th from Saturn**: Indicates a profession in iron and steel.
- **Sun in 10th from Saturn**: High-profile position or prestigious role.
- **Saturn Retrograde with Mars and Venus in 11th from Saturn**: Native earns significant name, fame and success.
- **2nd from Saturn aspected by Jupiter**: Possible involvement in an educational institution.
- **Saturn in its 2nd round touching the 6th house from Jupiter**: Potential disturbance to reputation or facing criticisms.
- **Transiting Saturn touching the 11th house from Venus or Venus**: Indicates a new job, appointment, or the start of a business.
- **Transiting Saturn touching Sun**: Likely to bring a promotion or professional advancement.
- **2nd House from Saturn in Libra or Taurus with Venus**: Likely involvement in jewelry or gold-related business.
- **Saturn and Mars in conjunction or trine**: Causes obstacles in appointments, job interviews, or professional advancements.
- **Saturn in 10th from Sun with Mars in 12th**: Indicates that the father may have been employed in a government position.
- **Saturn aspecting Mars**: Suggests that the development or progress of a brother may not be smooth.
- **Saturn in Gemini or Virgo (3rd or 6th house)**: Suggests a tendency toward business rather than traditional employment.

- **Mars and Rahu ahead of Saturn**: Points to a business related to vehicles, travel, or tourism.
- **Moon and Saturn adjacent to Mercury**: Indicates difficulties or delays in completing one's education.
- **Rahu in 2nd to Saturn**: Often points to a low-paying job.
- **Aspecting planets to Saturn or 2nd house from Saturn**: Helps reveal the type of working environment.
- **Saturn next to Sun, Mercury, or Venus**: Signifies a good income and employment with favorable benefits.
- **Venus in 2nd to Saturn with Sun and Mercury in 4th**: Suggests employment in government treasury or financial institutions.
- **Venus in 12th from Saturn**: Indicates potential involvement in money lending.
- **Sun and Mercury in 7th from Saturn**: Points toward employment in a wealthy or well-established company.
- **Saturn in Aries or Scorpio with no planet in 2nd or 12th**: Indicates instability in life, frequent changes in profession.
- **Saturn touches Sun and Mercury before Venus**: Benefits from the father's wealth are likely.
- **Mars in 3rd from Saturn with Ketu in 4th**: Points to significant struggles in life.
- **Saturn + Jupiter, with Ketu in 3rd and Mars in 7th**: Bank employment is possible and the native may later change profession or pursue astrology.
- **Mars in 7th from Saturn**: Indicates a lower-paying job.
- **Moon in 2nd and Ketu in 3rd from Saturn**: Native has a Sanyasi (renunciant) tendency.
- **Retrograde Saturn with Mercury and Venus in 11th**: Brings good reputation, fame and financial gains.
- **Saturn in Scorpio with Ketu and Mercury in 12th**: Indicates spiritual abilities.

- **Saturn in Sagittarius**: Points toward a career in banking.
- **Saturn + Mercury in Virgo**: Indicates a career as an advocate.
- **Saturn + Mercury**: Tends to favor educational pursuits.
- **Saturn + Venus**: Suggests a happy married life.
- **Saturn + Moon**: Points to employment in a foreign land.
- **Saturn in 3rd from Jupiter**: Likely job loss before age 30.
- **Saturn + Moon in Cancer in a female chart**: Indicates flat or underdeveloped breasts.
- **Moon and Mercury in 3rd from Saturn**: Suggests grocery or retail business.
- **Saturn + Mars in Taurus**: Indicates a profession as an accountant.
- Saturn conjunct Mars - Creates a cynical nature.
- Saturn conjunct Ketu in Mars' sign - Profession connected with machinery.
- Saturn in trine with Venus - Happy marriage.
- Saturn trine Ketu and Mercury - Intellectual nature.
- Saturn in trine with Moon and Ketu - Practices Sahaj Yoga (patience).

House Placement from Jupiter

- **5th House to Venus**: Problems with children.
- **6th House**: Gift of wealth.
- **10th House**: Career success.
- **2nd House**: Compulsive lying; wealth when away from family.

Rahu: The Karmic Catalyst

Rahu, unlike other planets, lacks an intrinsic nature and instead absorbs the qualities of the Rashi (sign) and any planets it conjuncts with in 1, 5, or 9 positions. Its behavior is heavily influenced by these associations. Rahu is often regarded as a force of *Kaal* (time) and is known for instigating significant beginnings and shifts in life's patterns, impacting areas like sleep, habits and lifestyle.

In a chart, Rahu represents illusions, hidden activities, obstacles and secrecy. It symbolizes work carried out in mystery, often linked to areas that are hidden or obscure in nature, such as detective work or dealing with unsolved mysteries. During transits, when Jupiter or Saturn crosses over Natal Rahu, it usually brings new beginnings, relieves previous difficulties and ushers in transformative changes in various aspects of life.

Rahu in Different Houses from Jupiter

1st House: Rahu in the 1st House makes the native imaginative, often lost in daydreams and building "castles in the air." Such individuals may exhibit confusion and a tendency to fantasize. Guru Chandal Yoga (Jupiter conjunct Rahu) can lead them into undesirable company until around age 24-25, though it can also amplify the benefits of a favorable planet, bringing significant gains.

2nd House: Rahu here can delay marriage, create family challenges and cause skin allergies. Money can be short-lived and the native might have a diplomatic but dry manner of speech. Relationships with family and relatives may feel distant or lack warmth and the spouse could also show tendencies toward daydreaming.

3rd House: The native may be the youngest sibling, with no younger siblings born after. Communication may be loud but lacks action, as Rahu dampens courage, making the native avoid confrontation. Frequent travels without clear purpose are likely, with Rahu introducing losses during these trips. Communication may feel detached and siblings might also exhibit illusory thinking.

4th House: The native may live in or eventually move to an L-shaped house. Female family members may experience health or mental issues. Academically, they may lean towards research-oriented fields, but malefic aspects can force educational travels. The mother might display imaginative or illusory tendencies and there could be ancestral roots in a distant location.

5th House: Rahu in the 5th House often brings bad habits like drinking, gambling and smoking. There may be delays in having children and children might have illusory or dreamy tendencies. The native's secrets remain hidden and problems here stem from past-life karma.

6th House: Health issues can arise, particularly allergies or lung-related problems. Open enemies tend to lack courage and will not dominate the native. Hardworking servants or helpers might be daydreamers and there's a potential for pet-related accidents, like dog bites.

7th House: Partners or friends may be illusory, unhelpful and dry in nature. Issues can arise in daily income and activities related to partners, who might be less educated or not dependable in times of need.

8th House: Rahu here compromises longevity unless supported by benefic aspects, which can improve lifespan and reduce difficulties.

9th House: The native may have a strong interest in mantras and spiritual studies. Rahu adopts Jupiter-like traits, endowing the native with public appeal and recognition, often leading to long-distance travels for spiritual or mantra-related studies.

10th House: Professionally, the native may experience instability and frequent job changes. Rahu's influence brings a desire for change, though actual transitions may lack support. Benefic aspects can bring stability to the career.

11th House: Rahu in the 11th House suggests limited friendships, often with people who are unhelpful or unreliable. Elder siblings may have a reserved or dry nature and gains are usually limited or unfulfilling.

12th House: Rahu here opens possibilities for foreign settlement, though the native may ultimately return to their homeland. There may be a lack of satisfaction in bed pleasures and   secret enemies tend to be ineffective or daydreamers.

Rahu in Different Signs

- **Rahu's Nature and Influence:**

Rahu initially presents challenges but can later provide gains, often giving more than other planets as it represents expansion.It is a friend to Venus and Saturn and yields good results in the signs of Mercury and Venus (Gemini, Virgo, Taurus and Libra). Problems from Rahu are generally tolerable, while those from Ketu are often harder to bear. Rahu brings research abilities, feelings of emptiness, hallucinations and digestive issues.

Aries: Risk of head injury; often associated with an east-facing house.

Taurus: Fortunate placement; increases Venusian qualities, with a good flow of money and a house facing south.

Gemini: Exalted position; suitable for careers in photography and media, though communication may be inconsistent.

Cancer: May cause heart issues and, in female charts, potential issues with breastfeeding due to reduced milk production.

Leo: Stomach issues, often gas-related.

Virgo: Affects the large intestine; potential for gastroenteritis or ulcers.

Libra: For females, can cause vaginal dryness; for males, difficulties with sexual performance and issues in the outer genital area.

Scorpio: For females, may lead to uterine issues; for males, potential kidney problems.

Sagittarius: Problems around the thighs and the upper part of the knees.

Capricorn: Causes dryness in the knees, affecting joint lubrication.

Aquarius: Issues with calves and veins.

Pisces: Problems in the feet, affecting mobility or comfort.

- **Aspect and Conjunctions:** Benefic aspects on Rahu can positively modify its effects, amplifying its attributes in favorable ways.

Rahu Secrets

- **Rahu + Venus + Moon**: In males, a high sex drive or desire is indicated.
- **Rahu + Venus**: Can lead to extramarital affairs.
- **Venus + Mercury + Moon**: In females, a high sex drive; Moon brings potential for blames or controversies.
- **Venus + Moon + Rahu | Venus + Mercury + Moon + Jupiter | Venus + Mercury + Moon + Rahu**: In a female chart, such combinations suggest a suspicious nature, potentially damaging married life, with the husband suffering due to the wife's negative traits. Guidance is advised.
- **Jupiter 7th from Mars**: Indicates a tendency toward high blood pressure.
- **Mars + Saturn + Mercury | Mars + Ketu + Saturn | Rahu + Mars/Saturn**: In a male chart, this combination shows fear of the wife, leading to situations where the wife may bully or dominate the husband.
- **Jupiter + Mars**: High blood pressure, a barbaric or aggressive nature and intense anger. Mantra chanting is recommended to mitigate.
- **Jupiter + Sun + Mars**: In both male and female charts, this combination fosters pride and a sense of superiority. It can lead to issues arising from arrogance, restlessness and tarnished reputation due to ego and passion. Such individuals become easily agitated when their vulnerabilities are exposed, feeling deeply unsettled when their weaknesses are touched.
- **Jupiter + Sun + Mars + Ketu**: Brings political gains.
- **Jupiter + Mars + Moon + Rahu**: Indicates a rowdy personality with broad knowledge in various subjects, often a "jack of all trades." They may develop drinking habits, but with proper guidance, they can become excellent mentors.

- **Saturn + Rahu**: Indicates a low-paying job, even for a skilled person. If Rahu has a lower degree, the native may adopt their grandfather's profession; if Saturn has a lower degree, they may enjoy a comfortable life despite a low-paying profession.
- **No Planet Between Saturn and Rahu**: With Rahu in the 3rd from Saturn, this results in frequent job changes; however, a benefic aspect on Saturn can stabilize the profession.
- **Sun in 2nd + Venus in 3rd with Rahu and Saturn**: Ideal for a business in chemicals or medical fields.
- **Saturn in Virgo with Rahu in Gemini or Saturn and Rahu Conjunction**: Suited for a profession in media, photography, or as a cameraman in the media industry.
- **Rahu in 10th from Saturn with Sun or Mars Aspecting Rahu**: Suitable for work in a detective agency.
- **Sun and Mercury in 2nd and Venus and Rahu 3rd from Saturn**: Points to a career in media, film, or fine arts. An exalted Sun enhances this, while a Mars aspect brings high skill levels.
- **Mars and Venus Between Rahu and Saturn**: Indicates high proficiency in surgery, possibly as a high-level surgeon.
- Rahu with Moon - Wavering mind.
- Rahu conjuncts any planet - Expands that planet's influence.

Rahu & Ketu : Health Issues

Rahu in Different Signs

Aries: Head-related issues, frequent headaches or migraines.

Taurus: Problems in the throat area, including tonsils and thyroid concerns.

Gemini: Shoulder-related discomfort or recurring pain.

Cancer: Lung issues, dryness in respiratory passages and persistent dry cough.

Leo: Gastric problems, digestive issues and potential spinal concerns.

Virgo: Issues in the intestines, liver complications, or digestive tract ailments.

Libra: Sexual health issues, such as dryness, low sperm count in males and similar concerns.

Scorpio: Problems related to reproductive organs, such as testicles, kidneys and uterus.

Sagittarius: Thigh-related pain or discomfort, impacting mobility.

Capricorn: Knee problems, including dryness and joint issues.

Aquarius: Calf muscle issues, vein-related problems in the legs.

Pisces: Vulnerability to accidents affecting the feet, potentially involving vehicles (e.g., getting run over).

Ketu in Different Signs

Aries: Prolonged migraines, dizziness.

Taurus: Throat issues, possibly dismantling the throat structure.

Gemini: Severe shoulder problems.

Cancer: Breast cancer, potential breast removal, heart issues.

Leo: Spinal problems, pancreas issues, ulcers.

Virgo: Intestinal concerns, possible removal of organs (e.g., appendix).

Libra: Effects of negative energies, issues with sexual health, especially severe for females who may feel paranormal molestation experiences.

Scorpio: Uterus complications, possible uterus removal, kidney issues.

Sagittarius: Thigh-related mobility issues, potentially fixed or painful movements.

Capricorn: Knee replacement (both genders).

Aquarius: Problems with arteries, veins, calves and legs.

Pisces: Foot issues leading to a noticeable change in gait.

Transit of Rahu & Ketu

Rahu Transit

In the **6th Round of Jupiter**, transits over Rahu and Ketu often indicate challenging times. Here are key points on the effects of Rahu, Mars and Ketu transits:

1. **Rahu's Transit**: Stays in each sign for approximately 1.5 years, completing a full cycle in 18 years.
    - When Rahu transits in the **1st, 5th, or 9th** houses from natal Mars, the risk of accidents increases.
    - If Jupiter aspects this combination, there is protective influence, reducing risk.
2. **Mars and Rahu Conjunction**:
    - Rahu will conjunct with Mars for roughly 1.5 years.
    - The most critical accident-prone period occurs when transiting Mars moves over natal Rahu or natal Mars, especially if it forms a **1st, 5th, 9th, or 12th** relationship with natal Mars.
    - Mars' transit over natal Mars in these houses with Rahu's aspect intensifies risk.
3. **Mars-Rahu-Saturn Combination**: Increases the likelihood of accidents or critical issues.
    - Benefic aspects offer some protection, but the natal promise (indications in the birth chart) is more significant than transiting influences alone.
4. **Ketu's Influence**:
    - Ketu represents detachment and often causes problems related to the sign or planet it's connected to in a chart.
    - In the **1st Round**, transiting Ketu over Saturn may not cause issues, but in the

2nd Round, it begins to create more challenges, often detaching or disrupting the aspects of life governed by Saturn.

Please Note : Both **transits** and **natal placements** must be analyzed together, with particular attention to aspects and the presence of protective influences.

1. **Saturn + Ketu**: Leads to detachment and lack of desire.
2. **Mars + Ketu or Venus + Ketu**: Challenges in marital life, often indicating discord or misunderstandings.
3. **Transiting Rahu over Mars**: Generally does not bring health issues to the husband; remedy can include blood donation.
4. **Challenging Combination for Profession**:
   - **Mars + Saturn + Ketu**: Signifies low-paid jobs and potential renunciation (Sanyas Yoga).
   - **Mars + Saturn + Ketu + Jupiter**: Can indicate a high religious role, such as a head priest and with additional benefics (Sun and Venus), it brings fame
   - **Ketu's Role in Relieving Pain**: In professions that involve healing or providing relief, Ketu can be a beneficial influence.
5. **Rahu's Transits**:
   - **Rahu over Sun**: Issues for father or negative impacts on name and fame.
   - **Rahu over Moon**: Mental unrest or depression and challenges for the mother.
   - **Rahu over Venus**: Brings new financial opportunities or income sources.
   - **Rahu over Saturn**: Indicates a potential change in job, career path, or overall life direction, initiating a new chapter.

Ketu Transit

1. **Ketu Transits Over Saturn**:
   - **1st Round (1,5,9)**: Health issues may arise.
   - **2nd Round**: Disruptions in education, career challenges like transfers or suspensions, mirrored when Saturn transits over Ketu.
2. **Ketu Transits Over Venus**: Indicates potential litigation, issues concerning wife or sister and financial loss.
3. **Ketu Transits Over Mercury**:
   - **1st Round**: Brings changes in education, such as subject or school transitions.
   - **2nd Round**: Strains relations with relatives and neighbors, along with possible litigation.
4. **Ketu Transits Over Jupiter**: Signals a life shift toward spirituality; resistance to this change and pursuing material desires instead can lead to significant difficulties.
5. **Rahu in Kalpurush Rashi**:
   - Generates strong desires related to the house (bhava) it occupies, leading the native to pursue these desires fervently.
   - Rahu simultaneously introduces obstacles to fulfilling these desires, creating a cycle of illusions and continuous pursuit without lasting satisfaction. This often tires the native, as the goals feel achievable but remain elusive due to Rahu's influence.

Ketu, as a karmic planet, symbolizes unfulfilled past life duties, fostering desires for the areas (bhava) where it is placed. However, Ketu's desires often encounter obstacles, leaving needs fulfilled but desires unfulfilled.

On the other hand, **Rahu** creates a sense of lack or scarcity in the respective house of the natal chart (D1), where the native feels incomplete, inferior, or deficient. Rahu also represents a past life curse specific to the sign and house it occupies, resulting in sorrow or dissatisfaction even if desires seem achievable but remain unfulfilled. For example, **Rahu in Venus's sign** leads the native to long for a beautiful spouse, but satisfaction in that area will remain elusive, causing a restless pursuit, sometimes even through extra-marital relations.

Curses and Remedies Associated with Rahu's Conjunctions:

1. **Rahu + Moon**: Mother's curse; feelings of lacking motherly love.
2. **Rahu + Saturn**: Curse from an elder brother or servant, lacking support.
3. **Rahu + Mars**: Curse related to a brother, strained brotherly relationships.
4. **Rahu + Venus**: Curse involving a female, leading to relationship troubles.
5. **Rahu + Sun**: Father's curse, often creating issues with fatherly relationships.
6. **Rahu + Sun** (specific impact): Challenges with male progeny; potential health risks or separation from the son to alleviate the impact.

Remedies for Ketu:

- Reading and distributing religious texts.
- Engaging in meditation and spiritual practices.

Ketu seeks to complete unfinished spiritual work and fulfilling these remedies can ease its impact.

Health

Body Parts as per Kaalpurush Kundli

Aries (1st House): Head, Brain, Face, Eyes.

Taurus (2nd House): Vocal Chords, Thyroid Gland, Throat, Neck.

Gemini (3rd House): Nervous System, Brain Cells, Lungs, Shoulders, Arms, Hands.

Cancer (4th House): Chest, Breasts.

Leo (5th House): Heart, Ribs, Spinal Column, Upper Belly.

Virgo (6th House): Digestive System, Intestines, Spleen, Waist.

Libra (7th House): Kidneys, Skin, Lower Spine.

Scorpio (8th House): Reproductive System, Sexual Organs, Excretory System, Bowels.

Sagittarius (9th House): Hips, Liver, Sciatic Nerve, Thighs.

Capricorn (10th House): Knees, Joints, Skeletal System.

Aquarius (11th House): Calves, Ankles, Circulatory System.

Pisces (12th House): Feet, Toes, Lymphatic System, Body Fat.

Diseases signified by Planets in different Signs

Aries

Sun: Head, brain, eye issues, headaches, hemorrhage, strokes.

Moon: Poor eyesight, unsteadiness, hair loss, insomnia.

Mars: Stress, bleeding, injuries, neurological problems.

Mercury: Convulsions, nervous strain, impotence, sweating.

Jupiter: Cerebral thrombosis, pyorrhea, lethargy, weak brain function.

Venus: Sinus issues, headaches, desire for alcohol, cold symptoms.

Saturn: Cold, catarrh, cerebral ischemia, dental issues, vertigo, tumors.

Rahu: Ear problems, brain fever, dizziness, headaches, hallucinations.

Ketu: Migraine, growths or tumors.

Taurus

Sun: Tonsillitis, diphtheria, polyps, cold-related sinusitis.

Moon: Throat issues, pharyngitis, tonsils, mouth ulcers, eye and urinary concerns.

Mars: Mumps, acne, neck pain, nose bleeding, swellings.

Mercury: Ear problems, stammering, laryngitis, pharyngitis.

Jupiter: Ringworm, catarrh, tonsils.

Venus: Diphtheria, headaches, tonsillitis, venereal issues.

Saturn: Throat growths, gum bleeding, kidney issues.

Rahu: Dental issues, throat infections, insomnia.

Ketu: Throat ulcers, growths, mumps, large carbuncles.

Gemini

Sun: Cold, cough, bronchitis, pulmonary issues, nerve problems.

Moon: Bronchitis, asthma, lung infections, rheumatic pains.

Mars: Lung ulcers, growths, infections.

Mercury: Asthma, nervous issues, joint pain in shoulders and hands.

Jupiter: Lung congestion, liver problems.

Venus: Skin issues, lung problems, ascites (water retention in the abdomen).

Saturn: Rheumatic pain, bronchitis, asthma, lung malignancy.

Rahu: Neck and shoulder pain, epilepsy, insomnia.

Ketu: Skin allergies, joint pain in the upper body, gastric issues.

Cancer

Sun: Measles, gas-related issues, swelling, skin eruptions.

Moon: Common colds, ulcers, weight gain, convulsions.

Mars: Hemorrhage, chest ulcers, tumors in the chest area.

Mercury: Nervous disorders, poor digestion.

Jupiter: Constipation, digestive problems, gas, jaundice, liver issues, ascites.

Venus: Gas, nausea, dizziness.

Saturn: Vomiting, liver problems, anemia, chest tumors, digestive issues.

Rahu: Heartburn, indigestion, chest pain, intestinal worms.

Ketu: Indigestion, urinary problems, risk of breast cancer, dyspepsia, piles.

Leo

Sun: Heart defects, spinal cord issues, back pain.

Moon: Cardiac issues, spinal infections, low blood pressure.

Mars: Angina, heart-related issues, swelling around the heart.

Mercury: Spinal cord disorders, tumors, weak heart.

Jupiter: Heart valve complications, joint or thigh pain.

Venus: Back pain, spine issues, heart problems.

Saturn: Infections in the spinal vertebrae, heart artery problems.

Rahu: Urinary and heart issues.

Ketu: Heart attacks, nerve disorders, indigestion.

Virgo

Sun: Hyperacidity, stomach ulcers, indigestion.

Moon: Food poisoning, bowel issues, indigestion.

Mars: Loose motions, irritable bowel syndrome, burning sensations.

Mercury: Diarrhea, food allergies.

Jupiter: Liver issues, jaundice, digestive ulcers.

Venus: Worm infestations and food-related diseases.

Saturn: Chronic intestinal problems.

Rahu: Chronic digestive infections, gas, burning sensations.

Ketu: Fevers, general weakness, intestinal concerns.

Libra

Sun: Nephritis, kidney diseases, skin issues.

Moon: Kidney swelling, migraines, venereal diseases, hysteria.

Mars: Kidney stones, brain hemorrhage, urinary problems.

Mercury: Urinary tract infections, backaches.

Jupiter: Diabetes, kidney and urinary issues.

Venus: Urinary disorders, effects on head and brain.

Saturn: Kidney and glandular issues.

Rahu: High diabetes, dental problems, fevers.

Ketu: Kidney stones, urinary blockages, dizziness.

Scorpio

Sun: Urinary stones, reproductive issues, bowel syndromes.

Moon: Tonsillitis, allergies, hydrocele, ovarian issues, psychic disturbances.

Mars: Hernia, piles, menstrual issues, kidney stones, tension.

Mercury: Testicular pain, menstrual issues, hearing issues.

Jupiter: Piles, prostate, uterus, diabetes, hydrocele.

Venus: Prostate, venereal diseases, uterine tumors, throat problems.

Saturn: Hernia, hydrocele, piles, sterility, menopause.

Rahu: Uterine issues, blood pressure, venereal diseases, surgeries (piles, hydrocele, hernia).

Ketu: Genital issues, blood pressure, drowsiness.

Sagittarius

Sun: Piles, fever, sciatica, fistula.

Moon: Fractures, skin allergies, sciatica, gout.

Mars: Pain in shoulders and legs, fractures, piles.

Mercury: Nerve disorders affecting thighs and hips.

Jupiter: Arthritis, gout, sciatica, joint pain.

Venus: Issues related to hips and thighs.

Saturn: Fractures in thighs or hips, persistent pain.

Rahu: Rheumatic and joint pain.

Ketu: Muscle twitching, pain in joints and shoulders.

Capricorn

Sun: Burning sensations in the legs, knee pain, lung issues.

Moon: Weakness in knees and legs, general pain.

Mars: Knee injuries, skin eruptions, lung problems.

Mercury: Allergies, gout.

Jupiter: Circulatory issues, skin ailments, liver problems, joint pain.

Venus: Cough, cold, lung disorders, leg pain.

Saturn: Arthritis, lung infections, blood impurities.

Rahu: Knee damage, weakness, pain.

Ketu: Issues with knee caps, lung and blood disorders.

Aquarius

Sun: Hematemesis (vomiting blood), swelling, varicose veins, palpitations.

Moon: Fluid retention in legs, leg pain, heart issues.

Mars: Fractures, vein-related skin issues, heart-related problems.

Mercury: Nerve weakness, general pain.

Jupiter: Ankle and joint pain, backache, heart discomfort.

Venus: Vein, leg and heart issues.

Saturn: Cramps, ankle and joint pain, spinal discomfort.

Rahu: Blood impurities, insomnia, diabetes.

Ketu: Calf muscle pain, chest discomfort.

Pisces

Sun: Eye problems, lung and uterine issues, fever.

Moon: Cold, cough, depression.

Mars: Bone fractures, corns, skin issues, diarrhea.

Mercury: Cramps, lung issues, memory loss, fears, anxiety.

Jupiter: Heart issues, acidity, leg and back pain.

Venus: Vein and cardiac problems.

Saturn: Corns, gland swelling, lung and intestine issues.

Rahu: Indigestion, weakness, lung problems, asthma.

Ketu: Neurological issues, weakness, asthma, muscle pain.

General Diseases Signified by Planets

Sun: Bile disorders, diarrhea, eye problems, headaches, fever, loss of appetite, heart disease, thirst and sunstroke.

Moon: Eye diseases, cold, cough, blood impurities, venereal diseases, skin diseases, lunacy, influenza, phlegm, smallpox, measles, mental disorders, epilepsy, typhoid, sinus issues, dropsy and swelling.

Mars: Accidents, blood defects, cuts, wounds, dog bites, piles, high blood pressure, heart disease, constipation, anemia and bile issues.

Mercury: Stomach disorders, skin issues (eczema, itches, scabies, ringworm, leucoderma), leprosy, intestinal problems, mental disorders, sore throat, tonsils, muteness and baldness.

Jupiter: Liver issues, jaundice, hernia and bronchitis.

Venus: Diabetes, reproductive or semen disorders, anemia, ovarian diseases, venereal diseases, uterine issues, eye diseases and phlegm.

Saturn: Rheumatism, arthritis, lethargy, gas troubles, speech defects, tooth problems, indigestion, ulcers and asthma.

Rahu: Accidents, sexual disorders, cataracts, tooth problems, leprosy, body aches, stammering, intestinal issues, rheumatism, pox, sudden death, violent deaths, homosexual inclinations, snake bites and insanity.

Ketu: General body aches, tumors, growths, wounds, leprosy, itching, suicidal tendencies, stomach aches, smallpox, piles, cancer, sudden death, skin rashes, insect bites and viral fevers.

Key Factors to Check for Health Issues

1. **Saturn's Placement and Combinations**: Saturn's conjunctions, especially with malefics (Rahu, Ketu), often indicate chronic health problems. Its position reflects karmic ailments from past life actions.
   - *Saturn + Moon + Rahu*: Indicates chronic, karmic diseases from past life.
   - *Saturn + Moon + Ketu or Jupiter + Moon + Ketu*: Signifies diseases that may resolve current-life karmic debts and are not carried forward.

2. **Moon's Influence and Aspects**: As Moon represents the mind and emotional health, malefic conjunctions, particularly with Saturn, Ketu, or Rahu, may lead to chronic or mental health issues.
   - *Jupiter + Moon + Rahu*: Indicates health suffering linked to present-life deeds.
   - *Mercury + Moon*: Throat or respiratory infections.
   - *Mercury + Ketu + Moon*: Growth in the throat area, with Venus involvement suggesting thyroid issues.

3. **Sixth House and Its Lord**: The sixth house governs health, disease and adversities. A strong malefic presence or challenging aspects here can indicate chronic ailments.
   - Malefics like *Saturn, Rahu and Ketu* here can highlight specific health vulnerabilities.
   - The sixth house lord's unfavorable placement may suggest persistent or impactful health concerns.

4. **Malefic Influences on Ascendant and Vital Planets**:
    o   Malefics (Rahu, Ketu, Saturn, Mars) impacting the ascendant, Sun, or Moon often indicate health challenges or specific illnesses affecting vitality and mental stability.

Planetary Combinations Indicating Specific Diseases

- **Rahu + Mercury + Mars**: Issues with the spinal cord.
- **Sun + Moon + Rahu + Saturn**: Chronic headache or migraine tendencies.
- **Venus's Influence**: Known as *Mrit Sanjeevani*, Venus is linked to healing potential.
- **Sun as Dhanvantri**: Sun represents general health and healing potential, often connected to medical assistance in a chart.

Ear Diseases:

- *Rahu + Mercury + Jupiter (Male) or Venus (Female)*: Indicates ear-related issues.

Teeth Issues:

- *Mars*: Governs teeth and afflictions to Mars can cause teeth problems due to Mars representing hard substances.
- *Saturn + Rahu + Mars*: Signifies dental decay, pain, or disfigurement.
- *Jupiter/Venus + Mars*: Indicates healthy teeth.
- *Venus + Mars*: Beautiful, well-formed teeth.

Eye Conditions:

- *Saturn/Rahu/Ketu + Sun/Moon*: General troubles with eyesight.
- *Saturn/Rahu/Ketu + Sun/Moon + Mars*: Causes regular irritation or burning in the eyes.
- *Ketu + Sun/Moon + Mars*: Suggests early-age cataracts or a need for eye surgery.

Breathing and Cold-Related Issues:

- *Moon/Venus + Jupiter/Saturn*: Prone to colds, obstructed breathing.
- *Saturn + Moon + Ketu*: Indicates bronchitis or asthma.

Uterus and Urinary Problems:

- *Moon + Venus + Ketu + Saturn/Jupiter*: Suggests uterus-related issues in females.
- *Rahu + Moon/Venus + Saturn/Jupiter*: Linked to urinary bladder problems or infections (UTI).

Kidney and Stone Issues:

- *Ketu + Moon/Venus + Saturn + Jupiter*: Indicates kidney problems.
- *Ketu + Moon/Venus + Saturn + Jupiter + Mars*: Presence of kidney stones.

Blood and Circulatory System Disorders:

- *Mars + Moon + Rahu*: Associated with blood impurities or mental disturbances.
- *Mars + Moon + Ketu*: Affects the circulatory system and can cause mental irritation.

Specific Transits and Health Impacts:

1. **Ketu and Saturn Axis**:
    - *Transiting Ketu over Natal Saturn or vice versa*: Indicates possible health issues, immobility, or situations requiring one to stay at home.
2. **Jupiter and Rahu Axis**:
    - *Transiting Jupiter over Natal Rahu or vice versa*: Changes in health, potential for immobility, accidents, or significant health challenges.
3. **Saturn in Ketu Axis / Jupiter in Rahu Axis**:
    - This combination, when both conditions are satisfied (Saturn-Ketu and Jupiter-Rahu or vice versa), suggests potential for physical immobility or significant illness due to the activation of *Karma Karaka* (Saturn) and *Jeeva Karaka* (Jupiter) in challenging placements.

Ayurvedic Tridosha and Planetary Influence:

1. **Vata (Air Element)**:
   - *Saturn, Mercury, Rahu*: These planets influence Vata dosha, each with unique expressions:
     - **Saturn**: *Mand Vaat* (slow Vata)
     - **Mercury**: *Sheeghra Vaat* (fast Vata)
     - **Rahu**: *Visha Vaat* (toxic Vata)
2. **Pitta (Fire Element)**:
   - *Mars, Sun, Ketu*: These planets affect Pitta dosha, as follows:
     - **Sun**: *Jwar Pitta* (fever or heat-related Pitta)
     - **Ketu**: *Varna Pitta* (skin-related Pitta)
     - **Mars**: *Teevra Pitta* (intense or sharp Pitta)
3. **Kapha (Water Element)**:
   - *Jupiter, Venus, Moon*: These planets affect Kapha dosha, with each having specific roles:
     - **Jupiter**: *Jeev Kapha* (life-sustaining Kapha)
     - **Venus**: *Dravya Kapha* (material or fluid Kapha)
     - **Moon**: *Sleshma Kapha* (phlegm-related Kapha)

Organ Health:

- **Jupiter and Liver**: Afflictions to Jupiter may lead to liver issues.
- **Moon and Lungs**: Afflictions to the Moon may lead to lung-related problems.

Combinations and Disease Indicators:

- **Venus + Moon + Ketu**: Linked to diabetes, uterus issues, urinary tract infection (UTI), kidney problems and indigestion.
- **Jupiter + Mars + Rahu**: May indicate smallpox.
- **Moon + Mercury + Mars + Rahu**: Associated with suicidal tendencies.
- **Moon + Rahu**: Hallucinations.
- **Rahu + Saturn + Mars**: Gastric problems, intestinal disorders.
- **Rahu + Jupiter + Mars** or **Saturn + Mars + Rahu**: Accidental death.

Cancer-Related Combinations:

- **Moon + Mars + Saturn + Rahu**: Breast cancer.
- **Mercury + Mars + Saturn + Rahu/Ketu**: Skin cancer.
- **Venus + Moon + Mars + Rahu + Saturn**: Uterus cancer.
- **Mars + Moon + Rahu + Saturn**: Blood cancer, bone marrow cancer.
- **Mercury + Rahu + Mars + Sun**: Mouth or tongue cancer.

Timing of Disease Activation:

Diseases tend to manifest when **transiting planets (Jupiter, Saturn, Rahu, Ketu)** align in a way that activates these natal combinations, especially during the **6th round of Jupiter's transit**. This specific timing often triggers the onset of health conditions represented by these planetary patterns in a natal chart.

Combinations

Wealth-Enhancing Combinations:

Venus (Wealth) + Mercury (Property) + Sun (Success) + Saturn (without influence of Mars, Ketu, Moon): This alignment creates a *Supreme Yoga of Wealth*, enhancing wealth, property and recognition.

+Rahu: This combination can still be favorable with Rahu, as it may increase expansion or innovation, but should avoid conjunction with Mars, Ketu, or Moon.

Effects with Additional Planets:

- **Jupiter + Venus**: Tends towards ordinary material conditions rather than immense wealth.
- **Saturn + Venus + Mercury + Sun + Jupiter**:
    - **+Moon**: May lead to a loss of material wealth.
    - **+Mars**: Involves litigation or legal disputes.
    - **+Rahu**: Wealth may be amassed through unconventional or possibly unethical means.
    - **+Ketu**: Leads to disputes or blockages in financial matters.

Important Note:

Saturn's Role in Material Gains: Saturn, in combination with other wealth indicators (Venus, Mercury, Sun), is essential for material benefits. Saturn's partnership with these planets without malefic interference strongly indicates the potential for stable and lasting wealth.

Profession

Key Planets and Their Influence on Profession:

Saturn: The primary significator of profession; stability and persistence in career.

Jupiter: Promoter, supporting growth, expansion and ethical standards.

Sun: Symbolizes recognition, government-related roles and authority.

Moon: Indicates variability, creative arts, food industry and changes or transfers.

Mars: Represents technical fields, power-oriented roles and potential hazards.

Mercury: Associated with commerce, knowledge, communication and land-based jobs.

Venus: Connected with wealth, luxury, arts and assets.

Rahu: Suggests foreign, unconventional, or shadow professions (e.g., photography).

Ketu: Low-profile roles, spirituality, or jobs with a hands-on, manual aspect.

Assessing Career Focus:

1. **Saturn's Connections with Other Planets**: Saturn's conjunctions or aspects with these planets shape the type and nature of one's profession.
2. **Directional Chart** (for Saturn placement):
   - **1st, 5th, 9th Houses**: Primary influences in career.
   - **2nd, 6th, 10th Houses**: Indicate actionable areas.
   - **3rd, 7th, 11th Houses**: Show areas of adaptation or change.
   - **4th, 8th, 12th Houses**: Represent the underlying background or unseen aspects of the profession.

Saturn and Aspects in Profession:

3rd Aspect of Saturn: Represents initial stages or foundational steps in a profession.

10th Aspect of Saturn: Reflects later stages, including peak accomplishments or results in one's career.

Strength of Saturn: Saturn's impact is weakened if there are no planets in the 2nd, 12th and 7th houses, potentially reducing career stability.

Key Combinations for Professions

Astrology and Spirituality:

1. **Astrologer**:
   - **Saturn + Sun + Mercury + Ketu**: Creates a renowned astrologer.
   - **Saturn + Mercury + Ketu**: A strong combination for an astrologer.
2. **Intuition and Sixth Sense**:
   - **Saturn + Jupiter + Sun**: Enhances intuitive power and sixth sense.
3. **Vastu and Astrology**:
   - **Saturn + Mercury + Ketu + Mars/Venus**: Combination for Vastu expertise and astrological skills.
4. **Healer**:
   - **Saturn + Venus + Jupiter + Ketu**: Indicates a person with healing abilities.
5. **Spiritual Astrology Guru**:
   - **Saturn + Jupiter + Mercury + Ketu + Mars**: A powerful combination for spiritual leadership in astrology.
6. **Preacher/Teacher of Occult Science**:
   - **Venus + Saturn + Mars + Ketu + Jupiter**: Reflects a teacher or preacher with expertise in occult sciences.

Each combination influences career direction, especially when Saturn interacts with these planets, guiding the native toward professions in astrology, spirituality, or healing practices.

Scientist

- **Virgo**: Indicates applied science and research-oriented skills.

- **Venus**: Signifies higher intelligence and creativity in scientific pursuits.
- **Mercury**: Intelligence and analytical skills.
- **Combination**: Virgo + Mercury + Venus + (Sun/Moon) + Rahu/Ketu.

Writer

- **Gemini**: Strong in communication.
- **Mercury + Ketu + Mars + Sun**: Combination of knowledge, skill in communication and ability to bring thoughts to light.

Politician

- **Sun (Exalted)**: Ruling nature and high status.
- **Jupiter**: Nobility and advisory skills.
- **Saturn**: Karma and discipline.
- **Mercury**: Intelligence.
- **Rahu/Ketu**: Hard work, secrecy and strategic thinking.
- **Additional Factors**: Sun in relation to an exalted planet or in a fiery sign, with optional Mars for courage.

Legal Head / Judge

- **Libra/Venus**: Signifies balance and law.
- **Ketu**: Argumentative skills and attention to detail.
- **Saturn**: Professional stability.
- **Jupiter**: Human dignity and advisory skills.
- **Sun**: Righteousness.
- **Mercury**: Intelligence.

Defense Personnel

- **Signs**: Mars (strength), Sagittarius (fearlessness), Aries (courage and adventure), Scorpio (secrecy and punishment).

- **Combination**: Mars + Saturn + Sun + Rahu/Ketu + Jupiter.
- **Aries Influence**: Reflects courage and an adventure-oriented mindset, with Sun and Mars for honor and Saturn for discipline.

IAS (Indian Administrative Service)

- **Signs**: Capricorn, Aries, Leo, or Libra.
- **Key Planets**: Venus (governance), Sun (government), Saturn (karma), Jupiter (wisdom) and Mercury (intelligence and policy-making).

Insurance Professional

- **Sign**: Pisces (Yogakshema, associated with insurance and security).
- **Planets**: Saturn + Rahu + Jupiter + Ketu + Venus.
- **Role of Planets**: Saturn (karma), Rahu (work related to uncertainty or after-death), Jupiter (advisor), Ketu (detachment or relief) and Venus (wealth/security).

Industrialist

- **Signs**: Virgo (intelligence and analytics) or Libra (trade and balance).
- **Planets**: Saturn (karma, discipline) + Mercury (commerce) + Venus (wealth) + Sun (success and leadership).

Doctor

- **Signs**: Pisces (healing, relief) or Leo (health and authority).
- **Planets**: Saturn (karma) + Jupiter (advisor, teacher) + Sun (medicine and health) + Ketu (mukti from disease).

Engineer

- **Planets**: Saturn + Mars (technical expertise and precision).

Stock Market Professional

- **Planets**: Venus + Rahu (risk, speculation and money management).
- **Note**: No inclination for speculation if Venus is combined with Moon (which tends toward caution and emotional attachment).

Combinations for Foreign Travel

1. **Primary Travel Indicators**
   - **Jupiter + Moon + Rahu** or **Saturn + Moon + Rahu** in 1st, 5th, or 9th houses or in conjunction: Indicates potential for foreign travel.
   - **Moon** represents travel, while **Rahu** is the significator of foreign lands.
2. **Specific Travel Reasons**
   - **Mercury + Rahu**: Travel for educational purposes.
   - **Venus + Moon + Rahu**: Travel due to spouse.
   - **Ketu**: Indicates short-term foreign travel, with the likelihood of returning home, unlike Rahu, which favors travel with the possibility of settling abroad.
3. **Timing of Foreign Travel**
   - When **transiting Jupiter** activates any of these combinations, it can signal the timing of travel.
4. **Professional and Educational Settlement Abroad**
   - **Saturn + Rahu**: Travel or foreign settlement for work or professional reasons.
   - **Exalted Moon** or **Moon-Jupiter exchange**: Foreign travel is likely.
5. **Female Horoscope Specifics**
   - **Venus + Mercury + Moon + Rahu/Ketu**: Travel for studies or advanced education.
   - **Venus + Saturn + Moon + Rahu/Ketu**: Travel for professional reasons.
   - **Disturbed Mercury**: May indicate visa issues or delays in travel arrangements.

Marriage Combinations

Male Chart Indicators

- **Early Marriage**: If **Jupiter** is linked to **Venus** by 1st, 5th, 9th, 2nd, 12th, or 7th positions from Jupiter.
- **Delayed Marriage**: If **Saturn** is linked to Saturn.
- **Marriage Difficulties**:
    - **Venus + Ketu**: Difficulty for the male in getting married; **Jupiter's aspect** may mitigate this.
    - **Venus + Rahu** in positions 1, 5, 9, or 12: Delay or denial of marriage and , if married, there may be issues with spouse's faithfulness.

Female Chart Indicators

- **Marriage Promise**: If **Mars + Venus** are conjunct.
- **Marriage Difficulties**:
    - **Ketu + Mars**: Difficulty in finding a match; **Jupiter's aspect** can alleviate this.
    - **Mars + Rahu**: Delay or denial; if married, the female may develop dislike toward her husband, but **Jupiter's aspect** can help.

Separation or Divorce Indicators

- **Separation**: **Venus + Ketu + Mars** indicates potential separation or strained relationships between husband and wife. **Jupiter's aspect** may bring compromise.
- **Divorce**: **Mercury + Ketu + Mars** signifies a strong likelihood of divorce without other mitigating factors.

Separation and Divorce

- **Venus + Rahu + Mars**:
    - ○ **Male Chart**: Indicates ill-treatment by wife, possibly leading to separation or divorce.
    - ○ **Female Chart**: Husband may be abusive or violent.

Indicators of Love Affairs

- **Mercury + Ketu** in the same sign or odd signs (1, 5, 9): Suggests a love affair.
    - ○ **Supported by Jupiter or Venus**: Potential for marriage.
    - ○ **Connected with Mars**: Indicates a break in the affair.
    - ○ **Connected with Moon**: Leads to accusations or blame.
    - ○ **Connected with Saturn**: Affair is likely to occur at the workplace.
    - ○ **Connected with Sun**: Affair becomes publicly known.

Pregnancy Before Marriage

- **Venus + Moon in Female Chart** with **Mars crossing Venus**: Implies a likelihood of pregnancy before marriage; if **Rahu** is involved, the affair may remain secret.
- **Venus + Jupiter + Moon** with Jupiter in between: The female will contemplate relationships but may avoid pregnancy.

Dual Relationships

- **Mercury + Venus + Mars**:
    - ○ **Female Chart**: Indicates dual relationships.
- **Mercury + Mars + Venus**:
    - ○ **Male Chart**: Indicates dual relationships.
- **Moon + Mars + Venus**:
    - ○ **Male Chart**: Indicates dual relationships.

Happiness and Multiple Relationships

- **Mercury + Venus + Saturn** in Female Chart: Suggests happiness in a relationship with a lover.
- **Jupiter or Saturn** connected with multiple **female planets**:
    - **Male Chart**: Likely to have multiple relationships.
- **Jupiter or Saturn** connected with multiple **male planets**:
    - **Female Chart**: Likely to have multiple relationships.

Matchmaking in BNN

The BNN system provides specific compatibility guidelines to assess harmonious alignment between a male and female chart. Here are the essential conditions:

1st Condition: Trine Compatibility Check

- **For the Female Chart**:
    - Check the **sign where Mars is placed** in the female's chart and note the trine signs (1st, 5th and 9th from Mars).
- **For the Male Chart**:
    - Ensure **Jupiter or Mars** is placed in one of the trine signs observed from the female's Mars position.
    - Then, check **Venus** in the male's chart and note its trine signs.
- **For the Female Chart**:
    - Check that **Jupiter or Venus** falls in the trine signs identified from the male's Venus position.

This trine compatibility suggests harmonious energy exchanges between significant relationship planets in both charts.

2nd Condition: 7th Lord Compatibility Check

- **For the Male Chart**:
    - Identify the **7th Lord from Jupiter** and check its position in the **D-9 (Navamsa)** chart. Note the Rashi (sign) and its trines.
- **For the Female Chart**:
    - Check that **Jupiter or Moon** in the female's natal chart falls within the same trine signs identified from the male's D-9 7th Lord.

This alignment supports compatibility and ensures that the partners have a natural flow of understanding and harmonious relationship energy.

Additional Checks:

Denial Indicators:

In the **Male Chart**: Check if the female's chart has a **Mars and Ketu combination** in the relevant Rashi, indicating denial (more prominent if **Ketu > Mars**).

In the **Female Chart**: Check if the male's chart has a **Venus and Ketu combination**, indicating denial of compatibility (more prominent if **Ketu > Venus**).

Mars, Mercury, Venus Combination:

A **Mars, Mercury and Venus** combination in one of the charts may indicate **lack of conjugal bliss** or challenges in mutual satisfaction in the relationship.

Combinations for Child Birth

Gender Predictions

- **Sun**: Indicates a male child.
- **Venus**: Indicates a female child.
- **Jupiter** connected with **Sun** (1, 5, 2, 12, 7 positions): Suggests a male child.
- **Jupiter** connected with **Venus**: Suggests a female child.

Child Birth Challenges and Denials

- **Rahu** connected with **Sun** or **Venus**: Potential denial of child birth or danger to the child after birth.
- **Ketu** connected with **Sun** or **Venus**: Indicates obstructions or challenges in child birth.
- **Sun + Venus** within **3°20'**: Possible denial of child birth.
- **Saturn** with **Sun** or **Venus**: Delay in child birth.

Fertility Issues

- **Moon + Venus** in Male Chart: Suggests reduced sperm count.
- **Moon + Venus** in Female Chart: Possible issues with ovaries, conception difficulties, or inability to conceive.

Influence of Malefic Planets

- **5th Lord from Jupiter** in **6, 8, or 12** houses or **5th House** occupied or aspected by malefics: Challenges in child birth.
- **Saturn + Mars**:
    - General: May indicate having one child less.

- In an odd sign: Indicates two male children, but one may result in miscarriage.
- **Moon + Ketu**: Indicates the likelihood of a female child or miscarriage.
- **Mars + Ketu** in Male Chart: Child birth within 13 months of marriage.

Other Indicators

- **Moon aspecting the 5th House**: Suggests the possibility of surrogacy.

Education Combinations

- **Mercury**: Primary significator of education.
- **Venus**: Represents expertise and specialization in studies.
- **Sun**: Symbolizes success in educational pursuits.
- **Jupiter**: Ensures completion and stability in education.

Obstacles in Education

- **Mars**: Hurdles related to math, machinery, arguments and competitive nature.
- **Ketu**: Challenges in fields related to medicine, law and spirituality.

Nature of Education by Planets

- **Rahu**: Involvement in foreign matters, exposure to deceitful elements, international studies.
- **Saturn**: Slowdowns or reluctance in learning, promotes practical or vocational studies.

Beneficial Combinations for Education

- **Mercury + Jupiter + Sun**: Ideal combination for meritorious education.
- **Mercury + Rahu**: Creates "Bahu Vidya Yog," enabling education in multiple fields, often achieving two or more master's degrees.
- **Mercury + Sun + Venus + Jupiter + Rahu**: Strong inclination towards research and higher studies, such as Ph.D.

Indications for Foreign Studies

- **Mercury + Moon + Rahu/Ketu**: Studies abroad or higher studies in foreign lands.

Education Challenges and Interruptions

- **Mercury + Mars + Ketu**: Indicates minimal education.
- **Mercury + Ketu**: Suggests potential breaks or interruptions in education.
- **Retrograde Mercury** or Mercury in exchange: Denotes educational setbacks or failure.
- **Mercury + Moon + Ketu**: Failure in studies due to involvement in romantic relationships.

Property Ownership and Characteristics

Venus in 1, 2, 3, 5, 7, 9, 11 from Jupiter: Indicates ownership of a house.

- **4th Lord from Jupiter in 1, 2, 3, 5, 9, 11**: Native is likely to own a house.
- **Ketu and Venus in 1, 2, 5, 9 (Ketu's degree higher than Venus)**: Native may face challenges in owning a house, possibly leading to the sale of property due to debt. It's advised not to take property solely in their name.

Specific Combinations for Property Types

- **Venus + Mercury**: Indicates a duplex, luxurious or well-furnished home in a commercial or upscale area.
- **Venus + Rahu**: Suggests ownership of a multi-story building, mansion, or large apartment; property may be in wife's name or native could own multiple properties.
- **Venus + Saturn**: Property purchase after marriage, possibly registered in wife's name.
- **Venus + Saturn + Sun**: Points to government-allotted property.
- **Venus + Mars**: Indicates an ordinary house.
- **Venus + Jupiter**: Beautiful and comfortable home, even if in exchange.
- **Venus in 2nd, 7th, 3rd, 6th, 9th, or 12th signs**: Likely to own a duplex or multi-story home.
- **Ketu in 2nd from Jupiter**: Native will prefer living on higher floors, avoiding the ground floor and may choose to use stairs frequently.

Retrogression of Planets

Retrogression occurs when a planet appears to move backward in the sky due to the relative motion between Earth and the other planet. This phenomenon has a significant impact on the planets' influence in an astrological chart, particularly for Jupiter and Saturn, which are considered the most impactful when retrograde.

Understanding Retrogression:

- **Rahu and Ketu**: Always retrograde and their retrogression is inherent to their nature, so it is not considered in the same way as for other planets.
- **Sun and Moon**: Never retrograde.
- **Retrograde Planets**: Jupiter, Mars, Saturn, Venus and Mercury can all experience retrogression.

Major Impacts of Retrogression:

Saturn Retrograde:

Symbolizes unfinished or incomplete karma from past lives. The native must address both past and present life karma, adding an extra burden.

Determining Past Life Karma: The nature of the past life karma can be understood by analyzing the sign of retrograde Saturn and its position relative to Jupiter (e.g., if Saturn is retrograde in a Mars sign and positioned 3rd from Jupiter, the past life karma may relate to siblings).

Degrees of Retrograde Saturn:

Saturn retrogrades over the same degree thrice (before retrogression, during retrograde motion and after turning direct).

This gives the native three opportunities to address and rectify the past life karma related to the house and sign where Saturn is placed.

Past Births for Karma Resolution:

Saturn in Enemy Sign: Indicates multiple past births are linked to the unfinished karma.

Saturn in Friendly Sign: Fewer past births involved.

Saturn in Own Sign/Exalted: Indicates that the native is close to completing their karmic cycle, likely in the last birth.

Key to Resolving Karma: Acceptance of past life karma without resentment or resistance is crucial for neutralizing the effects of retrograde Saturn.

Jupiter Retrograde:

Relates to pending karma in areas like religious duties, public activities, social obligations and responsibilities tied to mentors or gurus.

Beneficial Aspect: If the native leaves their birthplace during Jupiter's retrograde phase, it can bring benefits (as Jupiter is often associated with the 12th house, representing places away from home).

Other Retrograde Planets:

Mars Retrograde: Indicates unresolved karma related to siblings, land, property, or (in a female's chart) issues related to the husband.

Venus Retrograde: Can improve relationships with girlfriends and signify pending karma related to wife, sister, or daughter.

Mercury Retrograde: Indicates unfinished educational karma, often pointing to lessons or learning from past lives that need to be revisited.

Combined Retrogression Effects:

- **Saturn, Mercury and Venus Retrograde**: When all three are retrograde in a chart, the native may experience an abundance of material comforts and benefits related to their significations.
- **Mars and Saturn Retrograde**: Tends to bring obstacles and struggles in life.
- **Saturn and Jupiter Retrograde Together**: This combination often brings a mix of problems and solutions, creating a dynamic where the native faces challenges but also finds ways to overcome them, leading to personal growth and abundance.

Retrogression adds an extra layer of karmic significance and emphasizes the qualities of each planet based on the elements of the sign where the retrogression occurs. Retrograde planets symbolize past life lessons that need to be addressed and signify areas where karma is being tested. Here's an in-depth look at retrogression based on the sign's element and house position:

Elements and Retrogression

Fire Signs (1, 5, 9 - Aries, Leo, Sagittarius): Creativity

Retrograde planets in fire signs stimulate the desire to *create* based on the planet's significance.

Example:

Venus Retrograde in Leo: Encourages the native to pursue creativity and financial gains through arts and beauty.

Saturn Retrograde in Fire Signs: Often found in creative fields or professions.

Jupiter Retrograde in Fire Signs: Suggests dedication to teaching or other roles that inspire others.

Earth Signs (2, 6, 10 - Taurus, Virgo, Capricorn): Stability

Earth signs emphasize materialism, patience, tolerance and grounding. Retrograde planets here push the native to focus on these qualities in their approach to the planet's significations.

Example:

Saturn Retrograde in Earth Signs: May indicate a life where material stability is tied to past karma. This could manifest as a focus on career stability, requiring resilience and a methodical approach.

Air Signs (3, 7, 11 - Gemini, Libra, Aquarius): Intelligence

Air signs emphasize mental clarity, communication and analytical thinking. Retrograde planets here encourage handling their significations with intellect and diplomacy.

Example:

Mercury Retrograde in an Air Sign: Emphasizes intellectual challenges or past life lessons involving communication, requiring careful and considered expression.

Water Signs (4, 8, 12 - Cancer, Scorpio, Pisces): Emotion

Water signs emphasize emotions, empathy and intuition. Retrograde planets in water signs signify karmic lessons involving emotional responses or unresolved emotional matters.

Example:

Mercury Retrograde in Water Signs: Points to emotional connections with family, particularly siblings, aunts, or uncles, where the native may need to work through past emotional ties.

Rules of Retrogression in Karmic Perspective

Rahu/Ketu: Always linked with past karma related to the house they occupy.

Aspects of Retrograde Planets: Considered from their natal position, not from a previous house.

Elemental Influence of Sign and Karma Load:

Exalted or Own Sign: Pending karma from the immediate past life, high chance of resolution in this life.

Friendly Sign: Karma spans over the past few lives (usually two to three). Likely resolved in this or the next life.

Enemy or Debilitated Sign: Represents karma accumulated over many lives. Resolution may require many more lifetimes.

Specific Planetary Impacts in Retrogression:

- **Mercury (R)**: Impact on communication, siblings and intellect; karmic influences linked to sister, maternal uncle, or daughter.

- **Saturn (R)**: Karmic duty linked to elder siblings, big brothers and social responsibilities.
- **Mars (R)**: Energy and aggression retrogression affects issues with siblings, health problems for the husband in a female chart, or difficulties in achieving fortune.
- **Venus (R)**: Karma related to relationships and finances; retrogression may indicate a deep karmic lesson with a wife or daughter.
- **Jupiter (R)**: As the significator of self, retrograde Jupiter points to a focus on self-development and personal growth as a karmic theme.

Retrogression as a Karmic Test:

Retrograde planets act as a red flag from the universe, prompting us to address specific karmic areas with greater focus. When a retrograde planet aligns with challenging aspects in one's chart, it serves as a reminder to pay particular attention to these areas. The journey through retrogression is a test from the universe, guiding the native to realign with the karmic lessons of their past.

Combustion

In astrology, combustion refers to a planet coming close to the Sun within a specific degree range, effectively overshadowing or diminishing the planet's external qualities while amplifying its inner significations. This state resembles refining metals in a furnace, where impurities are burned away, leaving only the pure qualities. Here's an overview of how combustion impacts different planets:

General Rule of Combustion

- **Combustion**: When a planet is in the same **Nakshatra** as the Sun.
- **Super Combustion**: When a planet is in the same **Quarter/Charan/Pad** as the Sun.

This distinction intensifies the effects of combustion, affecting the external and internal significances of each planet as follows:

Combustion Effects on Each Planet

Mercury (Immune to Combustion)

Internal Significance: Heightened intelligence, sharper wit.

External Significance: Education or learning processes might be disrupted, symbolizing a purification where unneeded learning habits are removed.

Venus

Internal Significance: Heightened beauty, love, artistic abilities and appreciation for fine arts.

External Significance: Issues in relationships with spouse, daughter, or sister; potential disruptions in fertility (sperm-related issues).

Note: If Venus's degree is higher than the Sun's, it is beneficial and signifies wealth and abundance. If Sun's degree is higher, it indicates potential disturbances in Venus's external significances.

Mars

Internal Significance: Amplified courage, energy, enthusiasm, recognition of bravery.

External Significance: Skill and relationship with siblings, particularly brothers, may face challenges.

Unique Recognition: When Mars is combust, the native may receive extraordinary recognition for bravery, potentially leading to honors such as bravery awards.

Jupiter

Internal Significance: Enhanced wisdom and respect for knowledge.

External Significance: Religious or philosophical aspects are not significantly disturbed, as the Sun shares similar pious qualities.

Impact: Jupiter's combustion purifies the spiritual and moral compass of the native, enhancing wisdom rather than diminishing external religious practices.

Saturn

Internal Significance: Amplified qualities of judgment, justice, honesty and loyalty.

External Significance: Potential disruptions in career or profession, with challenges to professional status.

Recognition: The native may become recognized for their sense of justice and loyalty, possibly in roles where these traits are essential.

Moon (Amavasya – New Moon)

Internal Significance: Extra intelligence and heightened mental acuity, as Moon combust with the Sun forms an Amavasya.

External Significance: Emotional visibility and expressiveness are suppressed but purified, potentially leading to introspective insights.

Combustion thus acts as a transformative force, emphasizing the internal significances while challenging or distorting external attributes, leading to a complex interplay of strengths and weaknesses for each planet in close proximity to the Sun. This phenomenon may lead to greater internal recognition or realization of the planet's essential qualities but also implies that external aspects, often involving relationships or career, may face challenges during such periods.

Past Life and BNN

Bhrigu Nandi Nadi suggests that our birth chart, with its specific planetary configurations, reflects not only our present life journey but also past karmic influences that continue to shape our current experiences. In this framework, each house and planet can represent connections to past, present and even future karmas. Here's a deeper exploration of these connections:

Key Houses for Understanding Past Life Karma - Jupiter is Jeev Lagna

9th House from Jupiter (or 5th house backward from Jupiter's current position):

This is considered the "past life Jupiter" or the *jeeva lagna* (soul's starting point) of past lives. It reflects past life attitudes, unfinished desires and responsibilities carried forward.

5th House from Current Jupiter:

This house, known as the "future jeeva lagna," reveals the karmic seeds being sown in this life, pointing to future incarnations.

6th House from Jupiter:

This is the 10th house from the past life *jeeva lagna* and symbolizes past life karma - essentially, unfinished actions and duties that now manifest as current life responsibilities and challenges.

10th House from Jupiter:

Represents present life karma, responsibilities and the actions undertaken in this life.

Indicators of Living Out Past Life Karma

Link between the 6th and 10th House Lords:

If these lords form relationships such as the 1st, 5th, 7th, or 9th, it suggests the native is reliving similar karmic patterns from a past life. This might mean encountering similar challenges, relationships, or responsibilities.

Influence of Retrograde Saturn:

Retrograde Saturn (Saturn in reverse) especially emphasizes unfulfilled karmic duties from past lives.

To interpret, take the past life Jupiter as the current ascendant (lagna) and examine Saturn's placements or aspects. A connection between Saturn and the past life lagna implies repeated responsibilities related to Saturn's significations.

Financial Indicators in Past Life

2nd House Lord of Past Life Lagna and Venus Connection:

A connection here indicates that the person had material wealth or prosperity in past lives, which could influence present attitudes toward wealth.

10th House Connection with Rahu, Ketu, Saturn, or Mars:

This combination points to financial hardship, struggles, or poverty in the past life, suggesting lessons about resourcefulness and self-sufficiency may be important.

10th House Connection with Moon, Venus, or Mercury:

Indicates a prosperous family and financial life in the past, which might suggest a familiarity with comfort or harmony in family dynamics in the current life.

Past Relationships and Sudden Death

8th House from Past Life Lagna or 4th House from Current Jupiter with Rahu or Ketu:

This placement indicates an untimely or sudden death in a previous life, hinting at compromised longevity that could influence the current life approach to health and security.

Sun in the 8th House from Past Life Lagna:

Indicates strained relationships with the father or authority figures in the past life.

Similarly, if the Moon occupies this position, the mother relationship may have been challenging; with Venus, issues could have arisen with a spouse; and with Mars, the relationship with brothers or husbands might have been marked by discord.

Present Life Karma and Rashi Sign Influence

6th House Rashi in Present Life Jupiter (indicating past life's 10th house):

If the 6th house falls in certain signs, it can suggest the soul's past life social role:

Pisces or Sagittarius (9/12): Indicates a past life as a *Brahmin*, or priestly figure.

Aries or Scorpio (1/8): Suggests a warrior or *Kshatriya* background.

Capricorn or Aquarius (10/11): Tied to a servant or service-oriented role.

Cancer, Gemini, Taurus, Virgo, Libra (4,3,2,7,6): Indicates a merchant (*Vaishya*) role.

Leo (5): Reflects a role associated with government or authority.

Karma-Driven Connections in Past and Present Life

Past Life Lagna's 10th House in Relation to Rahu, Ketu, Saturn, or Mars:

This suggests the native may have struggled with ethical choices, possibly involving illicit activities.

Venus Connection in the 2nd House:

If the 2nd house (material wealth) of past life Jupiter is linked to Venus, the individual was likely financially prosperous.

Overall Insights

Astrological analysis of past life karma isn't deterministic but offers a potential view into the purpose and opportunities within the present life. Retrograde and combust planets also point toward repeated lessons or skills the soul is refining across incarnations.

More such insights will be covered in my next book on Karmic Astrology

Karmic Influence Planet

Identifying the Karmic Influence Planet from the Birth Mahadasha Lord

1. **Determine the First Mahadasha Lord**: At the time of birth, each individual is under a specific planetary Mahadasha period. This period is governed by one of the planets according to the planetary sequence in the Vimshottari Mahadasha cycle.
2. **Counting Five Planets Backward**: From this first Mahadasha lord, count five planets backward in the sequence of Mahadashas. The fifth planet backward is identified as the *Karmic Influence Planet*, which will play a central role throughout life.
3. **Significance**: The themes, lessons and significations associated with this planet will influence key events, relationships and the native's primary life challenges and opportunities.

Order of Mahadasha in the Vimshottari Sequence

In the Vimshottari Mahadasha system, the planets follow a specific sequence, each governing for a set number of years:

1. **Ketu** – 7 years
2. **Venus** – 20 years
3. **Sun** – 6 years
4. **Moon** – 10 years
5. **Mars** – 7 years
6. **Rahu** – 18 years
7. **Jupiter** – 16 years
8. **Saturn** – 19 years
9. **Mercury** – 17 years

Example of Identifying the Karmic Influence Planet

Suppose the first Mahadasha at the time of birth is governed by **Mars**. To find the Karmic Influence Planet:

- Begin with Mars and count five planets backward in the Vimshottari sequence: Mars → Moon → Sun → Venus → Ketu.

The fifth planet backward is **Ketu**, which becomes the Karmic Influence Planet. This planet will subtly guide or dominate the native's life themes, influencing events, relationships and personal growth. The native will often find themselves continuously dealing with situations that reflect Ketu's qualities, such as spirituality, detachment, or letting go of material attachments.

Once identified, the *karmic influence planet* defines a unique path for the individual, reflecting a karmic focus carried over from previous lives. Its influence permeates multiple areas and the native finds that life situations, relationships and work continuously involve themes or *karaktatwas* (significances) related to this planet.

Impact of the Karmic Influence Planet

Here's how each planet, when acting as the controlling force, manifests across life themes and how lessons arise from it:

Ketu:

Lessons in detachment, spirituality and releasing material attachments. The person may encounter situations that challenge their grip on material desires, pushing them toward introspection, spirituality, or a non-attachment approach.

If accepted, life becomes peaceful; resisting detachment brings dissatisfaction with worldly achievements.

Venus:

Themes of relationships, beauty, luxury and pleasure dominate. The person may work in artistic fields, deal with wealth, or have relationship-centered life paths.

Accepting Venus's lesson of valuing true love and harmony over excess indulgence can bring balance; attachment to superficiality might lead to inner emptiness.

Sun:

A focus on leadership, recognition and authority. The native might experience life situations that test their ego and sense of self-worth.

Embracing humility and a balanced self-esteem leads to growth; excessive pride may lead to repeated ego conflicts.

Moon:

Life revolves around emotions, nurturing and family. The person may encounter circumstances requiring emotional resilience and compassion.

Accepting emotional depth brings inner strength; resisting emotional openness can create loneliness and disconnection.

Mars:

Themes of energy, courage and conflict. The native often deals with assertive, challenging scenarios that test courage and determination.

Embracing constructive energy use (sports, constructive challenges) leads to fulfillment; resisting may lead to impulsive conflicts or burnout.

Rahu:

Focus on ambition, unconventional paths and material pursuits. Rahu tests the native with desires and illusions, often pushing them toward power, status, or fame.

Accepting and channeling ambition ethically brings success; indulging in deception or shortcuts can bring downfall.

Jupiter:

Centered around wisdom, knowledge and spirituality. The individual may find purpose in teaching, guiding, or lifelong learning.

Embracing humility in wisdom sharing brings fulfillment; arrogance or misuse of knowledge can lead to isolation or loss of respect.

Saturn:

Revolves around discipline, hard work and responsibility. Saturn's influence brings repetitive tasks, challenges and duties that may feel burdensome.

Accepting responsibilities brings strength; resisting Saturn's lessons results in stress, delays and health issues.

Mercury:

Focus on communication, intellect and business. The individual may work in fields involving writing, speaking, or analysis.

Embracing clarity and ethical communication brings success; gossip, dishonesty, or mental restlessness lead to setbacks.

The Lesson of the Karmic Influence Planet

The Karmic Influence planet demands recognition of its lessons. By learning and applying the principles associated with this planet:

- **Acceptance and Adaptation**: Leads to peace, success and inner harmony.
- **Resistance or Complaint**: Creates discomfort, obstacles, or repeated challenges.

This karmic focus, once accepted, aligns the individual with their soul's journey, helping them evolve. The universe, in essence, offers continuous opportunities to balance and integrate the energy of the controlling planet, guiding the native toward growth and fulfillment in alignment with their past life karma.

Transits & Progression

In BNN (Bhrigu Nandi Nadi), predictions are based on the transits of planets instead of the dasha system, which is common in other branches of astrology. Transits are categorized into two main types: **fast-moving planetary transits** and **slow-moving planetary transits**. Each type impacts life differently and both are crucial for accurate prediction.

1. Fast-Moving Planetary Transits

The fast-moving planets include the Sun, Moon, Mercury, Venus and Mars. These planets move quickly through the signs:

- **Sun**: Takes about 30 days to transit each sign.
- **Moon**: Takes approximately 2.5 days per sign.
- **Mercury**: Stays in each sign for about 30 days, **Venus**: Transits each sign in about 30 days.
- **Mars**: Takes roughly 45 days per sign

These fast-moving transits influence day-to-day life events, moods and short-term occurrences. They bring minor but noticeable shifts that can be felt in the near term, affecting activities, relationships, communication and immediate actions. While they don't generally dictate major life events, their transits trigger shifts when they activate natal planets or create significant aspects with slower-moving planets.

2. Slow-Moving Planetary Transits

The slow-moving planets - Saturn, Jupiter, Rahu and Ketu - play a more profound role as they impact major life changes and milestones:

- **Saturn**: Takes approximately 2.5 years to move through each sign, bringing sustained influence on stability, discipline and karma.
- **Jupiter**: Stays in each sign for about 1 year, associated with growth, expansion and major opportunities.
- **Rahu and Ketu**: Each spend about 18 months in a sign, often associated with karmic influences, unexpected changes and lessons.

These slower transits bring impactful transformations, marking phases of growth, struggle, or achievement that can set the course of one's life path. Since these planets move slowly, their effects are often deeply felt and signify turning points or significant life events, such as career changes, marriage, or health challenges.

Jupiter Progression (Virtual Transit)

In BNN, the concept of Jupiter's progression - also called virtual transit - is used to predict specific timing of events across the different rounds of Jupiter's journey through the zodiac. Jupiter's progression is divided into "rounds":

- **1st Round**: 0–12 years - Childhood, foundational experiences
- **2nd Round**: 12–24 years - Early adulthood, education, family influence
- **3rd Round**: 24–36 years - Career building, independence, personal growth
- **4th Round**: 36–48 years - Family life, career peak, stability
- **5th Round**: 48–60 years - Legacy, contribution, reflection
- **6th Round**: 60–72 years - Health and retirement, karmic returns

Each round of Jupiter progression influences the themes for that stage of life. For example, in the 3rd Round (24–36 years), Jupiter's transit over natal planets might trigger career opportunities, whereas in the 5th Round (48–60 years), it could relate to legacy and personal fulfillment.

Transit : Fast Moving Planets

Transit of Sun Over Natal Planets

Sun over Natal Sun: Brings success, strengthens vitality, boosts learning and earnings. Issues may arise with government if the natal Sun is afflicted.

Sun over Natal Moon: Affects father's travels and possible blames; good period for mother and sisters regarding learning and earnings. Native may plan travel or changes for recognition. Limited government support.

Sun over Natal Mars: Increases determination and work ethic but can lead to blood-related health issues, high fever and headaches. Potential conflicts with siblings and favorable time for husband's gains (in female chart). Possible home repairs.

Sun over Natal Mercury: Supports educational success, better communication and property gains for the father. Female natives may reconnect with friends. Gains in intellectual pursuits.

Sun over Natal Jupiter: Elevates status, creates opportunities to connect with influential people and fosters spiritual involvement. Favorable period for native and family.

Sun over Natal Venus: Brings financial strain, possible health issues for the wife, or marriage. Heightens desires for luxury and perfection but may disrupt finances. Health concerns for diabetics; father's focus may shift to pleasurable activities.

Sun over Natal Saturn: Causes delays, financial pressure and   stress. Native experiences low confidence, yet success is achievable through hard work. Potential conflicts with father and issues for father's health.

Sun over Natal Rahu: Favors gains from speculations or unconventional means. Native may lean towards irreligion or experience laziness; father's energy may decrease.

Sun over Natal Ketu: Brings a sense of detachment and contemplation. Concerns arise related to children; father may have spiritual inclinations or divine thoughts.

Transit of Moon over Natal Planets

On Natal Sun: Heightens ego issues, promotes contemplation of short travels or job changes and a strong focus on gaining recognition. May shift perspectives on professional matters and foster spiritual aspirations.

On Natal Moon: Overthinking phase, future-focused with artistic and sensual distractions. Desire for diverse entertainment and possible encounters with the opposite sex.

On Natal Mars: Heightened restlessness and urgency; quick to temper. Minor injuries or fever may occur due to exertion and frequent movement.

On Natal Mercury: Emphasis on learning, earning and networking. May deepen relations with someone of the opposite sex, potentially leading to blames. Possible allergic reactions.

On Natal Jupiter: Mind filled with noble or divine aspirations, celebrations involving women and the desire to enrich wisdom through short trips.

On Natal Venus: Focus on pleasures and luxuries, with a risk of making planning errors, overindulgence, or financial losses.

On Natal Saturn: Discomfort at work, contemplation of career change, potential blame at the workplace. May take a short trip for relaxation.

On Natal Rahu: Illusions and eccentric thoughts, potentially unethical pleasures involving the opposite sex and possible susceptibility to hallucinations or involvement with shadowy ideas.

On Natal Ketu: Reflective, melancholic mindset due to past events. Inclination toward spirituality or the occult, with potential for disagreements with female family members.

Transit of Moon and Female Menstrual Cycle

The relationship between the **transit of the Moon and the menstrual cycle** of females is a fascinating insight derived from Bhrigu Nandi Nadi (BNN) astrology. It provides a compelling connection between astrology, human biology and the ancient wisdom of Vedic seers. Let's delve into this concept in detail, breaking down its significance, working mechanism and real-world implications.

How the Concept Works

1. Connection Between the Moon and the Menstrual Cycle: The Moon is a planet closely associated with emotions, cycles and water content in astrology. It also has a natural rhythm of approximately 28 days, which mirrors the average menstrual cycle for most women. In astrology, the **Moon's influence** extends to physical functions and its impact on the menstrual cycle has been observed to be consistent over thousands of female horoscopes.

2. Role of Mars in Female Horoscopes: In female horoscopes, **Mars represents the physical body**, blood and vitality - critical elements related to the menstrual cycle. When the Moon, representing cycles and regular rhythms, interacts with Mars, the connection triggers menstrual activity due to Mars' control over the blood flow and bodily functions.

3. Transits of the Moon Over Natal Mars:

- **Direct Transit:** When the Moon transits directly over the sign where Mars is placed in a female's natal chart, it can trigger the onset of the menstrual cycle. This connection is because Mars, as a fiery planet, governs blood-related matters and the Moon's transit activates its influence.
- **Aspects:** The Moon's 7th aspect (opposite sign) to Mars also holds significance. For instance, if Mars is in Aries, then when the Moon transits Libra (the opposite sign), it could also be a trigger point for the menstrual cycle.
- **Timing:** This predictive model uses a range of **±1 to 2 days** to allow for variations in an individual's natural cycle. For example, if today the Moon is transiting Taurus and a female's Mars is placed in Taurus or Scorpio, there is a high possibility that her cycle might begin around this date.

4. Example Calculation:

- Suppose today the Moon is in Taurus.
- If a female's natal Mars is also in Taurus or its opposite sign Scorpio, her menstrual cycle could start today or within 1-2 days.

This observation is **astoundingly accurate**, with an 80-90% success rate among females who have regular cycles without health complications affecting their periods.

A Lasting Legacy of Vedic Knowledge

The scientific approach of ancient seers, who were able to identify such precise patterns, speaks to the depth of **Vedic knowledge and its understanding of human nature**. This method, among others, reflects that:

- The **science of astrology** isn't about mere fortune-telling; it's an in-depth study of human life, karma and cosmic influence.

- Every planetary transit isn't random but a key in the **grand design** that governs our lives and actions.

By engaging with these principles and observing them in real-life scenarios, practitioners and students can deepen their understanding of astrology and appreciate the scientific structure embedded in this ancient knowledge. Through such methods, BNN astrology brings forth the wisdom of our seers, emphasizing that **life events are influenced by the universe's design** - a design we're slowly rediscovering and understanding through astrology.

Transit of Mars over Natal Planets

Transiting Mars over Natal Sun: Native becomes stubborn, power-driven and argumentative. May experience heat-related issues, mental stress, or confrontations with enemies at work. Possible injuries to children or father's professional obstructions.

Transiting Mars over Natal Moon: Hasty, restless and prone to mental tension. Increased anxiety, risk of travel-related incidents and possible dry mouth or acidity. May impact mother's health; siblings might travel.

Transiting Mars over Natal Mars: Accident-prone, with heightened energy, stubbornness and stress. Strong but potentially reckless decisions, with peace at home disturbed, especially if the native is a husband.

Transiting Mars over Natal Mercury: Overconfident in communication, leading to misunderstandings and disputes. Educational and relational hurdles. Unrest and disputes with friends or relatives and husband may spend time with friends.

Transiting Mars over Natal Jupiter: Blood pressure issues, acidity, or ulcers. Increased stubbornness, tension and danger from fire or sharp objects. Professionally strained and potential entrapment if Rahu is also involved. In female charts, husband experiences changes and recognition.

Transiting Mars over Natal Venus: Gains from foreign sources, reconnection with relatives and social interactions with opposite sex friends. Possible indulgence in sensual pleasures, home repairs and family arguments.

Transiting Mars over Natal Saturn: Disturbances in professional life, impatience, discomfort at work, disputes with superiors and risk of accidents or losses.

Transiting Mars over Natal Rahu: Overindulgence in sensual pursuits and danger to siblings. Intense jealousy, suppressed anger, energy loss and vehicle-related issues.

Transiting Mars over Natal Ketu: Desire for power, feeling of immobility, stubbornness, cramps and   injuries. Health concerns and body limitations may require attention.

Transit of Mercury over Natal Planets

Transiting Mercury over Natal Sun: Enhances intelligence and communication, leading to recognition and success in interactions. Helps in gaining support from friends, successful media use and brings gains from property for the father.

Transiting Mercury over Natal Moon: Encourages artistic pursuits but may distract from studies, leading to diplomatic or cunning behavior. The native might face criticism or emotional disappointment, possibly through a romantic relationship and may experience travel.

Transiting Mercury over Natal Mars: Disturbs studies and increases irritation. Leads to illogical behavior, disputes with siblings or uncles and potential health issues affecting bones and skin. In female charts, husband may meet with a female friend.

Transiting Mercury over Natal Mercury: Strengthens the native's natural intellect and social skills, especially enhancing friendships with the opposite sex. Quick decision-making ability and sharp business intellect.

Transiting Mercury over Natal Jupiter: Encourages knowledge gains and brings success in interviews or meetings. Interactions with noble people, potential romantic encounters and benefits for younger relatives away from home.

Transiting Mercury over Natal Venus: Brings gains from property and pleasant social interactions, possibly involving celebrations at home. Financial and business gains, with a focus on pleasurable relationships.

Transiting Mercury over Natal Saturn: Strengthens commercial skills and brings auspicious gains, especially in the professional realm, where the native is recognized as skilled. Friendship and cooperation at work, especially with the opposite sex.

Transiting Mercury over Natal Rahu: Promotes innovative thinking in commercial and communication areas, possibly related to foreign skills. Encounters fake friends or misleading advice and relatives may experience health issues.

Transiting Mercury over Natal Ketu: Brings potential breaks in education, property disputes and an unfavorable period. The native may feel distracted or disconnected from friends and social circles, with differences of opinion with siblings.

Transit of Venus over Natal Planets

Transiting Venus over Natal Sun: Encourages a display of luxurious lifestyle, resulting in short-term gains and celebration at home. Brings financial gains and luxury items, socialization with women and status enhancement.

Transiting Venus over Natal Moon: Indicates potential health issues for a daughter or wife, disputes among female family members, financial drains due to speculation and overall unrest and uneasiness in domestic matters.

Transiting Venus over Natal Mars: Heightens passion and sensual pleasure, possibly resulting in pregnancy in female charts. Financial gains for siblings, improved residence or black money usage, cooperation from the spouse and financial gains for the husband in female charts.

Transiting Venus over Natal Mercury: Brings prosperity in land and property matters, with celebrations and opportunities for wife to gain property. Adds extra income resources and chances for pleasurable meetings with friends of the opposite gender.

Transiting Venus over Natal Jupiter: Financial gains, family celebrations, disputes, luxury item gains and divine works or blessings. The wife may meet a mentor or spiritual guide, creating a fortunate period.

Transiting Venus over Natal Venus: A fortunate period focused on pleasure and entertainment, with possible plans for extra income and fortune improvement. Pleasurable and celebratory moments at home.

Transiting Venus over Natal Saturn: Financial gains with prospects for purchasing or financing a residence, potential for loans or loan clearances, organized work, fund releases and effective planning for smooth business functioning.

Transiting Venus over Natal Rahu: Unexpected financial benefits, possible vehicle or electronic purchases, a chance for sudden marriage with someone from a different community or place and foreign-related gains. Challenges arise for the native's spouse.

Transiting Venus over Natal Ketu: Difficulties in financial matters and disputes needing legal attention, struggles to recover money owed and potential house troubles or disputes with the spouse.

Jupiter Progression

In the Bhrigu Nandi Nadi (BNN) approach, predictions are primarily driven by the transit and progression of planets rather than traditional dasha systems. Here, **transit** and **progression** play distinct roles, especially with Jupiter's progression, which is uniquely used for predicting significant life events across different stages of life. Let's break down these elements in detail:

Understanding Transit vs. Progression

Transit:

A transit is the actual, real-time position of a planet in the zodiac.

All planets, when transiting certain positions in relation to a natal chart (such as being conjunct, opposite, or in a trine to natal planets), are believed to activate the results of that specific natal planet. Transits are continuous and are used to predict events based on the real-time motion of planets, especially the slow-moving ones like Saturn, Rahu, Ketu and Jupiter, as they influence long-term events in life.

Progression (Specific to Jupiter):

Progression is a method used solely for Jupiter in BNN, recognizing Jupiter's unique influence on the overall development of life events.This is also know as **Virtual Transit of Jupiter.**

While transits reflect the current position of planets, progression looks at Jupiter's movement in "rounds" (each round being one full cycle through the zodiac), with each round relating to different life stages and areas of life.

Jupiter completes one round every **12 years** by passing through all 12 zodiac signs, making it an essential indicator of life events across various ages.

Rounds of Jupiter's Progression

Jupiter's progression over time is divided into six rounds, each covering a span of 12 years. Each round is associated with different houses in the natal chart and specific aspects of life, based on Jupiter's transit through the signs.

Jupiter's Six Rounds:

Round	Age Range	Associated House	Life Events Predicted
1st	0-12 years	1st House	Self, health, early education and identity
2nd	12-24 years	2nd House	Family, finances, values and social behavior
3rd	24-36 years	3rd House	Siblings, communication, courage and travel
4th	36-48 years	4th House	Home, property, peace of mind and mother
5th	48-60 years	5th House	Children, creativity, speculation, past karma
6th	60-72 years	6th House	Health, service, debts and obstacles

Explanation of Each Round:

1st Round (0-12 years, 1st House):

This round is associated with the self and foundational years, highlighting early education, health and personality development.Events related to self-identity, childhood experiences and how others perceive the individual are emphasized.

2nd Round (12-24 years, 2nd House):

This phase covers growth into adolescence and young adulthood, focusing on family, finances and social behaviors.Events may include early financial learning, family dynamics, the influence of family values and the start of one's personal earning journey.

3rd Round (24-36 years, 3rd House):

In this period, communication, sibling relationships, short-distance travel and mental courage are emphasized. Individuals may experience more active relationships with siblings, more frequent travels and development in communication skills and social connections.

4th Round (36-48 years, 4th House):

This round is related to home, domestic comfort and emotional peace.Focus areas include home-building or property investments, responsibilities related to the mother or nurturing figures and an emphasis on attaining peace and security within the household.

5th Round (48-60 years, 5th House):

Associated with children, creativity and outcomes of past karma.Events may include interactions with children, speculative gains and opportunities for creative pursuits. It may also reflect the consequences of actions taken in earlier life stages.

6th Round (60-72 years, 6th House):

Focuses on health, service to others, managing debts and overcoming obstacles. Health concerns may become more prominent and individuals may experience a stronger need for routines and addressing unresolved matters from past rounds.

Progression as a Predictive Tool in BNN

Each time Jupiter transits over or aspects a natal planet in one of these rounds, it activates specific events, known as **activation periods**.

Activation periods vary with each round, reflecting how the significance of Jupiter changes as life progresses. For instance:

1st Round might activate events like early education or learning basic skills.

4th Round would lean toward property, peace of mind and establishing a stable home.

6th Round typically reflects issues related to health or addressing life's unfinished tasks.

Progression Timing:

The progression system adds an extra layer to transits by indicating not just the general potential of a planet, but when specific events tied to a house are likely to unfold.

For example, if natal Jupiter is in a particular sign, during each subsequent round, its progression through the signs will highlight specific areas of life, providing insights into timing for various milestones.

Key Takeaways for Progression in BNN:

Post-72 Years:

Jupiter's free will influence is believed to diminish after 72 years, indicating that subsequent life events are more about experiencing the results of past actions and decisions.

Combined Transit and Progression Influence:

Transits over natal placements reveal immediate effects, but Jupiter's progression contextualizes these by age-related themes, allowing for nuanced predictions.

Each round's events are also influenced by the interaction between transiting Jupiter and other slower-moving planets like Saturn, Rahu and Ketu, which may modify or intensify results.

In Bhrigu Nandi Nadi (BNN) astrology, **Progression** is a method where we study the **virtual transit of Jupiter** through a horoscope to determine the timing of life events. This virtual transit is unique because it does not involve the actual movement of Jupiter but rather assigns each house of the horoscope to a specific age based on Jupiter's position in the natal chart. The technique identifies which house influences each year of the native's life, progressing round by round as Jupiter completes cycles of 12 years.

Here's how we set up the virtual transit (progression) of Jupiter, dividing the life events into six rounds of 12 years each.

Jupiter Progression Table

1. **Starting Point**: Note the house placement of natal Jupiter. The first house in the progression begins here.
2. **Round**: Each round spans 12 years, covering each house sequentially for one year.
3. **Application**: We repeat this structure for six rounds, each round beginning in the house following where the previous round started.

Jupiter Progression Rounds Explained

Round	Age Range	House Representing Each Year	Explanation
1st Round	0-12 years	1st House (0-1), 2nd House (1-2), 3rd House (2-3), ... up to 12th House	Initial development, early childhood events and family
2nd Round	12-24 years	2nd House (12-13), 3rd House (13-14), ... up to 1st House	Adolescence, education, early relationships, skills
3rd Round	24-36 years	3rd House (24-25), 4th House (25-26), ... up to 2nd House	Career establishment, personal life and family growth
4th Round	36-48 years	4th House (36-37), 5th House	Stabilization in career,

		(37-38), ... up to 3rd House	investments, mid-life changes
5th Round	48-60 years	5th House (48-49), 6th House (49-50), ... up to 4th House	Mentoring role, children's achievements, planning for retirement
6th Round	60-72 years	6th House (60-61), 7th House (61-62), ... up to 5th House	Retirement, health, family legacies, spiritual pursuits

Example Application with an Illustrative Horoscope

Let's assume **Jupiter is placed in the 3rd House** in the natal chart. Based on this placement, each house will represent the following ages in the native's life:

House	1st Round (0-12 yrs)	2nd Round (12-24 yrs)	3rd Round (24-36 yrs)	4th Round (36-48 yrs)	5th Round (48-60 yrs)	6th Round (60-72 yrs)
3rd House	0-1	12-13	24-25	36-37	48-49	60-61
4th House	1-2	13-14	25-26	37-38	49-50	61-62
5th House	2-3	14-15	26-27	38-39	50-51	62-63

6th House	3-4	15-16	27-28	39-40	51-52	63-64
7th House	4-5	16-17	28-29	40-41	52-53	64-65
8th House	5-6	17-18	29-30	41-42	53-54	65-66
9th House	6-7	18-19	30-31	42-43	54-55	66-67
10th House	7-8	19-20	31-32	43-44	55-56	67-68
11th House	8-9	20-21	32-33	44-45	56-57	68-69
12th House	9-10	21-22	33-34	45-46	57-58	69-70
1st House	10-11	22-23	34-35	46-47	58-59	70-71
2nd House	11-12	23-24	35-36	47-48	59-60	71-72

In BNN astrology, Jupiter's progression, or virtual transit, activates certain planets based on each round (cycle) of 12 years. The progression of Jupiter is considered to have specific activation points, depending on which house it starts in for each round and the planets associated with that house. Here's a breakdown of how planets are activated in a given round and an example of how this method can be applied to interpret results.

Step-by-Step Guide to Determining Planetary Activation in a Round

Each Jupiter round activates planets based on the house it begins in for that round. For example, during the second round (12–24 years), the progression begins from the 2nd house from natal Jupiter's position. Here's the process for determining which planets are activated:

1. **Check the Planet in the Starting House**: Identify any planet in the house where Jupiter's progression starts for that round. For the second round, this is the 2nd house from natal Jupiter. The planet(s) in this house will be the primary focus for that round.
2. **Identify Trine Planets**: Check for planets in the trine houses (1, 5 and 9 positions) from the starting house. These planets gain importance and are likely to produce significant results.
3. **Identify Aspecting Planets**: Look at the planets aspecting the starting house. These planets also become activated and influence the results in that round.
4. **Analyze the House Ruler**: Determine the lord (ruler) of the starting house's zodiac sign. This planet will be active in the round and should be checked for any aspects or conjunctions.
5. **Conjunctions with Rashi Lord**: Examine any planets conjunct the rashi lord of the starting house, as these planets will also play a role.
6. **Aspecting the Rashi Lord**: Planets aspecting the rashi lord of the starting house are also activated.
7. **Exchange with 2nd Lord**: If there is an exchange of houses involving the 2nd lord (for the second round), this will also bring prominent results from both houses involved in the exchange.

Retrograde Jupiter

When Jupiter is retrograde in the natal chart, the starting point often becomes a topic of debate in astrology due to different perspectives on interpreting retrograde motion. Here's a breakdown of the varying viewpoints and the rationale behind each approach, along with why selecting the house where Jupiter is placed as the starting point may be the most practical method:

Starting from the 12th House (Previous House):

Rationale: Some astrologers consider the retrograde motion as a backward movement, implying that Jupiter's progression might "start" from the house before the one it occupies. Readers can check on their respective horoscopes and match their life events, in few cases it is seen that in Retrograde case especially when Jupiter's degree is less than 15 degrees, results match when previous house is taken as 1st house.

Taking the Current House Where Jupiter is Placed (Preferred Approach):

Rationale: By starting from the house where Jupiter is located, this method respects Jupiter's placement as the focal point of influence in the chart. Retrograde or not, Jupiter's position reflects the area where its effects are most active and relevant to the native's life. In this way, the house Jupiter occupies becomes the starting point of progression without additional layers or complications.

Advantages: This approach keeps the progression straightforward, following the natural house order. It aligns with the principle that Jupiter's retrograde motion does not diminish the house it occupies but rather may deepen its influence, adding introspection rather than altering its placement.

Understanding the Role of Jupiter and Saturn in Life's Journey

Jupiter's Transits and Free Will (0-72 Years)

- **Jupiter Transits and Free Will**: Until the age of 72, Jupiter's transits signify opportunities to exercise free will in matters related to the planet it activates. For instance, when Jupiter transits over Venus, it brings opportunities to enhance one's values around wealth, relationships and comforts.
- **Accumulation of Karma**: Actions taken by exercising this free will contribute to the native's karma, which accumulates up to the age of 72.
- **End of Free Will**: Post-72, Jupiter's influence wanes in terms of creating new karma through free will. Instead, it is a period of reaping the accumulated results of choices made up to that point.

Saturn's Influence Post-72 Years

- **Saturn's Role**: After 72, Saturn takes over, shifting focus from creating new experiences through free will to reaping the outcomes of prior actions.
- **Jeev and Experience**: Jupiter as the significator of Jeev (life energy) continues to experience the results provided by Saturn after 72. Whatever Saturn brings - be it comfort or adversity - Jupiter as Jeev feels it fully.
- **Example**: If Saturn transits over Venus in this stage, there might be financial or relational stability. However, if Jupiter is in an uncomfortable position or under stress, the native may not fully enjoy these benefits.

Key Planetary Influences in the Horoscope

1. **Jupiter - Jeev Karak**:
   - Jupiter, as the Jeev Karak, influences how we feel and interpret experiences as good or bad. The strength and position of Jupiter dictate how the native will internally react and adapt to external situations.
2. **Sun - Atmakarak**:
   - The Sun, representing the soul (Atmakarak), embodies willpower, courage and self-confidence. A strong Sun equips the individual to face challenges and adversity with resilience and inner strength, regardless of external circumstances.
   - **Significance**: A powerful Sun indicates the ability to navigate life's difficulties and reach one's goals with determination.

Importance of Transits in Shaping Life

- **Jupiter Transits**: Jupiter's transit helps shape how we experience life's ups and downs, influencing our sense of fulfillment or discomfort with what we receive.
- **Saturn's Long-Term Effects**: Saturn's transits represent the reality of outcomes and responsibilities, especially prominent after 72.
- **Rahu and Ketu Transits**: Rahu and Ketu's transits bring sudden changes and significant turning points, offering unexpected opportunities or challenges in life.

Together, Jupiter and Sun act as pillars, with Jupiter setting the course of experience and Sun providing the strength to face them. Saturn, Rahu and Ketu transits then punctuate the journey with karmic experiences and turning points, each transit playing a specific role in shaping the journey and fulfilling karmic cycles.

Jupiter Transit & Rounds of Jupiter

1st Round of Jupiter

Age calculation starts from the house Jupiter is posited, that house is taken as 0-1 years. In the first round of Jupiter, covering the ages from 0 to 12 years, the transit impacts self-development, physical growth and early life experiences. This period often reflects the physical and foundational experiences in a child's life. Here's how Jupiter's transit in this first round can impact a native's life:

Key Observations in the 1st Round of Jupiter:

Jupiter's Sign Placement and Dispositor:

Identify the sign in which natal Jupiter is placed.Find the dispositor (the planet ruling the sign where Jupiter is placed). When Jupiter transits over its dispositor, it triggers significant events, possibly related to early learning, growth spurts, or foundational changes.

Mars as Body:

If Jupiter transits over natal Mars during this period, health issues might arise, especially related to physical injuries, accidents, or ailments typical for young, active individuals. If Mars is in a fiery sign, the risk of burns, high fevers, or even minor shocks increases.

As Mars represents the body and physical energy, this can also indicate heightened activity or moments where the child's physical stamina or resilience is tested.

Rahu's Placement in Jupiter's Initial Four Signs:

If Rahu is positioned within the first four signs from natal Jupiter, this early Jupiter round is likely to bring health challenges or environmental stresses on the native. Issues might include general susceptibility to illness or minor, unexplained health discomforts.

Jupiter over Venus (Sanjeevani Yoga):

In the above horoscope during 3 -4 years of age native suffered severe head injury but was saved.

If Jupiter transits over Venus during this round, it forms a protective influence known as Sanjeevani Yoga. This helps counterbalance health issues, bringing healing, recovery, or strengthening the child's resilience. Venus's qualities bring nurturing, comfort and protection.

Jupiter Transit Over Malefics (Rahu, Ketu, Saturn, Mars):

Health-related challenges are likely when Jupiter transits over malefic planets like Rahu, Ketu, Saturn, or Mars. The severity depends on the native Jupiter's strength, which acts as a buffer to mitigate or increase these health concerns. A double activation, where both transiting and natal Jupiter are impacted by malefics, indicates higher intensity.

2nd Round of Jupiter (Ages 12-24): Focus on Family, Finance and Speech

In this round, Jupiter's transits influence family dynamics, financial stability and communication. Here's how it plays out with key planets:

Family (Significator: Moon)

Jupiter Transit over Moon: Brings positive family experiences, harmony and emotional support within the family structure.

Jupiter Transit over Rahu or Saturn: Can create disruptions or misunderstandings within the family. It might lead to detachment, familial challenges, or a lack of support from family members.

Finance (Significator: Venus)

Jupiter Transit over Venus: Increases financial stability, often bringing wealth, gains, or enhanced financial security.

Jupiter Transit over Ketu: Negatively impacts finances, potentially causing financial strain, unexpected expenses, or reduced earnings.

Speech (Significator: Mercury)

Jupiter Transit over Mercury: Enhances communication abilities, making the native articulate and effective in speech. It's beneficial for any profession involving speaking, writing, or negotiation.

Jupiter Transit over Mars: May cause conflicts due to blunt or aggressive communication, leading to misunderstandings or arguments.

3rd Round of Jupiter (Ages 24-36): Focus on Siblings and Travel

In this period, Jupiter's transits activate themes related to siblings and travel, reflecting in the native's relationships and opportunities for movement.

Siblings (Significator: Mars)

Jupiter Transit over Mars: Generally positive for siblings, fostering harmony, cooperation and support. Siblings may experience growth or success.

Jupiter Transit over Rahu: Creates difficulties for siblings, which could manifest as health problems, disputes, or misunderstandings. This transit might also impact the relationship quality with siblings.

Travel (Significator: Moon)

Jupiter Transit over Moon: Encourages travel and movement, often for beneficial purposes like career advancement, personal exploration, or spiritual pursuits.

Jupiter Transit over Rahu: Negatively impacts travel plans, potentially leading to delays, obstacles, or unpleasant travel experiences.

4th Round of Jupiter (Ages 36-48): Focus on Happiness, Property, Vehicle, Mother, Farmland, Commercial Property, Building and Foreign Settlement

During this round, Jupiter's transits influence aspects related to home, happiness, property acquisition, relationships with the mother and potential foreign settlement.

Below are the specific areas activated by Jupiter's transit over key planets and how the presence of enemy planets affects outcomes:

Happiness (Significator: Venus | Enemy: Ketu)

Jupiter Transit over Venus: Brings periods of joy, comfort and enhanced personal well-being. The native may experience happiness through relationships, luxuries, or creative pursuits.

Jupiter Transit over Ketu: Can lead to challenges in finding peace and contentment, as Ketu's influence may introduce detachment or dissatisfaction with material pleasures.

Property (Significator: Mars | Enemy: Rahu)

Jupiter Transit over Mars: Encourages property acquisition or renovations. Good for purchasing new properties or land.

Jupiter Transit over Rahu: Could create obstacles or confusion in property matters, leading to disputes or unexpected challenges in acquiring or maintaining property.

Vehicle (Significator: Venus | Enemy: Ketu)

Jupiter Transit over Venus: Favors the purchase of vehicles, home improvements and other luxury items.

Jupiter Transit over Ketu: May bring issues related to vehicle or transport, such as breakdowns, accidents, or unexpected expenses associated with vehicles.

Mother (Significator: Moon | Enemy: Rahu)

Jupiter Transit over Moon: Brings favorable circumstances for the mother and strengthens the relationship with her. The native may experience emotional support from family and maternal figures.

Jupiter Transit over Rahu: Could lead to health issues for the mother or emotional challenges within the family, possibly creating distance from maternal relatives or family discord.

Farmland (Significator: Saturn | Enemy: Ketu)

Jupiter Transit over Saturn: Supports stability in agricultural or land-related pursuits. Good for long-term investments in farmland or agricultural properties.

Jupiter Transit over Ketu: May create challenges or obstacles in acquiring or maintaining agricultural land, leading to losses or disputes over land use.

Commercial Property (Significator: Mercury | Enemy: Mars)

Jupiter Transit over Mercury: Enhances opportunities in business properties or commercial real estate investments. Favorable for ventures in commercial spaces, offices, or rental properties.

Jupiter Transit over Mars: May bring difficulties with commercial properties, such as disputes, regulatory challenges, or accidents related to business ventures.

Builder Apartment (Significator: Venus | Enemy: Ketu)

Jupiter Transit over Venus: Indicates favorable periods for acquiring or investing in apartments, especially luxury or high-end real estate.

Jupiter Transit over Ketu: May create difficulties in real estate matters, delays, or issues in apartment deals, especially if Ketu causes detachment or unfulfilled desires.

Foreign Settlement (Significator: Moon)

Jupiter Transit over Moon: Can enhance the likelihood of foreign settlement, travel, or connections abroad. The native may consider opportunities outside the homeland, possibly relocating or engaging in international projects.

5th Round of Jupiter (Ages 48–60): Focus on Children, Habits and Purva Punya (Past Life Merits)

This round of Jupiter's transit highlights the influence on children, the emergence of new habits and the fruits of past life karma (Purva Punya). Events and experiences related to these areas can be particularly prominent and the intensity will be influenced by planets activated in Jupiter's progression.

Children (Significator Planets: Sun, Mars for Male Children; Moon, Mercury, Venus for Female Children)

Male Children (Sun, Mars | Enemy Planet: Rahu)

Jupiter Transit over Sun or Mars: Positive developments regarding male children, such as achievements, progress, or support. They may bring pride and joy to the native.

Jupiter Transit over Rahu: Possible challenges or issues related to male children, such as disagreements, health concerns, or misunderstandings.

Female Children (Moon, Mercury, Venus | Enemy Planet: Ketu)

Jupiter Transit over Moon, Mercury, or Venus: Favors well-being and success of female children, fostering harmony and positive experiences.

Jupiter Transit over Ketu: May bring challenges or separative experiences related to female children, such as distance, misunderstandings, or difficulties in their personal lives.

Note: The impact of Jupiter's transit over these planets may be heightened if they are active in progression, making it a period of particular focus and influence on children.

Habits (Significator: Saturn | Enemy Planet: Mars)

Jupiter Transit over Saturn: New habits may form during this transit, influenced by Saturn's themes of discipline and commitment. Depending on the native's disposition, this can be a time of adopting beneficial habits, such as meditation, spirituality, or disciplined work routines. However, if Mars is also prominent, it may bring the risk of impulsive or stress-related habits.

Jupiter Transit over Mars: May encourage active or competitive habits but can also bring about conflict-driven behaviors if not moderated. Physical or demanding activities may become more attractive.

Purva Punya Bhava (Fifth House) – Rewards of Past Life Merits

Planets in Benefic or Exalted Signs: When Jupiter transits over benefic, exalted, or planets in their own signs, it brings favorable outcomes as blessings of past life karma. These transits promote positive growth, recognition and blessings, especially in relationships, wealth, or spiritual pursuits.

Planets in Debilitated or Enemy Signs: Jupiter's transit over debilitated planets or those in enemy signs may bring challenging results. This period can highlight areas where unresolved past karma may cause setbacks or difficulties, urging the native to address unfinished karmic obligations.

Planetary Exchange: If there is an exchange of signs, Jupiter's transit can amplify the benefits. These areas may show improvements or favorable results twice during Jupiter's transits, signaling doubled blessings and support.

6th Round of Jupiter (Ages 60–72): Results of Past Negative Actions (Paap Karmo ke Phal)

The 6th round of Jupiter's transit reflects the consequences of negative or unresolved past actions, often manifesting in challenges related to debts, diseases and enemies. This is a crucial period, especially when Jupiter progresses over malefic planets or benefics in debilitation or enemy signs. While debilitated planets and malefics bring challenging results, exalted and own-sign planets provide relief and resilience during this phase.

Key Areas of Focus: Debts, Diseases and Enemies

Mars: Mars governs disease, enemies and potential surgical interventions. During this round, Jupiter's transit over Mars, especially if Mars is debilitated, can bring health issues or conflicts that may require surgical treatment.

All Malefics: In the 6th round, malefics such as Saturn, Rahu and Ketu play significant roles. Jupiter's transit over these planets may activate challenging karmic outcomes in the form of physical health issues, mental strain, or hidden adversaries.

Planetary Impact on Health and Karma

Rahu: When Jupiter transits over Rahu, the native may face hallucinatory experiences, delusions, or diseases that are difficult to diagnose. Rahu's influence can cloud clarity, causing confusion or unexplainable health issues that may be challenging to treat.

Ketu: Jupiter's transit over Ketu can manifest as severe, even life-threatening diseases. Ketu's role as a "karaka of detachment" in this round may bring detachment from the physical body itself or critical health concerns that require serious attention.

Saturn: Jupiter's transit over Saturn often indicates chronic or long-term health issues. Saturn's nature signifies persistence and endurance, meaning any disease that arises may be slow to resolve, requiring sustained care and patience.

Venus (in Debilitation): If Venus is debilitated, Jupiter's transit can result in health issues that necessitate prolonged medical treatment or dependency on medications. Venus in this state may also point to issues with lifestyle diseases related to indulgence or excess.

The Role of Planetary Strength

Exalted and Own-House Planets: If Jupiter transits over exalted planets or those in their own houses, positive results can counterbalance the difficulties. These planets provide strength, support and resilience, enabling the native to overcome challenges with greater ease and to manage health issues more effectively.

Debilitated and Enemy Sign Planets: Transits over debilitated or enemy-sign planets can increase karmic burdens. These placements indicate vulnerability in health or heightened conflicts, reflecting the consequences of unresolved or negative karmic actions.

Key Takeaways of the 6th Round of Jupiter's Transit

Debts, Disease and Challenges: The native may experience the outcomes of past karma, particularly unresolved or negative actions. The focus often involves health complications, difficulties with adversaries, or debt-related issues.

Karmic Closure: This round often brings the culmination of lifelong karmic patterns, with the native beginning to face and resolve accumulated karmic debts. The period is seen as a time of "karmic accounting," where the results of both positive and negative actions reach a final settlement.

Resilience and Recovery: Jupiter's transit over positive or benefic planets provides relief, while difficult transits demand endurance. This period emphasizes the importance of health management and resolution of pending conflicts.

In this final active phase of Jupiter's progression, the native experiences the full spectrum of karmic results, primarily those related to unresolved debts and challenges. Positive planetary placements bring resilience, while negative configurations signal the need for acceptance and perseverance.

Jupiter Transits over Natal Planets and Their Effects

Jupiter Transit over Natal Sun:

During this period, native may encounter issues related to government, powerful authorities, or influential individuals. With effort and assistance from someone knowledgeable or an authoritative figure, these issues can be resolved. Seeking advice from a subject matter expert may be beneficial.

Jupiter Transit over Natal Moon:

Native may experience challenges or blames from adversaries, as well as cold-related health issues. There could be travel, a change in residence, or devotional inclinations, especially for the mother or mother-in-law. If expecting a child, it may indicate the birth of a female. Interaction with the opposite sex may also increase.

Jupiter Transit over Natal Mercury:

This is generally a favorable transit. For students, it enhances knowledge and success in exams or competitions. It brings prosperity for younger siblings and cooperation from knowledgeable individuals. Gains in land-related deals, successful professional meetings or trainings and enhanced communication - both verbal and written - are expected. Native may also experience new connections with the opposite sex or strengthen friendships.

Jupiter Transit over Natal Venus:

This transit enhances affluence and assets, leading to a rise in comfort and enjoyment (sukha). It's an auspicious time for celebrations and buying luxury items. In a male horoscope, it often indicates marriage. Results may also include wealth, family harmony and the possibility of marriage or the birth of a daughter.

Jupiter Transit over Natal Mars:

This transit brings haste, stubbornness and distances the native from close ones, often due to a power-driven approach. Tensions, blood pressure and a strong desire to exert control may arise. Success is likely in construction or technical activities and one of the native's brothers may gain societal recognition. In female charts, this transit can indicate marriage prospects if single and for married women, the husband may receive a promotion.

Jupiter Transit over Natal Jupiter:

An excellent period for self-development, bringing name, fame and personal growth. Decisions may include family expansion, with an opportunity for childbirth planning. This transit activates the 5th and 9th houses, which can bring forth results from past karma.

Jupiter Transit over Natal Saturn:

Employment and promotions are likely, bringing an increase in workplace authority, fame and status. This transit is generally favorable for career growth, though if natal Mars is linked to Saturn, obstacles may arise in getting a job or promotion. For Aries ascendants, as the 11th house acts as a *badhak* (obstacle), positive results may be reduced.

Jupiter Transit over Natal Rahu:

This transit may lead the native into a "maya jaal" (illusionary web) with health issues, possible hospitalization, or medication needs. If natal Jupiter has low immunity, the intensity of health problems may be high; otherwise, effects may be minimal. There is a risk of food poisoning, adverse medicine reactions, or misguided decisions driven by illusions or lust. The transit can obstruct Jupiter's typical good effects, luring the native into circumstances that would be better avoided.

Jupiter Transit over Natal Ketu:

This transit enhances divine knowledge and occult powers, while often restricting materialistic gains. Ketu, being obstructive like a "black hole," draws the mind toward spirituality rather than material pursuits. This combination may lead to joint pains due to opposing energies, potentially causing nervous debility and health concerns. Ketu obstructs worldly desires, guiding the native toward spiritual awakening, while Rahu seeks to deepen material attachments and illusions.

Saturn Transit Effects on Natal Planets

Saturn Transit over Natal Sun:

This period can bring stress and opposition, especially in professional areas. Although recognition may come from the parental side, difficulties with higher-ups, bosses and possibly disputes with father or son are likely. Saturn's malefic nature impacts health and when combined with Sun's role in immunity, it may reduce overall resilience. Professional relationships, especially with authority figures, may become strained, as Saturn challenges Sun's natural authority and ego.

Saturn Transit over Natal Moon:

Changes in profession, transfers and potential blames are common, alongside feelings of tension and increased expenses. Cold-related health issues may arise. If natal Moon is weak, there could be risky associations or scandal. The native's mother may experience health issues as well and Saturn's influence may heighten the native's emotional or psychological stress.

Saturn Transit over Natal Mercury:

For students, this transit favors educational achievements and learning gains, albeit with delays. It brings new opportunities for knowledge expansion, such as training or educational ventures. Business-related progress and land purchases are possible and younger siblings might also experience career advancements or growth.

Saturn Transit over Natal Venus:

This period may activate marriage prospects, romantic relationships, or affairs. It can bring affluence, potential birth of a daughter and increase in assets, influencing both the 2nd (wealth) and 7th (relationships) houses. Venusian themes of comfort, pleasure and material growth are likely to emerge, with Saturn possibly adding a serious or commitment-oriented approach to these areas.

Saturn Transit over Natal Mars:

This transit often brings mental tension and harassment at work. The pressure from higher-ups and an ego-driven approach could create workplace friction, as Saturn's humbling influence clashes with Mars's assertiveness. If Mercury aspects are present, there may be a focus on technical education or skill-building. This period may also prompt thoughts of job changes; if unemployed, youth may find physically demanding job opportunities.

Saturn Transit over Natal Jupiter:

Saturn's influence on Jupiter brings growth and stability to the native's profession, often leading to promotions, new status and significant career advancements. Known as a transformative transit, it marks a major life turn, opening up new avenues and establishing long-term goals. However, it can also trigger gastric issues, as Saturn's restrictive nature impacts Jupiter's expansive qualities.

Saturn Transit over Natal Saturn:

This transit tends to slow down life's momentum, bringing increased workload, efficiency challenges and periods of lethargy or exhaustion. The native may feel burdened and life may seem to "slow down" as Saturn emphasizes responsibility and self-discipline. Health issues, especially nervous or stress-related, may arise, with pressures building from multiple directions.

Saturn Transit over Natal Rahu:

There is a risk of involvement in hidden or ethically ambiguous activities. Saturn's aspect may encourage work in foreign environments, or even secretive or "shadow" work. This period may bring a sense of detachment and Vaat-related disorders (joint pain, stiffness) may occur. Saturn over Rahu can also indicate an increased likelihood of needing to perform last rites for a family member.

Saturn Transit over Natal Ketu:

This transit is often associated with feelings of dejection and conflicts at work, potentially leading to litigation or legal disputes. There is an aimlessness, with the native potentially seeking spiritual solace by visiting holy places. The quality of job roles may feel compromised, with possible frustrations and losses in various areas of life.

Saturn Transit Aspects

- **Aspects:** 1st, 3rd, 7th, 10th
- **Important Aspects:** 1st and 3rd are the most significant, often indicating areas where Saturn's influence is strongest in terms of challenges, delays and responsibilities.

Jupiter Transit Aspects

- **Aspects:** 1st, 3rd, 5th, 7th, 9th, 11th
- **Important Aspects:** The 1st, 5th, 9th and 7th aspects are key, representing areas of growth, wisdom, expansion and benevolence. These aspects typically bring positive changes, opportunities and learning experiences.

Rahu-Ketu Transit Aspects

- **Aspects:** 1st, 5th, 9th, 12th
- **Important Aspects:** The 5th and 9th aspects are particularly impactful. They often indicate karmic influences, unexpected events and transformative experiences, focusing on desires (Rahu) or detachment (Ketu).

Rahu Transit Over Natal Planets

Rahu over Natal Sun:
This creates a *Grahan* effect, obscuring the natural light and vitality associated with the Sun. It can result in health risks or dangers to the father or son. If the father is no longer present, then special attention should be given to the son. Support from government or authoritative bodies may be obstructed, with potential covert moves or conspiracies against the native. Rahu's influence brings deception, mystery and illusion, often leading the native towards atheistic or non-religious thoughts.

Rahu over Natal Moon:
This transit can endanger the mother, daughter, or mother-in-law, bringing confusion and clouded judgment. Decisions made during this time might be error-prone, leading to potential losses, especially in foreign dealings. Rahu's foreign and heterogeneous nature can disrupt the mind, introducing foreign elements or influences that could lead to a feeling of disconnection or misunderstanding.

Rahu over Natal Mercury:
Rahu's transit over Mercury may disrupt education and impact communication. There could be issues or risks for younger siblings and friends, as well as skin allergies. Problems may arise in land or property matters, potentially leading to litigation. However, if Mercury is well-supported by beneficial planets in the natal chart, this transit could bring opportunities for foreign meetings, educational pursuits, or business collaborations, particularly in media, foreign training, or client work.

Rahu over Natal Venus:
Rahu's transit over Venus enhances material benefits and may lead the native to live in illusions related to Venusian

matters like relationships, aesthetics and luxury. Although it doesn't diminish Venus's benefits, it can distort perception, often creating a sense of disillusionment. This period can bring sudden wealth, home renovations, a new vehicle (since Rahu is associated with wheels), or other unexpected gains. However, it can be challenging for women homemakers, as it may cause emotional strain or hallucinations. Rahu's separative influence on Venus can also lead to marital discord or even separation.

Rahu over Natal Mars:
This transit heightens the risk of accidents or issues related to blood and if the Sun is involved, there's a potential risk of heart problems. For siblings, particularly brothers, it indicates health issues or danger. In a female chart, this transit can pose significant risks to the husband's health, potentially signaling a dangerous situation.

Rahu over Natal Jupiter (Jeeva Sankat Yoga):
This transit can bring intense fears of death, health crises, or encounters with toxic influences such as poisoning, wrong medications, or food poisoning. Snake bites, diagnostic challenges, or even the death of a close relative could occur. Rahu, as a symbol of illusion and destruction, casts a shadow over Jupiter, creating confusion, tempting the native toward indulgent or wrongful associations (Guru Chandal Yoga). While Jupiter's positivity can support high ambitions, Rahu disrupts stability, pushing the native towards breaking life's established patterns or circles. This combination can also bring both success and denial, offering opportunities that might have hidden downsides.

Additional Notes on Rahu and Ketu's Effects:

- **Rahu for New Beginnings:** Rahu is often associated with breaking patterns and creating new beginnings, while Ketu is related to the accumulation or residual impact of habits from past lives.

- **Death-Related Concerns:** A combination of Rahu with Jupiter, Ketu with Saturn and the Sun in trine with the birth sign, coupled with Moon-Mercury connections, can potentially indicate life-threatening periods.
- **Rahu on Sun and Mercury (Budh Aditya Yoga):** Rahu's transit over Sun and Mercury can expand intellectual and creative capabilities, often increasing the native's recognition or influence. However, this can also lead to an inflated ego or misjudgment if not well managed.

Rahu Transit Over Natal Saturn

Encounters with Difficult Individuals:
During Rahu's transit over Saturn, the native may face shrewd or deceitful people and may feel compelled to interact with them without alternative choices. The period can bring repetitive tasks and the resurfacing of unresolved issues or events from the past, which may feel burdensome.

Focus on Clearing Pending Work:
This transit encourages the native to focus on clearing up any outstanding or unfinished business. It emphasizes the need to address matters related to the houses occupied by or ruled by Rahu and Saturn (especially in relation to Jupiter's position), bringing events connected to these houses into prominence.

Tantra and Mantra Interest (Siddhi):
For natives with this transit or a similar Rahu-Saturn conjunction in their natal chart, there may be a strong attraction towards occult practices, including tantra and mantra. This combination often enhances intellectual abilities, making the native multi-talented, but also inclines them towards finding unconventional or "shortcut" means of earning money.

Opportunity for Karmic Cleansing:
This transit serves as a significant opportunity to shed past karma and move towards a more spiritually aligned path. It is a favorable period for the native to submit to spiritual or divine guidance, clear old debts (both physical and karmic) and adopt a more honest, pure way of living.

Note on Transits of Saturn, Rahu and Ketu

The effects of transits involving Saturn, Rahu and Ketu often recur, with similar events happening each time. Although the context, location and conditions may vary, the underlying themes repeat, allowing for karmic resolution and growth through these cyclical experiences.

Ketu Transits Over Natal Planets

Ketu Over Natal Sun:

Spiritual Inclination and Restrictions: The native or the father may visit holy places, reflecting a turn towards spirituality. This transit may also impose limitations or setbacks in the son's progress.

Government and Legal Orders: Ketu, the significator of litigation, may bring authoritative instructions, possibly from government or legal institutions, requiring compliance. These may feel restrictive but are intended to guide the native.

Health Impact on Father: Father may experience health issues, prompting further focus on the spiritual.

Ketu Over Natal Moon:

Turn to Charity and Spirituality: The native may become more god-centered, involving themselves in charitable actions and seeking peace.

Mental Restlessness and Health Concerns: This transit often brings mental unrest, especially if unresolved emotional issues are present. Blood-related health issues could arise.

Philosophical Outlook in Family: Mother or mother-in-law may adopt a philosophical outlook, facing life with greater spiritual insight.

Ketu Over Natal Mercury:

Bondage in Partnerships and Legal Challenges: Ketu's influence can bring disputes or difficulties in partnerships.

Legal entanglements or proceedings are likely due to Ketu and Mercury's connection to legal affairs.

Intellectual Blocks: Mental clarity may feel obstructed, with challenges in decision-making or understanding.

Health and Educational Disturbances: The transit may bring nerve issues, potentially leading to nerve blockage, particularly if the Moon is also involved. Skin-related problems can arise and if Mars is present, land disputes may become a source of conflict. Educational disturbances may affect younger natives.

Ketu Over Natal Venus:

Challenges in Relationships with Females: This transit may strain relations with female family members like the wife, elder sister, or sister-in-law.

Legal and Financial Blockages: Financial restrictions and family disputes may arise, especially in issues involving women. For female natives, legal issues or blockages in relationships may occur.

Family and Financial Disputes: Family harmony could be disrupted due to disputes, especially involving material or financial matters.

Ketu Over Natal Mars:

Health and Familial Tensions: This transit may bring issues related to blood or the nervous system and the native's adamant nature may lead to family tensions, especially with siblings. In female horoscopes, the husband may face career or personal obstacles, leading to marital discord. If Mercury is also involved, land-related issues or disputes may arise.

Ketu Over Natal Jupiter:

Spiritual Growth and Physical Ailments: Native tends to become more philosophical and may withdraw from worldly interests, neglecting appearance and social obligations. For those involved in research, this transit can bring a depth of understanding in metaphysical fields. Health issues may include nervous weakness or body pains, as both planets relate to spiritual liberation and reduce material desires.

Ketu Over Natal Saturn:

Professional Setbacks and Spiritual Restlessness: This period may bring professional dissatisfaction, as the native might struggle to find meaning or peace at work. Social reputation can suffer, potentially making the native feel like a subject of ridicule. If Mars is also involved, the native might consider resigning or changing careers.

Rahu Over Rahu:

Life-Altering Changes and Gains: This transit can initiate major shifts in the native's life, such as changes in residence, career, or personal circumstances. It often brings unexpected tensions but opens doors for awakening and transformational opportunities. There may be material gains, yet accompanied by digestive issues like stomach disorders. This period can bring valuable insights and lead to significant life changes.

Reverse Transit (Rahu Over Ketu or Ketu Over Rahu):

Breaking Patterns and New Opportunities: This unique transit brings a chance to reset and break through old patterns. The native may encounter obstacles but will also have the opportunity to overcome them and experience growth. This period is a test of alertness and awareness and success depends on recognizing and seizing the opportunities that arise. While Rahu over Rahu is better for material growth, this reverse transit focuses on life balance, offering gains through endurance and perseverance.

Ketu Over Ketu:

Family Discord and Inner Transformation: This transit may cause misunderstandings or disputes within the family. There is a potential for introspection and reassessment of personal values and priorities. Although challenging, it can bring the native closer to understanding life's impermanence and may deepen spiritual resolve.

Deferred Results in Transit

When Saturn or Jupiter transits over a natal planet and that planet's results are not manifesting (for instance, if Saturn or Jupiter transits over natal Venus and expected events like marriage or financial gains do not occur), this delay is often due to planetary deferral mechanisms. Key factors and scenarios that influence this deferral or delay in results are as follows:

1. Deferral Due to Next-Sign Strength

- **Next Sign Influence**: If the next sign from the natal planet's position is its **own sign** or **exalted sign**, the planet's results may defer until Jupiter or Saturn reaches that next sign.
- **Deferred Timeframe**: For Jupiter, the deferral may be by **one year**; for Saturn, it can delay results by **2.5 years**.

2. Deferral Based on Specific Houses

- **Venus**: If Venus is positioned in the 1st, 6th, or 11th house, results related to Venus (marriage, wealth) may experience delays.
- **Mars**: If Mars is in the 12th, 7th, or 10th house, Mars-related results (like energy, courage, property matters) may be delayed.
- This delay concept applies to all seven planets except **Rahu** and **Ketu**, which lack ownership of signs, exaltations, or debilitations.

3. Delays in Conjunctions and Aspects

- **Conjunction with Rahu or Ketu**: When any planet is conjunct with **Rahu, Ketu, or Mars** and Saturn or Jupiter transits over this conjunction, the benefic results of the conjunct planet may be delayed or deferred.

- **Power of Rahu and Ketu**: In conjunctions involving **Rahu-Mars** or **Ketu-Mars**, Rahu and Ketu tend to dominate, thereby giving their own results instead of allowing Mars to manifest its outcomes. Mars' effects are overshadowed, resulting in deferral of Mars-related results, which may manifest only after the influence of Rahu or Ketu subsides.

4. Influence of 7th Aspect

- Even if a planet is not in direct conjunction but rather under the **7th aspect** of transiting Saturn or Jupiter, there can still be delays in that planet's outcomes. This occurs because the aspect has a limiting or restrictive influence on the natal planet, much like a conjunction, particularly in cases where Saturn is involved.

Examples of Deferral in Planetary Results

- **Jupiter over Venus in the 6th House**: If natal Venus is in the 6th house and Jupiter transits over it, typical Venusian results (like marriage or financial gains) may delay until Jupiter moves into the next sign. If the next sign is Venus's own sign or exaltation, the delay may last an additional year.
- **Saturn Transiting Mars in 12th House**: If natal Mars is positioned in the 12th house, Saturn's transit may not immediately bring expected results like courage, energy, or resolution of property matters. Instead, Mars's effects may defer until Saturn exits the sign or reaches Mars's own or exalted sign.

Additional Insights on Delayed Activation

- **Deferred Benefic Results**: When Jupiter and Saturn both aspect or conjunct a natal planet, benefic results may defer if that planet is either weakened by position or in a Rahu/Ketu or Mars conjunction. The activation is likely postponed until transiting Jupiter or Saturn leaves the aspect or conjunction, shifting to more favorable conditions.
- **Rahu and Ketu's Amplified Power**: If Rahu or Ketu is conjunct a planet, especially in conjunction with Mars, Rahu or Ketu often takes precedence in giving their specific results. This can lead to intensified effects related to Rahu (material illusions, obsessions) or Ketu (detachment, spirituality), leaving Mars's typical outcomes (such as courage or conflict resolution) unmanifested until later transits.

Exchange of Planets

When two planets exchange signs, it amplifies their impact, causing their results to manifest twice during transits. This occurs because whenever **Jupiter or Saturn** transits over any sign ruled by either of the exchanging planets, it triggers both planets, resulting in dual activation. As a result, the exchange brings about a recurrence of outcomes, making it beneficial and more impactful in the life of the native.

Key Points of Planetary Exchange Effects

Dual Activation:

In a **Jupiter and Venus exchange**, whenever **Jupiter** or **Saturn** transits a sign ruled by Jupiter (Sagittarius, Pisces) or Venus (Taurus, Libra), it activates both Jupiter and Venus's results. This is a more potent effect compared to a single planetary placement since it ensures both planets' significations manifest twice in the individual's life.

Increased Benefits with Multiple Exchanges:

More exchanges in a horoscope create a stronger, more favorable configuration. When multiple pairs of planets exchange signs, it adds layers of benefits and stability to the native's life. **Exchanges between benefic planets**, like Jupiter, Venus and Mercury, enhance overall harmony and success.

Even **exchanges involving neutral or unfriendly planets** yield better results due to the mutual activation and repeated outcomes, provided the exchange involves a friendly planet.

Example of Favorable Exchanges with Enemy Planets:

Suppose **Saturn and Mars** are in Leo (ruled by the Sun) while **Venus and the Sun** are in Capricorn (ruled by Saturn). Despite the **natural enmity** between Mars and Saturn and between the Sun and Venus, the mutual exchange of signs with a friendly planet (Sun with Venus, Saturn with Mars) brings balance and mitigates negative effects. The dual activation through transits strengthens the influence, making the results ultimately favorable.

Adverse Effects with Enemy Encounters:

However, if these exchanging planets subsequently meet an **enemy planet in transit**, the outcome can diminish or even reverse the initial benefits. For instance, if **Jupiter and Venus** exchange signs but **later conjunct a malefic like Rahu or Ketu**, the favorable effects may be curtailed or altered, leading to challenges instead of the expected benefits.

Direct & Indirect Transits

In astrology, the influence of transiting planets (especially slower-moving ones like **Jupiter, Saturn, Rahu and Ketu**) impacts multiple levels in a chart. This is seen in two ways: **direct transits**, where a planet activates a natal planet it directly passes over and **indirect transits**, where a transiting planet also activates the signs ruled by the planet it's transiting over. Here's how this works:

Direct Transit

Direct transit occurs when a transiting planet moves directly over a natal planet, activating that planet's significance.

For example, **Jupiter transiting over natal Mars** activates Mars directly, bringing themes of energy, courage and action to the forefront.

Indirect Transit

In an **indirect transit**, the transiting planet also activates the signs (rashis) ruled by the natal planet it's passing over, bringing additional houses into focus.

For instance, if **Jupiter transits over Mars**, it activates **Aries and Scorpio** (Mars' signs). We then examine where these signs are located in relation to **natal Jupiter** and the bhavas (houses) where these signs fall will also become activated, bringing results related to those houses.

Example

If **Jupiter transits over natal Mars**:

- **Direct Activation**: Mars is activated, bringing focus on energy, physical vitality and assertive actions.

- **Indirect Activation**: Aries and Scorpio houses from natal Jupiter also get activated, so if Aries is the 2nd house from natal Jupiter and Scorpio the 9th, the effects could influence finances (2nd house) and higher learning, fortune, or travels (9th house).

Specific Effects by Planet Type

Jupiter and Saturn: Both **Jupiter** and **Saturn** transiting a house or planet bring additional impacts.

Jupiter will generally bring **positive growth** or expansion, highlighting beneficial developments related to the house, the planet it transits and its lordships.

Saturn, in contrast, will **solidify** or **challenge** the area it activates, demanding patience, discipline, or adjustments related to that house, the transited planet and its lordships.

Rahu and Ketu:

Rahu and **Ketu** bring **intense and often karmic effects** in the bhava (house) they transit from natal Jupiter.

Rahu tends to bring obsession or illusion, magnifying the importance of that bhava or bringing hidden aspects to the surface.

Ketu brings detachment, spiritual insight, or a sense of incompleteness, often creating a break in that area.

Levels of Activation in Transit

For **transiting Jupiter, Saturn, Rahu, or Ketu** over any house, three main layers of activation occur:

- **Karak (Natural Significations)**: The core significations of the house, like the 10th house signifying career, status and authority.

- **Planets in the House**: Any planets placed within that house will become active and bring their themes to the forefront.
- **Lordships of Planets in the House**: The houses ruled by any planet in the house will also become activated, bringing additional dimensions based on those house significances.

Example of Multi-Layered Activation

Jupiter Transiting the 10th House:

- Activates **10th house significations**: Career, authority and public reputation become prominent.
- Activates **planets in the 10th house**: Suppose Venus is in the 10th house, so themes of harmony, relationships and luxury will become part of the career focus.
- Activates **lordships of Venus**: If Venus rules the 4th and 9th houses, those houses (home, inner happiness, luck and spirituality) will influence the 10th house matters, possibly bringing harmony in career with the support of family or a feeling of purpose.

House Impact Based on Transiting Planet

- **Jupiter**: **Positive activation**, generally beneficial outcomes related to planet, bhava (house) and lordships.
- **Saturn**: **Stabilizing or challenging activation**, demanding patience and attention to any weak areas in planet, bhava and lordship.
- **Rahu and Ketu**: Tend to bring **karmic results**; **Rahu** magnifies and distorts, while **Ketu** brings detachment and breakage.

Understanding the Influence of Gunas and Planetary Alignments on Karma and Life Experiences

In Chapter 18 of the Bhagavad Gita, Krishna describes three types of karmas (actions) according to their alignment with the **gunas** (qualities of nature): **Sattva (goodness), Rajas (passion) and Tamas (ignorance)**. Each action's quality is determined by the attitude, intention and consciousness behind it:

Sattvic Karma (Action of Goodness):

Defined as any action performed according to scriptural guidance, without attachment and without personal desires or the expectation of reward.

Characteristics: Selfless, motivated by duty and harmonious. It brings peace and positive results.

Rajasic Karma (Action of Passion):

Driven by personal desires, enacted with pride and often stressful.

Characteristics: Self-centered and aimed at gaining recognition, status, or wealth. It creates restlessness and fluctuation.

Tamasic Karma (Action of Ignorance):

Arises from delusion and ignorance, often disregarding personal capacity or the consequences to oneself and others.

Characteristics: Careless, impulsive and destructive, resulting in confusion or harm.

Planets and Their Gunas

Each planet embodies one of the three gunas, impacting the native according to its nakshatra placement and alignment within a chart:

Sattvic Planets: **Mercury and Jupiter**

Nakshatras of these planets are also sattvic, giving good results in dasha periods, especially when aligned with each other's nakshatras.

Rajasic Planets: **Sun, Venus and Moon**

Rajasic planets are dynamic, focused on creativity, love and ambition. They give good results in dasha periods when placed in rajasic nakshatras (like their own nakshatras or those of other rajasic planets).

Tamasic Planets: **Saturn, Mars, Rahu and Ketu**

Representing harsh lessons, grounding experiences and karmic learning, tamasic planets deliver optimal results in their own or other tamasic nakshatras.

Results Based on Planet-Nakshatra Alignment

Sattvic Planets:

- **Good Results**: In Sattvic nakshatras (Mercury in Mercury or Jupiter nakshatra)

- **Average Results**: In Rajasic nakshatras (Mercury and Jupiter in Sun, Venus, or Moon's nakshatra)
- **Bad Results**: In Tamasic nakshatras (Mercury and Jupiter in Rahu, Ketu, Saturn, or Mars' nakshatra)

Rajasic Planets:

- **Good Results**: In Rajasic nakshatras
- **Mixed/Average Results**: In Sattvic nakshatras
- **Bad Results**: In Tamasic nakshatras

Tamasic Planets:

- **Good Results**: In Tamasic nakshatras (Saturn in Mars or Rahu's nakshatra)
- **Bad Results**: In Sattvic nakshatras (e.g., Saturn in Mercury or Jupiter nakshatra)
- **Extremely Bad Results**: In Rajasic nakshatras

Dasha Period and Results Timing

The timing within dasha periods is key:

- **Sattvic Planets**: The middle part of the dasha tends to show the strongest results.
- **Rajasic Planets**: The beginning of the dasha period is most impactful.
- **Tamasic Planets**: The end of the dasha period holds the most significant outcomes.

Concept of Jeeva and Sharira

Each house has a **Jeeva (life force)** and **Sharira (body)** representing its core karmic energy and material manifestations:

- **Jeeva**: The lord of the nakshatra in which the house lord is placed.
    - E.g., if Mercury is in Venus' nakshatra, then **Jeeva** for Mercury is Venus.
- **Sharira**: The nakshatra lord of Jeeva, indicating the body or physical manifestations of the house.
    - E.g., if Jeeva (Venus) is in Mercury's nakshatra, then **Sharira** is Mercury.

Special Cases:

- If Jeeva is in its own nakshatra, it becomes both Jeeva and Sharira.
- If in its own sign, then **both Jeeva and Sharira** are represented by a single planet, intensifying its influence.

Varshphal

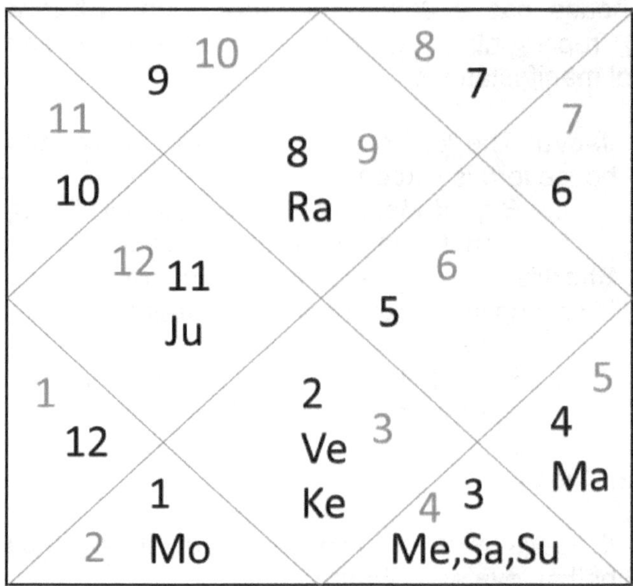

Varshphal in BNN (Annual Horoscope Analysis)

The *Varshphal* or annual horoscope approach in BNN focuses on analyzing the year's horoscope based on the native's age, Jupiter's progression and remedies. This process involves calculating the year's lagna (ascendant) using Jupiter's position in the natal chart and identifying appropriate remedies to balance planetary influences.

Steps to Determine the Annual Lagna:

1. **Calculate Completed Age**: Determine the year in progress based on the native's age.
2. **Identify Jupiter's Position**: Starting from Jupiter's natal placement, count forward by the number of

completed years. The resulting sign from this count serves as the lagna (ascendant) for the year.

- **Example**: For calculating the 50th year in progress:
- Start from Jupiter's natal position.
- Count 50 signs forward from this position.
- The 50th sign becomes the lagna for that year.
- In the above case it is the 12th sign and falls in the 5th house, this sign now represents the 1st house for the year.
- Numbers in Red are the new Rashi as per the Kalpurush Kundli
3. **Interpret with the Kal Purush Kundli**: Treat this sign as the 1st house in a modified Kal Purush Kundli, allowing you to make predictions based on the planetary influences in this layout.

Varshphal Annual Chart: Do's and Don'ts Based on Planetary Directions and Influences

Directions : Signs as per the Varshphal
1, 5, 9 - East | **2, 6, 10** - South | **3, 7, 11** - West | **4, 8, 12** - North
House Placement : All houses to be seen from the new Lagna as per Varshphal

Rahu

Direction-Based Caution: Check Rahu's position in the chart by house and apply directional meaning:

- **Do Not:** Start any repair, renovation, or construction work from the direction indicated by Rahu.
- **House Significance:** Rahu's house from Jupiter in the Varshphal suggests problems related to that specific house.

Ketu

- **Direction-Based Caution:** Avoid travel in the direction indicated by Ketu. Avoid clutter in this area of the house to ensure positive energy.
- **House Significance:**
- **2nd House:** Potential for family-related issues or even death.
- **3rd House:** Problems with siblings.
- **4th House:** Concerns for the mother.
- **5th House:** Potential issues with children.
- **10th House:** Problems in career.
- **12th House:** Spiritual inclinations, potentially indicating moksha (liberation).

Venus

- **Direction-Based Opportunity:** Travel or leisure trips are favorable in Venus's direction.
- **Special Positions:**
- **In Lagna or 7th House in a Male Chart:** Indicates marriage prospects.
- **Avoid:** Heavy white furniture within the house.

Saturn

- **Direction-Based Actions:** Start any new venture, profession, or establishment in the direction indicated by Saturn. This direction is auspicious for activities that are intended to last or be impactful over a lifetime.
- **House Significance:**
- **6th House:** Workers, servants, or laborers may leave unexpectedly. Visit or worship at a temple dedicated to Goddess Kali; if Saturn is retrograde, perform rituals or darshan in an anticlockwise manner.
- **10th House:** Success in job-related matters is likely.

Mars

- **Direction-Based Influence:** Especially significant in marriage direction for females. If in the 7th from Jupiter, it indicates a strong possibility of marriage that year.
- **Specific House Effects:**
- **2nd House:** Potential for accidents involving male family members; recite the Hanuman Chalisa before leaving home.
- **3rd House:** Be cautious during short travels.
- **6th House:** Avoid places with heavy tool usage to prevent accidents.
- **8th House:** Recitation of the Maha Mrityunjaya Mantra is advised for protection.
- **10th House:** Benefits from the government or authority figures.
- **11th House:** Favorable time to invest in land or property.
- **12th House:** Risk of injuries to feet; exercise caution.

Mercury

- **Direction-Based Influence for Education & Business:** If in the 6th, 8th, or 12th house, indicates educational or business challenges.
- **Special Guidelines:**
- **Watery Signs (4, 8, 12):** Buying and releasing a parrot is recommended.
- **2nd, 6th, or 10th House:** Consider keeping a pet parrot for prosperity and clarity in communication.

Sun & Moon

- **Eyesight Caution:** Placement in the 6th, 8th, or 12th house can lead to potential eye issues.

Saurabh Avasthi, CoFounder – Astrometry

Meet Saurabh Avasthi: Illuminating Lives Through Wisdom and Insight

Saurabh Avasthi stands as an exceptional figure, weaving together the realms of wisdom, transformation and self-discovery. With a multifaceted journey that spans diverse disciplines, he emerges as a luminary in the realm of holistic coaching and psychological astrology.

Bridging Psychology and Astrology: A Trailblazer in the Field

Saurabh Avasthi wears the crown of being the nation's sole practitioner of Psychological Astrology. Through his unparalleled insight, he delves into the depths of astrology, transcending conventional boundaries. His profound understanding of the human psyche has brought forth a unique perspective that goes beyond predictions – it's about unraveling the intricate tapestry of the mind.

A Catalyst for Transformation and Empowerment

With a legacy of coaching and mentoring thousands, Saurabh's expertise extends beyond astrology. As a seasoned practitioner of Graphology, he deciphers the nuances of written expression. He has become the most sought-after guide in the realm of Vedic Numerology, unraveling the cosmic code of numbers for those who seek clarity and purpose.

Navigating the Mind's Labyrinth

Saurabh's credentials extend to the realm of neuro-linguistic programming (NLP). As a certified Master Practitioner, he explores the intricate connections between language, behavior and transformation. His journey also extends into the realm of hypnotism, where he harnesses the power of the subconscious mind to facilitate change.

Pioneering Research and Unveiling Horoscope Insights
In a quest to understand the intricate interplay between neurocognitive behavior, neuroplasticity and astrological patterns, Saurabh Avasthi is at the forefront of pioneering research. He envisions a future where science and spirituality harmonize, offering profound insights into how our horoscopes may shape our cognitive journeys.

From Corporate Heights to Holistic Calling
Saurabh's journey is an embodiment of transformation. After two decades of thriving in the corporate world, steering the realms of Sales and Marketing for esteemed entities such as Colgate Palmolive, Vodafone, Hindustan Times and Askmebazaar, he embarked on a path fueled by passion. His corporate acumen now synergizes with his spiritual calling, creating a unique blend of practicality and profound insight.

Analytics that Illuminate Pathways
Beyond his spiritual endeavors, Saurabh Avasthi also illuminates pathways through data. He spearheads the realm of Data Analytics with his venture, pdobia (predictive date of birth insights and analytics), fusing ancient wisdom with modern analytics to unveil hidden patterns and potentials.
In essence, Saurabh Avasthi is not merely a coach or an astrologer – he's a torchbearer of transformation, an alchemist of the mind and a guardian of profound insight. His journey is an invitation to unravel the mysteries of the self and embrace the boundless potential that resides within.

Meenakshi Awasthi, CoFounder – Astrometry

Discover the Multi-Faceted Magic of Meenakshi Awasthi
Meenakshi Awasthi is a force of inspiration, seamlessly blending diverse realms into a harmonious tapestry of wisdom, healing and empowerment. With a journey that traverses the intricate pathways of education, passion and profound insight, she stands as a guiding light for those seeking clarity and transformation.

Education Meets Creative Expression
An accomplished Chartered Accountant by education, Meenakshi's journey expands far beyond the numbers. With a passion that ignites her creativity, she is a Qualified Fashion Designer, adding an artistic flair to her repertoire. Yet, her journey doesn't stop here.

A Journey into the Mystical
Meenakshi Awasthi seamlessly embodies the mystical arts. As a Pranic Healer, her touch radiates healing energy, as a Palmist, she deciphers the intricacies of one's life imprinted on their hands and as a Face Reader and Tarot Reader, she unravels the unspoken stories etched on visages and cards.

A Renowned Guide and Teacher
Meenakshi's proficiency extends to the role of a revered teacher. She imparts the art of Palmistry, Face Reading and Tarot Card Reading through specialized workshops. In her quest to bring holistic wellness, she delves into EFT (Emotional Freedom Technique), Switchwords, Chakra Healing and Balancing, Crystal Healing and Cord Cutting. Notably, she shares her wisdom through free Meditation sessions, creating spaces of tranquility and rejuvenation for all.

Healing the Mind, Body and Soul

Her journey towards healing is marked by milestones of accomplishment. Meenakshi's expertise spans Basic and Advanced Psychotherapy, Psychic Self Defence, Pranic Facelift, Crystal Healing and the esteemed levels of Arhatic and ACPH in Pranic Healing. Her dedication to these practices exemplifies her commitment to fostering holistic well-being.

Illuminating Paths of Positivity
Meenakshi's transformative journey took a courageous turn when she chose to leave a thriving fashion business behind. Her passion for guiding and helping people embarking on their life journeys led her to explore the realms of Palmistry and Tarot. For over five years, she has been a beacon of hope, guiding individuals out of the shadows of depression and agony. Through her unparalleled mastery in predictive palmistry and profound understanding of Tarot, she illuminates the way to positivity and light.

A Healer's Touch, a Guide's Insight
Meenakshi Awasthi has not only identified the precise areas that need healing but has also nurtured countless souls through Pranic Healing and compassionate counseling. Her journey is a testament to the power of passion, the magic of insight and the boundless potential of healing.
Step into the realm of Meenakshi's wisdom and let her illuminate your journey with light, healing and guidance.

Discover Astrometry: Where Wisdom Meets Innovation

Welcome to Astrometry, your portal to a world of wisdom and innovation. Founded by Saurabh Avasthi and Meenakshi Awasthi, Astrometry is not just an institution; it's a transformative journey. With a comprehensive range of courses, groundbreaking software and a unique consultation platform, we're redefining holistic learning.

Courses That Transform Lives
Astrology: Decode cosmic influences shaping destinies.
Numerology: Unveil the secrets hidden within numbers.
Tarot Card Reading: Tap into the mystic world of symbolism.
Graphology: Master the art of handwriting analysis.
Palmistry: Read the narratives etched on your hands.
Face Reading: Decode personality from facial features.
Philosophy: Embark on a quest for meaning.
Spirituality & Meditation: Connect with your inner self.
Psychology & NLP: Understand the human mind.
Healing Modalities: Harness energies for well-being.
Our Innovative Software
Seamlessly integrating astrology and numerology.
Simplifying complex calculations for accurate insights.
Empowering seekers to navigate life's journey.
Astrometry Talk - Your Bridge to Wisdom
Connect with experts in astrology, numerology and more.
Seek solutions and share your wisdom.
Earn through consultations while making a difference.
Holistic Education & Support
Blend of education, technology and opportunities.
Empower yourself personally and professionally.
Enhance your life with knowledge from Astrometry.

Join us at Astrometry and unlock your potential.
Where knowledge meets prosperity.

Courses in Astrology
Parashari Astrology
Nadi Astrology
Grad Astrology Courses (Integrated Course
of Nadi and Parashari Astrology)
Ayurveda (Medical) Astrology
9 Days 9 Planets
Zodiac and Human Behavior
Nakshatras - Stellar Insights
Mantra Siddhi
Remedies
Yantra Siddhi
Astro Vastu
Moksha Karma and Astrology

Courses in Numerology and Business Science
Essence of Numerology
Advance Predictive Vedic Numerology
Name Numerology
Mobile Numerology
Business /Corporate Numerology
Logo Designing
Visiting Card Designing
Wristwatch Analysis
Business Coach - Integrated Business
Training

Courses in Graphology
Master Practitioner Graphology
Signature Analysis
Doodles and Scribbles
Parenting and Child Behavior
Success and Handwriting
Love Betrayal and Handwriting
Money Consciousness and Handwriting

Courses in Palmistry
Predictive Palmistry

Street Smart palmistry
Palmistry and Relationships
Palmistry and Health
Palmistry and Money
Palmistry and Career

Courses in Tarot Card Reading and Face Reading

Tarot Card Reading - Basic to Advance Level
Spreads and Spells
Predictions without learning the meaning
Face Reading
Face Reading basic
Face Reading Advance
Body Language

Other Courses

7-Days 7-Chakras
SwitchWords
Advance Crystals Course
Basic Crystal Course
21- Days Gratitude Course
Animal Totem
Vedic Switchwords
Dowsing
Sigil
Zibu Symbols
Ram Shalaka Prashnavali
Durga Prashnavali

COURSES IN HEALING MODALITIES

Pranic Healing Basic
Pranic Healing Advance
Psychotherapy
Angel Healing Basic
Angel Healing Advance
EFT
Cord Cutting

Crystal Healing
Chakral Healing
Akashic Records
Auto Writing
Access Bar Healing

COURSES IN PSYCHOLOGY

NLP Practitioner Course
Brain : Understanding the Cognitive
Journey
Neuro Plasticity : Rewiring Your Brain
Memory and Cognition
Personality Theories
Motivation and Emotions
Self - Hypnosis
Covert - Hypnosis
Psychology for Self Help
Art of Asking Questions
Anger Management
Time Management
Stress Management
Leadership Styles
Habits Formation and Change
Limiting Beliefs
Elicitation of Values
Applied Psychology
Psychology for Manifestation
Psychometric Tests and Workshops
Your Vision Statement
Wheel of Life
Goal Setting
Discovering Personality Types
Discovering Passion

COURSES IN PHILOSOPHY

Introduction to Indian Philosophy
Vedas and Upanishads
Samkhya Philosophy + Yoga Philosophy

Nyaya and Vaisheshika Philosophy
Mimamsa Philosophy
Advaita Vedanta Philosophy
Jain Philosophy
Buddhist Philosophy
Carvaka Philosophy
Contemporary Indian Philosophical
Thought
Comparative Study of Indian and Western
Philosophies

COURSES IN SPIRITUALITY

Mindfulness Meditation
Transcendental Meditation
Guided Visualization
Breath Awareness Meditation: Ana Paan :
Vipassana Meditation
Chakra Meditation
Sound Bath Meditation
Lessons & Learning From
Bhagwad Geeta
Ashtavakra Geeta

MASTER ALCHEMIST PROGRAM
2 Years Integrated Learning Program
(Includes all the above courses)